3/99

MTV'S
MUSIC TELEVISION

# THE REAL WORLD™

## THE ULTIMATE INSIDER'S GUIDE

BY JAMES SOLOMON

WITH ALAN CARTER



PRODUCED BY POCKET BOOKS
DESIGNED BY RED HERRING DESIGN
MTV BOOKS / POCKET BOOKS
BASED ON MTV'S *THE REAL WORLD*
PRODUCED BY BUNIM/MURRAY PRODUCTIONS INC. IN ASSOCIATION WITH MTV

**EDITOR:** Greer Kessel
**ART DIRECTION:** Carol Bobolts, Deb Schuler and Robin Rosenthal, Red Herring Design
**DESIGN ASSISTANT:** Adam Chiu
**PHOTOGRAPHY EDITOR:** Janet DeMatteis
**DIRECTOR OF PRODUCTION, BUNIM/MURRAY:** Scott Freeman

**SPECIAL THANKS TO:** Lisa Berger, Brian Blatz, Andrew Blauner, Eduardo Braniff, Mary-Ellis Bunim, Lynda Castillo, Craig Cegielski, Gina Centrello, Tom Colamaria, Lisa Feuer, Janine Gallant, Robert Garcia, Jim Johnston, Jeff Keirns, Mark Kirschner, Andrea LaBate, George Lentino, Steve Lichtenstein, Claire McCabe, John Miller, Jon Murray, Donna O'Neill, Ed Paparo, Luigi Porco, Janice Potter, Renee Presser, Gary Pyle, Billy Rainey, Donna Ruvituso, Matthew Saal, Adam Salvatore, Laura Scheck, Robin Silverman, Donald Silvey, John Solomon, Dave Stanke, Liate Stehlik, Jennifer Stipcich, Van Toffler, Kara Welsh and Nancy Willen.

**PHOTOGRAPHY:** BOSTON— Courtesy of Peter Costello, Courtesy Annabel Delgado, Courtesy Elka, Ewing Galloway, Courtesy Jason, Courtesy Kameelah, Courtesy Montana, Courtesy Jon Murray, Courtesy Billy Rainey, Michael Walls; MIAMI—Courtesy Bunim/Murray Productions, Courtesy Cynthia, Courtesy Annabel Delgado, Dimitri Halkidis, Courtesy J. Mark Harrington, Courtesy Billy Rainey; LONDON—Courtesy Amanda Bernstein, Courtesy Bunim/ Murray Productions, Ewing Galloway, Peter Fox, Courtesy Lars, Courtesy Jon Murray, Courtesy Team UniDial/Express Racing; SAN FRANCISCO—Courtesy Bunim/Murray Productions, Lori Dorn, Ewing Galloway, Courtesy Scott Freeman, Courtesy Judd, Ken Probst/Outline; LOS ANGELES—Courtesy Bunim/Murray Productions, Ewing Galloway, Courtesy Glen, Courtesy Jon, Jeff Kravitz, Courtesy Tracy Mostovoy, Courtesy Jon Murray, Photofest; NEW YORK—Brian Bigalke/John Russell, Courtesy Bunim/ Murray Productions, Dimitri Halkidis, Ewing Galloway, Photofest, Jay Strauss.

Maps ©1997 by Rand McNally, R.L. 97-S-55

The cover of *Keepin' It Real* by Kevin Powell is reprinted by permission of the publisher, Ballantine Books, a division of Random House, Inc.

**AN ORIGINAL PUBLICATION OF MTV BOOKS/POCKET BOOKS**

POCKET BOOKS, A DIVISION OF SIMON & SCHUSTER INC.
1230 AVENUE OF THE AMERICAS, NEW YORK, NY 10020



ISBN: 0-671-01534-6

First MTV Books/Pocket Books/trade paperback printing November 1997

10 9 8 7 6 5 4 3 2
Pocket and colophon are registered trademarks of Simon & Schuster Inc. Printed in the U.S.A.

# Contents

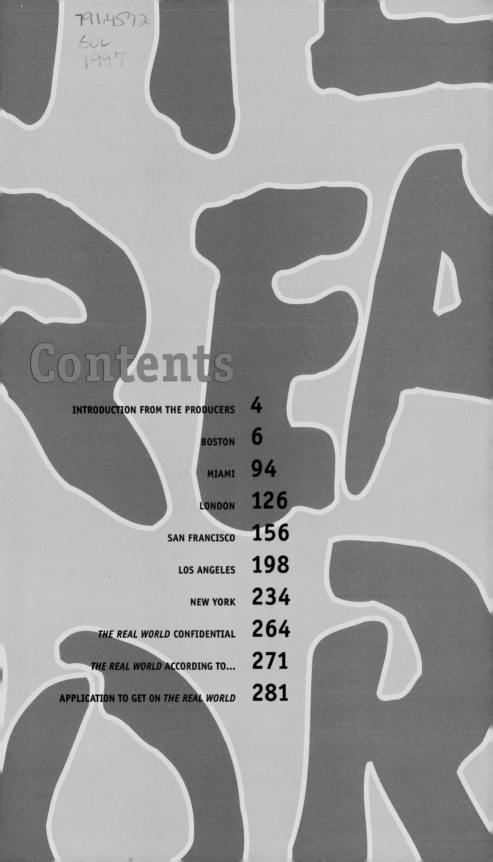

# So, you wanna be on *The Real World*?

The first year. That first season we had to beat the bushes and persuade the suspicious ("The Cast is OUT THERE...") in order to find people; everyone put on their in-line skates and pointed them downtown, hoping the casting flyers would adhere to metal poles, the posters to brick walls. We called on MTV, who agreed to carry our message: "seeking six strangers to live together in a loft, rent-free, and let their lives be taped for twelve weeks."

We, as partners, agreed. We needed diversity. We needed relatable kids from urban to suburban, financially challenged to wealthy, white-yellow-black-brown and in-between, gas jockeys to disc jockeys.

**Drama would come from diversity. Growth would come from diversity. Humor would come from diversity. Heck, diversity would come from diversity.**

Funny and relatable, dramatic and intelligent that first cast was, and future casts continued to be. We don't even have to hang up posters anymore, applicants seek us out.

But now the armchair critics (and Web-talk critics) abound. "Stereotypes!" they cry. "The Naïve Ingenue, the Token Black, the Token Hispanic, the Token Native American, the Homosexual, the Wild Card, the Male Hottie, the Suffering Poet, the Athlete, the Babe, the Intellectual, the Bad Girl, the Antihero, the Punk, the Rich Kid, the Poor Kid, the Sensitive One, the Insensitive One"....We cry back: "How can all of these be stereotypes? Do we really have slots to fill? Are they really the same every year? Was Flora really Puck in disguise?"

Introd

# Do YOU think we just fill slots?

Viewers usually recall the "larger than life" cast members who shook up the households and weren't afraid to express their true feelings. Pedro, Julie, Heather, and yes, Puck and Flora. But they also remember cast members who represented a relatable dilemma: Tami deciding to have an abortion, Rachel learning to live with an HIV-infected roommate, Mike learning to live without Ranch dressing (just checking to see if you're still paying attention), Cynthia feeling inadequate in the piranha-filled Miami house, or Elka having to choose between her father's values and her own hormones.

**The truth is, there are no stereotypes, just interesting people and relatable stories. Each cast member is unique; they're REAL.**

And we're always searching for more, so YOU should apply!

Don't assume that you're not "______" enough. Just be yourself. Be 100 percent yourself. Make a tape. Tell us why you feel good about yourself (or why you don't). Tell us why YOU should be on *The Real World*. All the details are in the back of this book.

But before you go there, start with the beginning and catch up on all the stuff you never knew about the different casts, starting with Boston.

Pictures...anecdotes...innermost thoughts—the real scoop is here.

And feel free to e-mail us at bmpmail@bunim-murray.com. We'd love to hear from you.

— Mary-Ellis Bunim and Jon Murray, Executive Producers

uction

CHARLES RIVER DAM
MUSEUM OF SCIENCE
HAYDEN PLANETARIUM
MIDDLESEX
CAMBRIDGE
Charlesbank Plgd
SUFFOLK
CHARLES
BLOSSOM
MASSACHUSETTS GENERAL HOSPITAL
CHARLES RIVER SHOPPING CENTER
CAUSEWAY
PORTLAND
MERRIMAC
CONGRESS
CITY HALL
COURT
CAMBRIDGE
LONGFELLOW BRIDGE
BEACON HILL
STATE HOUSE
BEACON
TREMONT
FEDERAL
FRANKLIN
Basin
Public Garden
Boston Common
River
BACK BAY
NEW ENGLAND COLLEGE OF OPTOMETRY
Charles
BEACON
COMMONWEALTH
ARLINGTON ST
BOYLSTON
STUART
CLARENDON
DARTMOUTH ST
HANCOCK TOWER
PUBLIC LIBRARY
HYNES CONV CEN
MASS
TPK
EXT
PRUDENTIAL CENTER
COLUMBUS
BERKELEY
HERALD
FRANKLIN INST OF BOSTON
Union Park
90
EAST
MASS. PIKE
ENTRANCE
Springfield
Boston
POINTS EAST ONLY

# Boston

## POP CULTURE LANDMARKS

TV shows set in Boston:
Banacek • Boston Common
Cheers • James at 15
St. Elsewhere • Spenser: For Hire

Movies set in Boston:
Blown Away • Celtic Pride • Coma
From the Hip • Love Story
Mrs. Winterbourne • Once Around
Soul Man • The Boston Strangler
The Brink's Job • The Good Mother
The Paper Chase • The Verdict
With Honors

## MUSIC

Some famous Boston bands:
Aerosmith • Belly • Boston
The Cars • J. Geils Band
Lemonheads • Mighty Mighty Bosstones
The Pixies • Throwing Muses
'Til Tuesday

Famous solo acts from Boston:
Juliana Hatfield • Donna Summer

## The Cast on BOSTON

SYRUS: "Boston was cool. People say Bostonians are rude and Boston is a very reserved town. Well, I enjoyed the city and Bostonians were very nice to me. No complaints."

JASON: "Everywhere I looked, people seemed pissed off and in a hurry. And I just knew that when they got where they were rushing to, they'd be pissed off there as well. Maybe it was the cold winter, but I never saw anyone really happy in Boston. I'm so much happier I'm no longer there."

KAMEELAH: "I didn't like Boston that much. I thought I'd have a lot of fun there because it's a college town. But all there was to do in Boston was drink, smoke and hang out in bars. It's so small. I walked the city in an afternoon."

ELKA: "There are like two things to do in all of Brownsville. In Boston, there was something different to do every day. I loved Boston. I imagined it would be some big, busy, not so attractive city. It was beautiful, especially covered with snow. It was the first time I'd ever seen snow."

SEAN: "Coming from the Midwest, I didn't think the people in Boston were very friendly. At least, not compared to where I come from. But I thought it was a fun city and I had a real good time."

MONTANA: "Coming from New York, Boston was quite a shock. I think Vaj said it best: '...it just doesn't pack the same punch.'"

GENESIS: "I really liked Boston, especially coming from such a small town. I thought it was a really exciting place. There was so much to do. Great shops. Fun clubs. And gorgeous gardens."

# Class

**Name: SEAN**
Birthdate: October 3, 1971
Hometown: Hayward, Wisconsin
Previous Stop: Living in St. Paul, Minnesota.
Previous Gig: Attending William Mitchell College of Law as a second-year law student.

**Name: JASON**
Birthdate: July 10, 1972
Hometown: Russellville, Arkansas
Previous Stop: Living in Boulder, Colorado.
Previous Gig: Managing a movie theater specializing in art-house films.

**Name: GENESIS**
Birthdate: April 19, 1976
Hometown: Gulfport, Mississippi
Previous Stop: Living with her girlfriend, Tammy, in Gulfport.
Previous Gig: Working at a local fitness club.

**Name: KAMEELAH**
Birthdate: September 20, 1977
Hometown: San Diego, California
Previous Stop: Living in Stanford, California.
Previous Gig: Attending Stanford University as a sophomore.

**Name: MONTANA**
Birthdate: April 13, 1975
Hometown: San Diego, California
Previous Stop: New York City.
Previous Gig: Working with disabled

# of '97

## The Boston Cast

**Name: KARMA**

**SEAN: "I never knew what its name was. I just called it 'Kitty.' But it was a kick-ass cat."**

**Name: SYRUS**
Birthdate: September 12, 1971
Hometown: Santa Monica, California
Previous Stop: Living in West Los Angeles.
Previous Gig: Working as a youth basketball coach and referee.

**Name: ELKA**

# the firehouse

## Firehouse Favorites

What was your favorite part of the Firehouse?

**SYRUS:** "The poolroom without a doubt, 'cause that's where I got to whip Sean's ass."

**SEAN:** "The poolroom was the tops for me, too, 'cause that where I whupped Syrus' ass. It was also the best place to kick back, listen to some good music and stop talking. Sometimes, it seemed like the only thing the seven of us ever did was talk, talk, talk. . . ."

**KAMEELAH:** "My bed. It was relaxing and it was mine!"

**ELKA:** "I loved my bed and I loved my sleep."

**JASON:** "My bed had a window next to it and I'd just stare outside and try to forget where I was. By far, the worst thing about the firehouse was the heat. It got really, really hot inside there the last few weeks of shooting. We had no air-conditioning and the hotter it got, the angrier we got."

**GENESIS:** "My purple blanket was my favorite. I called it 'The Purple Whoopster.' I adopted it the first day and it rarely left my side. I slept with it. I sat with it. I cradled it. It has cigarette burns. Tear stains. Cat hair. I wore that damn thing out."

**MONTANA:** "I had this favorite throw rug that looked like a tiger, which kept me company many a lonely night. We called it 'Cost-oom' because one of Sean's Wisconsin friends thought it was a costume. With his Midwestern accent it came out sounding like he was saying 'Cost-*oom*.'"

# "There was green mold growing on the urinals."

## FOUL OR FINICKY

SYRUS: "Everyone else in the house, except Elka, kept their area jacked up. **That house was so filthy I didn't think humans were capable of doing stuff like that. I'm talking cat feces in our kitchen trash, ladies' underwear left around our living room and feminine hygiene products openly exposed to everyone. That's just not right.**

"I think it was some peoples' way of saying, 'F**k you!' Well, as far as I'm concerned, you're definitely beneath me if you don't try to clean. If you're not being clean, then I'm going to be mean. Cleanliness is Godliness...and Syrus. That's all I've got to say!"

ELKA: "I'm a neat freak. You could've bounced a quarter off my bed. But that house was filthy. F-I-L-T-H-Y! There was green mold growing on the urinals."

SEAN: "I messed up my own areas, but I kept the common spaces clean. When I tried to get the others to do so as well, several of them were at my throat. So, I just said, 'F**k it!' Kameelah and Genesis were the biggest offenders, at least as far as the dishes were concerned. And Jason left his gum around the house, not to mention his dirty underwear."

GENESIS: "Sean and I had one huge fight the entire time we were in Boston and it was over cleaning house. He tried to take on this 'Big Daddy' role by telling us what to do. Listen, I was neurotically neat before I got to Boston, but that place turned me into a slob. Or rather, my housemates did."

MONTANA: "I'm slobby, but not slovenly. I leave clothes and books laying around, but never bowls of rotting pistachio ice cream like some people who will remain nameless."

KAMEELAH: "I kept my own room messy 'cause that's how I like to operate. But I always tried to keep the general living space clean, especially 'cause you're dealing with six different sets of germs. Jason, on the other hand, is nasty. The only time he considered changing his sheets was when he started to break out in hives. And I don't even think he bothered to in the end."

JASON: "I was the biggest slob in the house. That's a well-known fact. I hate cleaning so much. I despise it. I have to make a lot of money because I hate it so much. Either that, or I'll end up living in sloth."

### BOSTON BEAUTY!

**2-storied brick Firehouse located in historic Beacon Hill. 3 bedrooms, 2 bathrooms. 2500 square feet. Spiral Staircase. Pool table room. Fireplace. Built-in garage for your fire trucks (or your fiery feuds).**

**History: Prior to the Real World, the Firehouse was used by safety inspectors of the Boston Fire Department. Now, the facility is either being turned into a community center or a private residence, pending a community review. None of the show's furnishings remain.**

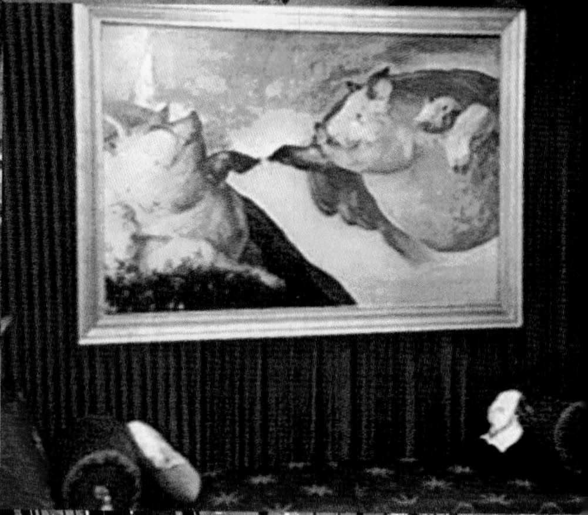

# Books & Games

**Ever wonder what the *Real World–Boston* cast was reading?** The following books were purchased by the producers (with each cast member in mind) to line the shelves inside the Firehouse:

- *The American Yoga Association Beginner's Handbook*
- *Blood Sport*
- *The Book of Virtues*
- *Candace Gingrich (The Accidental Activist: A Personal and Political Memoir)*
- *Daily Reflections for Highly Effective People*
- *Driven to Distraction*
- *Generation Ecch*
- *Gone With the Wind*
- *A Kwanzaa Keepsake*
- *Life Without Father*
- *Loose Lips*
- *The Official Cheerleaders Handbook*
- *A Penny Saved*
- *Reasonable Doubts*
- *Terms of Endearment*
- *The Road Less Traveled*
- *Thinner at Last*
- *30 Days to a Good Job*
- *Schindler's List*
- *Straight Jobs, Gay Lives*
- *The Man of the House*
- *The Ultimate Elvis*
- *When Someone You Love Is Depressed*
- *White Boys, River Girls*
- *Woman Make the Best Friends*

**...And a few board games, too:**

Balderdash • Catch Phrase
Channel Surfing • Clue
Risk • Scattergories • Taboo
Trivial Pursuit Genus III

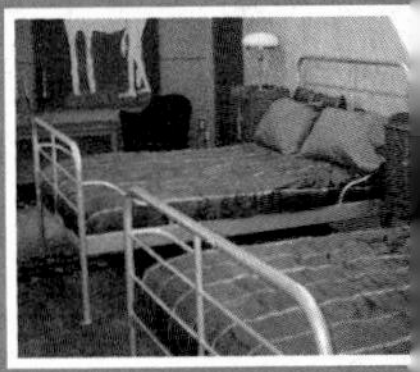

## FINDERS KEEPERS

**ELKA: "I just took a couple of mugs, and some frames, and some towels, and some candles, and a lot of books. That's it. There wasn't that much to take."**

**SEAN: "I took a picture frame, but I didn't have room for anything else. Oh yeah, I did nab the *Real World* banner from our competition with *Road Rules.*"**

**JASON: "I swiped a couple of books and a pillow with Einstein's face printed on it. I was looking for Shakespeare, but I think someone snaked him."**

**KAMEELAH: "I took a few picture frames, some books and the pillow with Beethoven's face on it. But I left everything else."**

**MONTANA: "I took my favorite security blanket, 'Cost-*oom,*' and some books."**

**GENESIS: "I stole my favorite purple security blanket, 'The Purple Whoopster.' When you've got the Whoopster, you don't need anything else."**

**SYRUS: "I didn't take anything, although I wanted to. I was just afraid they'd draw-and-quarter me if I did [laughing]."**

## ERIKA
*of Road Rules*
Sean's mission.

## SEAN
Arrived as logroller; Rock 'n' rolled with Syrus; Chopped Kameelah; Axed Genesis; Shimmied with Montana; Smooched Erika; Came small town; Left big time.

## JENNIFER
Syrus' best shot.

## SYRUS
Arrived as ball player; Played at night; Slept at After School Program; Dunked Kameelah; Fouled by Montana; Defended Montana; Soared with Sean; Made passes to many; Made catch with Jennifer; Came a free agent; Left signed.

## SHELTER, INC.
Montana's second chance.

## MONTANA
Arrived from Big Apple; Lived with Vaj; Leaped at others; Flirted with Sean; Flinged with Matt; Flopped with Matt; Flipped back to Vaj; Ratted on Syrus; Rescued by Syrus; Fired from center; Inspired by shelter; Came confused; Left clearer.

## VAJ
Montana's thing.

## MATT
Montana's fling.

## THE AFTER SCHOOL PROGRAM

Failed at first; Finished strong; Elka directed; Jason journaled; Sean rolled; Syrus hooped; Kameelah muraled; Genesis morale-d; Montana fired.

## GENESIS

Arrived as inexperienced lesbian; Experienced drag queens; On the town with Adam/Eve; On-line with men/women; Dialed Tammy: Dumped Tammy; Clicked with Kameelah and Jason; Clanged with Sean and Syrus; Came fearful; Left fearsome.

**ADAM/EVE**
Genesis' shepherd through the club underworld.

**TAMMY**
Genesis' exodus.

## KAMEELAH

Arrived as Stanford scholar; Researched "List"; Tested limits; Argued with Montana; Adopted Genesis; Passed on Sean; Pieced out Syrus; Skirted Elka; Flirted with Jason; Liked Doug; Loved by kids; Came determined; Left determined.

**DOUG**
Kameelah's favorite listing.

## JASON

Arrived with journal; Vibed with Genesis; Chilled with Syrus; Flirted with Kameelah; Betrayed by Timber; Betrayed Timber; Taught writing to kids; Spoken worded to cast; Came in pain; Left in peace.

**TIMBER**
Jason's spoken woman.

## ELKA

Arrived as innocent; Initially homophobic; Embraced Genesis; Graced her mother's memory; Bonded with partyers; Bonded with homebodies; Befriended a drag queen; Rooted for Vaj; Played with kids; Abstained with Walter; Came closed; Left open.

**WALTER**
Elka's Babe.

"I originally applied to *Road Rules,* which I preferred to *Real World* because of the traveling. After a series of interviews in Austin, they told me I'd reached the final round of interviews in L.A. I was really excited. Then they said, 'By the way, we've decided to switch you over to *Real World.* We think that you'd fit better in that puzzle.' If the truth be told, I was a little bit disappointed. But then again, I was just happy for any good news.

"My mother was diagnosed in January 1996 with lymphoma, which is cancer of the glands. She was hospitalized throughout much of the casting process. Reaching the final round was one of the last things I got to tell her. She died shortly before I was scheduled for my final interview in Los Angeles, so I seriously thought about dropping out. I talked about it with my father. I thought about it alone in my room for many, many hours. I knew my mother didn't want me to put my life on hold. I knew she wanted me to pursue my dreams and not be stuck in sorrow. My mother always taught me: 'You finish what you start.' So, I went out to L.A. for my interview and gave it my all.

"Of course, my mother's death affects me all the time. Perhaps, getting away from my house in Brownsville and going to Boston helped me cope. Or maybe it was just a way of delaying the bereavement period. But either way, the *Real World* experience encouraged me to keep a positive outlook on the future and continue to pursue my dreams.

"*The Real World* was everything I expected. I thought we'd have a beautiful house, which it was, and my roommates would be completely different from me, which they were. I expected we'd get to do wonderful things and go on a marvelous vacation, which we did. And I figured the cameras would be a nuisance from time to time, and they were.

"And *yes,* I *did* expect there'd be a gay person in the house. I knew that was something MTV tends to do. I was prepared, but I was still apprehensive about it. I'd been raised as a Christian to believe that homosexuality is wrong. And I'd also been taught to try and convince gay people to change their ways. Well, I quickly realized that's impossible. It's like trying to convince me to like women.

**"I don't agree with homosexuality, but I now accept it. I'm not some Bible-belt Christian who doesn't like homosexuals. That's how I arrived. But that's not how I left."**

**"Genesis opened my eyes and now I'm far more informed, open-minded and accepting.** Perhaps, I surprised some people at my willingness to accept Genesis. Perhaps, I even surprised Genesis. **But I'll tell you, I've had a lot more shocking things happen in my life than living with a lesbian."**

# Elka

IF *REAL WORLD* WAS MADE INTO A MOVIE, WHO WOULD YOU WANT TO PLAY YOU?
"I'd like Liv Tyler to play me. I think I see a lot of her in me. She plays innocent, naïve girls, who are slightly confused about the ways of the world, but still have strength and confidence. And she has brown hair."

WOULD YOU DO IT AGAIN?
"No. It was too emotionally draining. I felt too much pressure from my family not to say or do certain things. I'd never put myself through that again. Never. Unless, I could swear a little more. And start a few more fights [laughing]."

**DREAM TEAM**

Name six people from the real world you'd wish to live with on *The Real World?*

1. MOM ("I just wish I could spend a little more time with her.")
2. GENESIS ("I'd love to get to know her even better.")
3. EDDIE VEDDER ("I've got every Pearl Jam album.")
4. DAVE PARK, *RW* Director*
5. BILLY RAINEY, *RW* Director*
6. CRAIG BORDERS, *RW* Segment Director*

*"These three pulled me through this experience and I'm sure they could do it again."

**"I came into the house thinking, 'I don't drink. I don't have sex. And I don't have homosexual friends.' That was my 'don't' list. I still don't drink. And I still don't have sex. But now I'm friends with a homosexual. And if people back home have a problem with my friendship with Genesis, or any other gay person, well...so be it.**

**"I'd really hate for people back home to say I've been 'corrupted.' That's not what happened at all. I just experienced new thoughts and beliefs. But it hasn't changed my morality.**

"I also wish I could say I don't smoke 'cause I really want to stop. I arrived in Boston thinking I wasn't going to smoke. But living in such a stressful house, where everyone did, made it very difficult to quit. I didn't want to smoke on camera because I didn't want to hurt my father. I'm the last person who ought to be smoking 'cause my mother died of cancer. I didn't want my dad to think I wasn't strong enough to quit. I didn't want to hurt him every time I took a drag on a cigarette. I guess, in many ways, I'm still Daddy's girl and I didn't want to disobey him.

**"The one thing I didn't expect before the show was how emotionally draining the experience would be. I really do feel like I survived *The Real World*. It was sink or swim. And just about everyone else in the house was a more experienced swimmer, so to speak. They were all older, more independent and, for the most part, more worldly than me.**

**"But I definitely feel like I came out on top. I learned a lot about myself and about the world outside of Brownsville and Christianity. I feel like I made the most out of this experience. I did all that I could. I took a lot of risks. In fact, it was all about risk taking. I laid myself out for people to loathe and criticize, or to respect and have compassion for. I allowed my emotions to be exposed and let people see what I'm about.**

"As for post-*Real World*, I plan to return to school and transfer in the near future to the University of Texas. I'd like to major in communications, perhaps TV broadcasting. Maybe, I'll be a TV anchor someday. That would be fun.

**"I have such fond memories of *The Real World* and the people I met. And I think I made my mother very proud. Perhaps, some things she would have wished I hadn't said or done. But overall, I'm sure she's smiling down on me 'cause I finished the show, made six new friends and let people know who I am and why I am the way I am."**

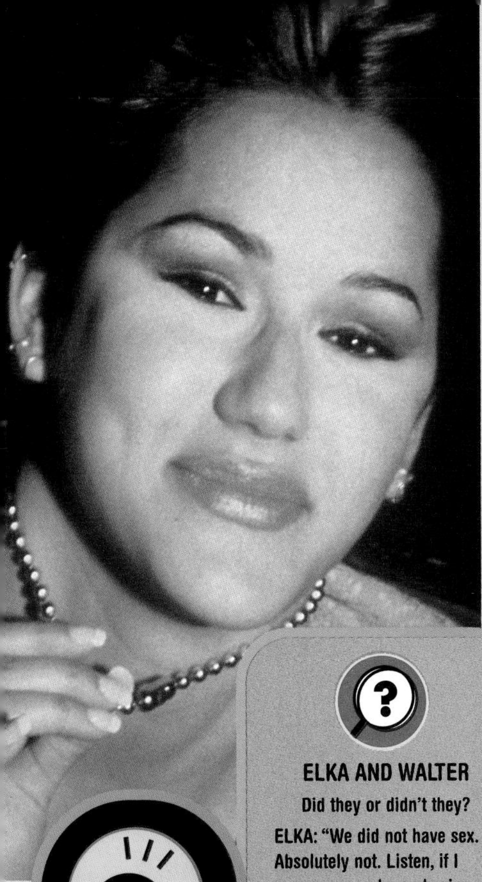

What advice would you give to future *Real World*-ers?

"Don't be scared of the criticisms and the put-downs. You're going to get that all your life. If it doesn't happen on *The Real World,* I promise it will happen to you in the real world."

### ELKA AND WALTER

Did they or didn't they?

**ELKA:** "We did not have sex. Absolutely not. Listen, if I were so gung-ho on having sex right now, my God, I would've had it with Walter in Boston. We had plenty of opportunities. But, I'm still against premarital sex, at least for now. Who knows, two years or even six months down the line. All I'm certain of is that two people should have sex only when their love for each other is strong and reciprocated. I know plenty of people who are married, but don't love each other at all. Should they be allowed to have sex just because they own a wedding certificate? I think love ought to be the determining factor."

**WALTER:** "No, we did not. It's a very special thing and we both felt it wasn't the right time or place to do it. I came to Boston to *see* Elka. Sex was the furthest thing from my mind, especially with all the cameras coming and going. When we feel it's the right time and place for it, then we'll have sex. But not before."

### SIGNIFICANT OTHERS

Name: WALTER
Age: 24
Job: Musician

**WALTER:** "I'd seen *The Real World* in Ireland about three years ago. It was the one with the Irish guy, Dominic. Most people that watch the show in Ireland think it's scripted. To tell you the truth, I didn't have a very high opinion of it myself.

"So, I was a little wary of it when Elka said she was planning to do it. I'm not a big fan of having our relationship aired on TV. I told her I didn't want to discuss any of my work or business over the phone. The most important stuff we discussed in letters. It was definitely a little annoying being followed everywhere by the cameras, especially since Elka and I hadn't seen each other for such a long time.

"I love Elka very much and I see marriage four or five years down the line. And then what? Living happily ever after."

**ELKA:** "Someday, I'd love to be able to marry Walter. I am very deeply in love with him and I think the greatest thing about it is that we fell in love with our minds—with letters and conversations long before any intimate experiences together. That's something I cherish about our relationship and I hope others respect as well.

"I think we might get engaged within the next two years. But college must be done before I'd even consider getting married. I don't want that type of commitment until I've completed my schoolwork. I don't know if Walter is going to be able to move to Austin or if his band will keep him in Las Vegas. But I do know, it's much nicer to finally be living on the same continent."

# About Elka

GENESIS: "I was real worried about Elka the first part of the show. She reminded me of myself when I was 18. She was paranoid about letting down her family, certainly to the point of limiting herself. I tried to tell her, 'You can't live life being scared of your father. He'll love you regardless of what you do.' But she had a hard time believing that, especially since her mother's death was so recent. She just wants so badly to live up to her mother's expectations.

"But I'm really, really proud of Elka. I think she grew up so much in Boston and let her true colors show. She became a very strong, beautiful woman before our very eyes. I think the two of us—the two girls from the South—arrived as girls, but left as women."

JASON: "Elka and I didn't get along at first. She really bugged me. I thought she was a perfect combination of arrogance, ignorance and youth. She'd experienced so little in Brownsville, but talked as if she knew so much. But over time, I grew to respect and really like Elka.

**"She grew up a lot during the show and she opened up a lot, too."**

SEAN: "Elka arrived very young and very sheltered. I think the way she was brought up–spoiled and babied–makes her even younger than she is. On top of that, she also struggles with the burden of trying to satisfy her dad and her late mother's wish that she be a lady at all times. What I think she really wants to be is the 19-year-old that she is.

**"When the camera wasn't on her, she'd smoke cigarettes and talk about sex. But when they were anywhere near, she'd switch into lady mode.**

"To Elka's great credit, she was the only person in the house who had good relations with everyone. Perhaps, that's because she never completely exposed herself to all of us, or at least, to the extent where we felt we really knew her. She was sort of everyone's friend, but no one's best friend."

SYRUS: "The first and best thing about Elka is her damn smile. A lot of times that big, huge smile with those dimples were what kept me going. She was great. She symbolizes fun and beauty in the purest form."

## "She symbolizes fun and beauty in the purest form."

## MONTANA: "I felt a lot like Elka's older sister. You don't always get along with your little sister, but you love and care for her very deeply.

"There were definitely times I couldn't stand to be around her. My biggest criticism of Elka is the tone she uses with waiters and other service people. If I'd ever talked to someone in my house or in a restaurant the way she does sometimes, my parents would've popped me in the mouth in a blink of an eye. She's so sweet that I really don't think she's even aware of the snippy and condescending way she sounds. I can forgive it. But I really didn't like being around it."

KAMEELAH: "Elka walked into the house and announced, 'I'm Catholic. I don't drink. I don't smoke. I don't have sex.' All four of those things were in doubt by the end of our stay. I think if she'd just come into the house and said, 'Oh yeah, I'm Catholic, but I struggle with that,' I'd have had a lot more respect for her. But instead, she came in with this hard-core stance, which she broke every time I turned around."

ELKA'S FATHER: "When Elka originally applied for *Road Rules,* I asked her, 'Isn't that the crazy show where all those kids live and fight with each other?' And she said, 'No, Dad. That's the stupid *Real World.*' Well, when Elka told me the producers had decided to cast her for *The Real World* instead, I said, 'Isn't that the show you told me was stupid?' And she said, 'No, Dad. It's not so stupid after all.'

"Elka's mother died on November 21, 1996. I was very reluctant to let her leave for Boston just two months later. It's hard for any father to give up his only daughter, especially when the other female in the house is gone. I was very proud of Elka for getting picked for *The Real World.* But I told her, I thought it was very selfish of her to even consider leaving her brother and me so soon after her mother's death.

"A few weeks later, I was watching *Monday Night Football* and a graphic appeared on the screen. It said that Miami Dolphin quarterback Dan Marino played in a Super Bowl 15 years ago...and 'hasn't played in one since.' A light bulb went off in my head. What if Elka was at home 15 years from now with three drooling kids in her arms, looking up at her reflection in the window and thinking, 'I once had an opportunity to be on TV, but my dad wouldn't let me'? Right then I decided, 'If Elka wants to do it, I'll support her.'

"Now, I'm really glad I did. On a scale of 1-10, I'd have to say *The Real World* experience was a 9+ for her. I can see how much confidence and maturity she gained. She's no longer the high school graduate that left here. She's turned into a woman and I'm very proud of her. And I know her mother would be very proud of her, too."

# Genesis

IF *REAL WORLD* WAS MADE INTO A MOVIE, WHO WOULD YOU WANT TO PLAY YOU?

**"Sharon Stone. I've always loved her. Sexually she has nothing to hide, which is the way I feel. She has a lot of grace and self-respect, and she doesn't care what anyone thinks of her."**

"So many people come up to me and say, 'Oh, my God. I don't know how you did it. I have so much respect for you guys.' Well, it really wasn't *that* hard. If you have nothing to hide, then it's not that difficult. I, for one, had the ride of my life.

"For starters, this was the first sense of family I've ever really known. My family back home just knows facts and figures about my past. But as for the person I am and the person I wish to become, no one knows me as well as some of the Boston cast and crew.

"This experience taught me so much. I was exposed to six new people with different opinions and lifestyles. They challenged me to be totally honest with them and, in turn, with myself. If I lied either way, I was defeating the whole purpose of being there.

"As for my honesty about being gay, I was terrified about telling the women in the house. That's why Jason, Syrus and I mutually decided to room together. I didn't want to pick a room with one of the girls and then have her freak out on me when she found out I was gay. So, when Jason and Syrus were really cool about it, the three of us just figured we could avoid potential problems by sharing a room.

**"Elka and Kameelah were the two roommates I was *the most* scared of telling. When Elka came home that first night and started asking me about my boyfriend, well, I just didn't have it in me to lie. Fact is she took it a lot better than I thought she would. I think she was really trying hard to accept me. She knew I had my own life to lead, just like she did—different strokes for different folks.**

**"I was extremely scared of Kameelah because she arrived with such an attitude. I thought she was the biggest bitch I'd ever seen in my entire life. I knew she was straight as soon as I met her. I thought, 'Oh, my God! I'm in trouble.' I delayed telling Kameelah the longest. But when she finally found out, that's when our relationship really started.**

"Before I came to Boston, I was living in a small town and was pretty content with what I had. I had no motivation to do better for myself. I was doing pretty well for Gulfport, which, in fact, wasn't that well at all. I was a college dropout. Dependent on my girlfriend. And barely 'out' to anyone but my family and closest friends.

"All of a sudden, I found myself surrounded by six new roommates, who were either in school or had already graduated. Everyone was very intelligent and very well-spoken. It was intimidating, at first. But it was a great motivator.

"Now, I want to go back to school. I've finally realized my relationship with Tammy was no longer in my best interest. And I realized I could no longer be satisfied with what I had. **If I hadn't come to Boston and met my roommates, I'd be nowhere. Two years from now, I'd still be in Gulfport going absolutely no place with my life.**

### DREAM TEAM

Name six people from the real world you'd wish to live with on *The Real World?*

1. KAMEELAH ("I love her to death.")
2. JASON ("He helped me find a lot in myself that I couldn't see.")
3. RuPAUL ("She's the most fabulous drag queen.")
4. HILLARY RODHAM CLINTON ("I think she's an extraordinary positive figure.")
5. HELEN STEINER-RICE ("She's a wonderful Christian poet.")
6. TORI AMOS, alternative rock singer

## "I'm not exactly sure where I'm headed now, but I know I can never look back."

"I guess that's why I applied to the show in the first place. It was the way for me to get out of my hole. For most people, getting away from Gulfport isn't easy. People leave, but they almost always come back. **It's just something about Gulfport. It's like the Bermuda Triangle of the South. It just sucks you right in.** Now when I go back home to Gulfport, I know it can only be for a short time.

"When *Real World* finished, I had nothing. No car. No apartment. No job. Nothing! I plan to move to a major city, probably Los Angeles, in the near future and go back to school. I studied meteorology before I dropped out. *The Real World* has whet my appetite to study film production when I go back.

"I hope that people look at the struggles I've been through and take comfort in their own struggles. Perhaps, they can even be encouraged to come out and be more of themselves. But I would be the last person to think that anyone should model themselves after me.

**"I guess what I want is what everyone else wants—to be happy. Before *Real World,* I thought I was. But I really wasn't, at all. It took a taste of *The Real World* to realize that."**

**2¢**

**What advice would you give to future *Real World*-ers?**

**"Don't worry about how things are going to be perceived. Just be honest with yourself and with others. That's all that you can control."**

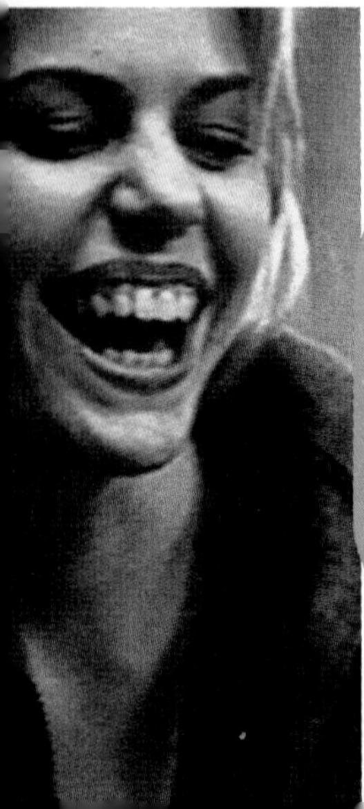

**?**

**WOULD YOU DO IT AGAIN?**
**"In a heartbeat, yes! I'd love to do it again. I'd do it with either the six I just lived with in Boston or a completely new set."**

# Gender Bending

"I know people are going to say lots of things about me:

"'She's not really gay.'

"'She's just confused.'

"'She's a bisexual.'

"'She likes older women 'cause she's searching for a mother figure.'

"Well, that's all bullcrap! I know exactly where I stand and exactly what I feel.

"I know beyond the shadow of a doubt that I'm attracted to women.

"I know that I like older women and it's not because I'm looking for a mother figure. If you're going to act like my mother, then I'm going to get rid of you. I don't want a mother; I want a lover and a friend.

"When it comes to men, I accept the fact that I love people genderlessly. But I can't call myself bisexual because I've rarely been attracted to men. I flirt with guys *only* when they know I'm gay 'cause they know it's completely in fun.

"I connect with cross-dressers and drag queens because there are very few feminine lesbians where I come from. In fact, I'm one of the most feminine lesbians ever to come out of southern Mississippi. I learned more girlie stuff from drag queens, like doing my hair and makeup, than from most women I know. We just have a great time together.

"The Boston gay scene was a revelation to me. There's just one gay club in the entire Mississippi Gulf Coast. So, I just couldn't believe how many gay and lesbian establishments there are in Boston. And the freedom they have, my God! When I saw a gay flag hanging over one of their stores, my first thought was, 'Take it down or else someone is going to burn your store down.' In Mississippi, if you put a gay bumper sticker on your car, you're likely to be pulled over and harassed by the cops.

"Listen, I hope people don't see me as screwed up in the head or confused about what I want. I know exactly what I want. I just want to be happy, to love and be loved."

## THE GARDEN of EDEN

**(Genesis and Adam/Eve)**

**Name: ADAM**
**Age: 22**
**Job: Record Store Salesman**

**Name: EVE**
**Age: "Any age you want me to be."**
**Job: Gender Illusionist**

**ADAM/EVE: "It was just meant to be.**

**"Don't you think the heavens just had to bring together a gender illusionist named Eve, with a *Real World* cast member named Genesis? You couldn't have scripted it any better.**

**"I knew Genesis was new to the scene the first moment I saw her. I've lived in Boston for six years and I've worked in just about all the clubs—gay and straight. I'm what we call 'a gender illusionist,' or drag queen. No, I'm not a woman trapped in a man's body. I'm an entertainer. Yes, I'm gay. But performing drag is what I love doing. Selling records is what I must do to earn a living.**

**"Genesis was someone who truly lived up to her name. She was the cause of so many new beginnings for me. She forced me to take a long, hard look at myself and see good things in me that I'd never seen. I only wish sometimes that she'd recognize how many wonderful strengths she has inside of her.**

**"The only bad thing I can say about my *Real World* experience is that I miss them all very much, especially Genesis. I had an absolutely wonderful time. I'd have to say *The Real World–Boston* was one big, happy Garden of Eden for me."**

**GENESIS: "Adam/Eve was the first gay person I met in Boston. He knew where to go, who to introduce me to and how to have a good time. And we had such a great time together, especially at the beginning when I wanted to go out a lot. Thanks to him, I got to see a whole new world that I never would've believed existed."**

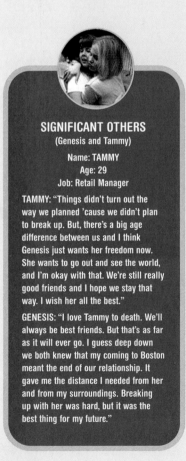

## SIGNIFICANT OTHERS

**(Genesis and Tammy)**

**Name: TAMMY**
**Age: 29**
**Job: Retail Manager**

**TAMMY: "Things didn't turn out the way we planned 'cause we didn't plan to break up. But, there's a big age difference between us and I think Genesis just wants her freedom now. She wants to go out and see the world, and I'm okay with that. We're still really good friends and I hope we stay that way. I wish her all the best."**

**GENESIS: "I love Tammy to death. We'll always be best friends. But that's as far as it will ever go. I guess deep down we both knew that my coming to Boston meant the end of our relationship. It gave me the distance I needed from her and from my surroundings. Breaking up with her was hard, but it was the best thing for my future."**

**"In Mississippi, if you put a gay bumper sticker on your car, you're likely to be pulled over and harassed by the cops."**

# About Genesis

JASON: "Genesis and I were friends from the first day. She keeps to herself, which I respect and do myself. A week might go by and we wouldn't say one word to each other. Just a mutual silent respect. But she's also very cool to talk to. If I had something to say, Genesis was a really good listener. And she speaks her mind. When she finally talks, she f**cking *says* it and says it *loud!* I feel really close to her, really close."

SEAN: "Genesis freaked me out. She seemed to be a very well-spoken person before and after the experience. But during our six months together, she sort of crumbled. All she did was sit around with her blanket, smoke cigarettes and talk on the phone or the computer.

"She and Kameelah didn't even bother to exchange pleasantries. God, we're living together. Be civil. At least say, 'Hello.' That really bugged me. Toward the end, I began to understand that Genesis' biggest problem is that she has very low self-esteem. Had I realized earlier, it might've changed the way I felt about her. I just took her silences as disinterest or dislike.

"But Genesis also helped destroy my stereotypical perception of the gay community. She brought a lot of drag queens to the house—the first ones I'd ever met. Now, I know a lot of really cool gay people—male and female—and I have her to thank for sharing that."

MONTANA: "I think Genesis is very insecure and afraid of confrontation. She'll let issues slide just to avoid conflict. I see Genesis almost as a little girl, confused about what she wants and where she fits in. She's very hard on herself. Her lack of confidence is almost sad to see. But her heart is very sweet and caring. She's very empathetic toward people experiencing bad times 'cause she's been through them herself. If something bad were to ever happen to any of us in the house, Genesis would be there to help out in any way she could."

KAMEELAH: "I think the world of Genesis. This experience changed her a tremendous amount, and all for the better. I think she's finally broken the cycle of dependent relationships, which have sucked the life out of her.

## "I think what we saw on the show was just the beginning of big, positive changes in Genesis' life."

# "If she'd been my roommate back home, I'd have been all up in her grill. I'd have said, 'Move the f**k out.'"

SYRUS: "I knew Genesis felt like an outcast 'cause she's gay. I tried to make her feel as comfortable as possible 'cause it makes no difference to me. But there was one thing about Genesis I couldn't get past. I realize some people are very moody and Genesis is one of them. But when you wake up in a house with other people living there, you ought to say, 'Hello,' 'Good morning,' or 'How you doing?' no matter how ugly you look in the morning. She never would. She'd f**king walk past you as if you didn't exist. I was, like, 'Hullo! Is this the *Twilight Zone?* Am I not here?' I can't understand that. Kameelah was the same way, too.

"And one night at dinner, Genesis said, 'I don't like none of you.' Straight up. Straight out. Just like that. I'm thinking, 'Whatever.' But because I'm a gentleman, I tried to bend over backward for her. Then, she says, 'The only cool people in the world are gay.' She says that in a house full of heterosexuals! When we still had a couple of months left. I'm thinking, 'What the hell is wrong with you, girl?' If she'd been my roommate back home, I'd have been all up in her grill. I'd have said, 'Move the f**k out.'"

ELKA: "I love Genesis. I'm proud to know her and to be her friend. And I'm very grateful to her for sharing her life and lifestyle. I just hope this experience gives her the confidence to be more comfortable with who she is. I hope that she's no longer afraid to show her true colors. I really hope she does well in life."

# Jason

"I walked into my *Real World* interview by accident. I was in a coffee shop in Boulder, Colorado and saw all these people next door with sunglasses on, striking poses. I asked them what they were doing and they said they were auditioning for *Real World*. Every single one of these guys had such attitudes. I thought, **'They're such schmucks! If those are the people trying out, I ought to audition and just be as honest as I can.'** Fifteen minutes after my interview, the casting agents called me back. I went through four more interviews later that night and met with Mary-Ellis, the producer, the next day.

"I think they picked me because I was very honest with them about my struggles and confusion about life. I guess you could call it a 'spiritual struggle' of sorts. I'm trying, like many people my age, to figure out where to go and what to do. I told 'em about spoken word and journaling—the books and books of journals I've compiled that describe my journey. I told 'em I'm not very good at covering up my feelings, which can be good and bad.

**"The main reason I did *Real World* was because I was bored with my life. I was tired of living in Boulder, where I had a s**tty job managing a movie theater. I'd seen enough episodes of the show to have an idea of what it would be like. Of course, you don't absolutely know until the camera is on top of you at the exact moment you're having a really bad fight with your girlfriend. You want them to go away...but they won't. That's when you find out what the experience is really like.**

"I definitely thought the experience would be a bit more glamorous than it was. It was much, much tougher than I expected it would be. Everything gets blown up. Even relationships outside the house take on much more pressure. There's just no escape. It was relentless and explosive. The cameras take your life and throw it down in front of you. They make you evaluate who you are and what you believe. **You better take a good, long look at all the bulls**t inside of you because the world is going to see**

?

**WOULD YOU DO IT AGAIN?**
**"Once a lifetime is enough for me!"**

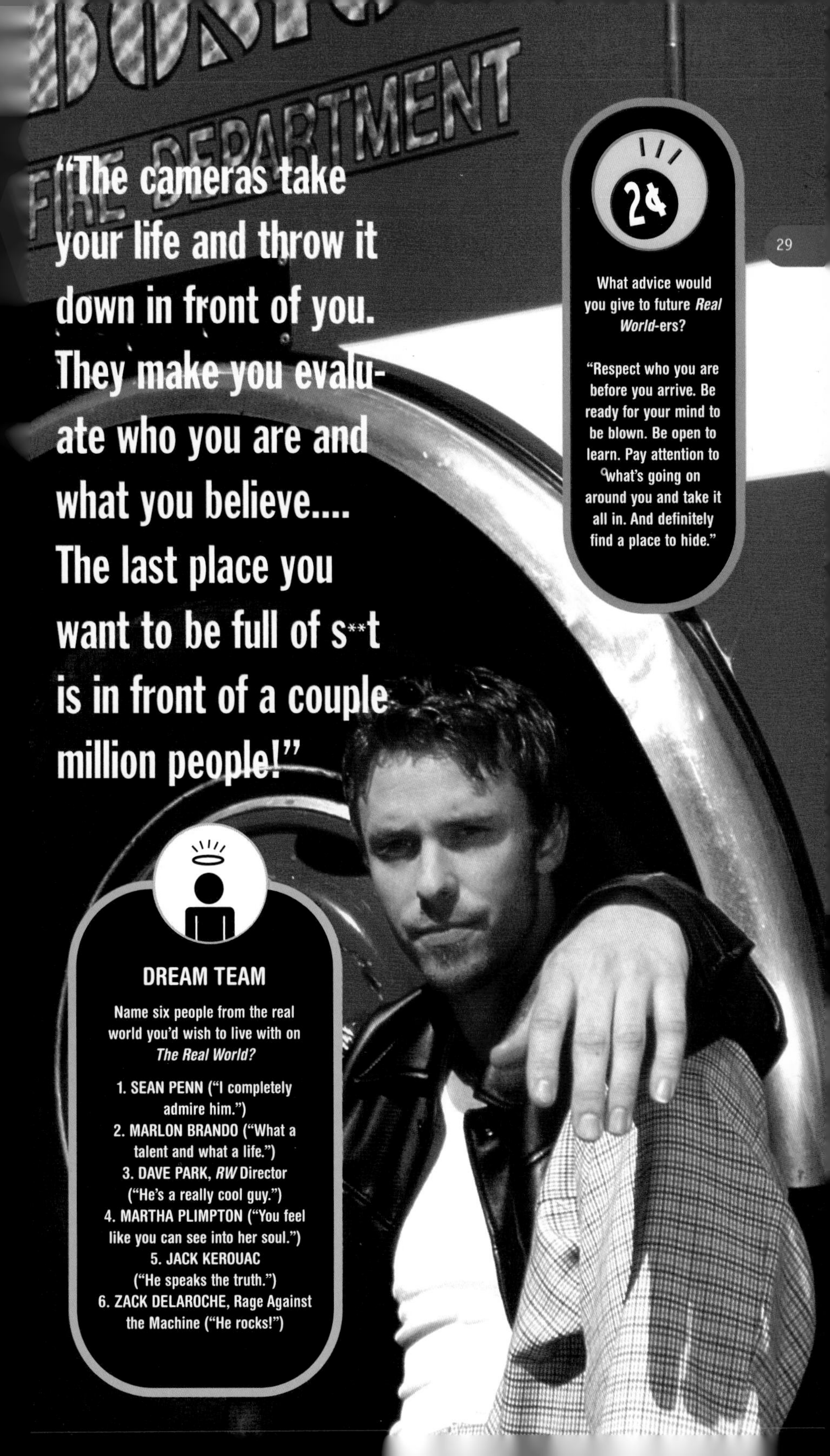


**"The cameras take your life and throw it down in front of you. They make you evaluate who you are and what you believe.... The last place you want to be full of s**t is in front of a couple million people!"**

What advice would you give to future *Real World*-ers?

"Respect who you are before you arrive. Be ready for your mind to be blown. Be open to learn. Pay attention to what's going on around you and take it all in. And definitely find a place to hide."

## DREAM TEAM

Name six people from the real world you'd wish to live with on *The Real World?*

1. SEAN PENN ("I completely admire him.")
2. MARLON BRANDO ("What a talent and what a life.")
3. DAVE PARK, *RW* Director ("He's a really cool guy.")
4. MARTHA PLIMPTON ("You feel like you can see into her soul.")
5. JACK KEROUAC ("He speaks the truth.")
6. ZACK DELAROCHE, Rage Against the Machine ("He rocks!")

**it. The last place you want to be full of s**t is in front of a couple million people!**

**"I learned a lot from this experience. I learned to appreciate the way I am and the person I've become. I also learned not to take myself so damn seriously and not to be so hard on myself. This journey teaches you how to be a really good friend to yourself because sometimes that's all you've got. It's taken me a long, long time to learn that.**

"Would I have done *Real World* any differently? No. But I wish I'd found my niche in the house a little sooner. It would've made things a lot more enjoyable. It took time to make friends and to work myself into the right situation. But there was nothing I could've done to speed that process along. So, no. No regrets.

"I'm not exactly sure where I'll be five years from now. Hopefully, I'll still be in touch with Kameelah and Genesis. I'd like to go to grad school, although for what I'm not exactly sure. Someday, I'd like to teach a course on cinema and spirituality. I plan to pursue my project on drive-in movie theaters and continue to journal. I journaled a lot during *The Real World*. Insanity inspires the best s**t and that experience was plenty insane."

IF *REAL WORLD* WAS MADE INTO A MOVIE, WHO WOULD YOU WANT TO PLAY YOU? **"Sean Penn. I f**king love him. I think he's the best actor of his generation."**

# Jason's

JASON: "I started journaling five years ago and I've filled 12 books and more than 1,000 pages. I started because it was the *only* way I felt comfortable communicating what was inside my head. I felt my thoughts were too crazy to tell people, so I'd just write them down. I write down all my observations, my hopes, my fears, my desires and my deepest, darkest thoughts.

"Here are some pieces I wrote down in my private journal, while I was on *The Real World:*

February 24, 1997
I hate this house. I need a person in a group, who is more like me. One, who also has a hard time in conversation...a person, who doesn't laugh easily. I can't relax here. I destroy myself with not knowing what to say.

February 29, 1997
This house, Boston, all this s**t is killing my thoughts. The way I think is fading. It's overwhelming...F**k!

April 6, 1997
Bus ride back from skiing—I had a few quiet moments of knowing my body and mind on this trip—one, under water at the pool, and another, coming down the slope on my board. Too much gets in the way of knowing what really, really counts (love, knowing yourself, friends, motorcycles and making love)...

Elka—I think we've been picking on her too much. Sometimes it seems damn cruel. Sean and Montana pick on her when someone's around to appreciate their wit, otherwise they're nice—kinda like s**thead friends in the 3rd grade.

# Journal

Syrus—Loving guy who truly cares for his friends—talks to fill the gaps of silence.

Montana—Crazy look in her eyes most of the time. Can't stand not to have mass amounts of attention and goes about getting this through her sexuality and humor—the latter being the only thing that works for me.

Genesis—Quietly trying to find her strength.

Kameelah—Strong, beautiful black woman, who takes great pride in her blood and skin—friend.

Sean—All-American-beef patty-feel good-Tom Cruise fan, who smiles and talks all the time. Good guy, smart but stupid in a naïve sense. Has not been through much emotional s**t and probably never will. (However, he is incredibly open to other people's ways, which I give him props for.)

Jason—F**ked up and a little scared of the way I see life. I've been trying since I was 17 to put the pieces together, so I could understand myself and other humans—and I've been doing this through these journal pages. I'll die someday and I don't want to live this life ashamed of what I have or haven't done. So, I just keep on livin' with my eyes wide open. But sometimes I'm as blind as everyone else.

May 24, 1997

Martha's Vineyard—I spent the whole day with just Kameelah and Genesis, and I'm not sure why it took me so damn long to find the peace of just the two of them. I feel close to them tonight. More than before and more than is possible with Sean, Montana, Elka or Syrus. It's not that they're any less intelligent, or boring, to be around. They just seem to talk a lot and say a little.

Last night, me, Genesis and Kameelah played, "You show me yours and I'll show you mine," because Genesis had never seen a penis before. I showed them mine. It was a glorious display, and I've been horny ever since.

Now, Kameelah just finished a shower, Genesis just finished a bath and they're toweling off a mere thick, cracked bathroom door away. (Did I mention that Kameelah showed me her boob, too, and she could feed the world!!)...

We're all sleeping in the same bed. But I suspect nothing will happen, as I'm dating Timber and it would be a bit awkward. And I really don't think anyone has the guts to instigate a ménage-à-trois. It would be interesting, though.

# About Jason

GENESIS: "Jason and I got along from the very first day. He's very, very smart and very moody. I think we knew how to balance each other out. He's in touch with his feelings, while I'm in touch with other people's feelings. He has a temper and I was able to cool him down. Sometimes, he'd have a fight and I could chill him out and show him the other person's point of view. We were always 100 percent honest with each other and respected each other's opinions entirely."

KAMEELAH: "Some people might look at Jason and think he's putting on some James Dean-like, ultracool act. Well, he really is an ultracool, genuine person. I'm not saying he's James Dean, but he's definitely not putting on an act. He's the real deal."

SEAN: "The first time I met Jason I thought he was such an a**hole. I'm sure he'd even consider his behavior toward me that first day as a little brash and abrasive. But the two of us ended up having a pretty cool relationship. He's a deep person with a lot of deep thoughts. He's very introspective and we had some cool conversation about our lives—where we're going and why we were put on this planet. No definitive answers, but a lot of food for thought."

ELKA: "Jason taught me a lot. He taught me how to think for myself. He taught me how to be confident when making decisions and not to regret the decisions I've made. And he taught me to follow my heart, no matter where it leads me."

MONTANA: "Jason is a complicated one. He's so moody, you never know how he's going to react.

**"He has this attitude that he *feels* more than other people feel. That he *sees* more than other people see.**

I just see that as arrogance. I felt like saying to him, 'If you only knew just how much you were like *everybody* else...' Jason is very talented, but he thinks he's so tripped out...and he's not."

SYRUS: "Jason was a real cool cat. He's in touch with himself and pretty deep. He's not the most positive guy, but there's a lot to learn from him. I hope our paths will cross again in the future."

## "Jason taught me a lot."

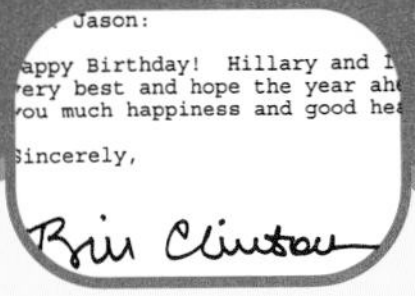

Jason:

appy Birthday! Hillary and I
ery best and hope the year ah
ou much happiness and good he

Sincerely,

Bill Clinton

## COUSIN BILL

**(Jason Comments on His Famous Relative)**

**JASON:** "I know everyone figures if you live in Arkansas you must be related to the President. Well, I really am. We're third cousins.

"I've only seen him once since he became President. That was back in December 1994 when Bill and Hillary, I mean, the President and First Lady, had a family Christmas party at the White House. I started drinking as soon as I got there and got pretty hammered. At one point, I stepped out and the Secret Service followed me. The agent stood behind me the whole time because there was a protest going on across the street. The whole thing was pretty wild.

"I saw Bill a lot more often when he was governor of Arkansas. He'd always stop to say 'Hello' or ask after my grandfather, even if he was in a big crowd. When I was eight, he caught me playing pinball inside his office, where he had this cool pinball machine. He was real nice about it and gave me a piece of coconut cake. In fact, I think he had one himself [laughing]. And when I applied to college, he wrote a letter of recommendation on my behalf. In fact, he heard I got accepted before I even told him. I guess you have your sources when you're the governor [laughing].

"I heard he's a fan of *The Real World,* so I tried to arrange a cast meeting with him and Chelsea at the volunteer's conference in Philadelphia. Unfortunately, it didn't work out. I guess the next time I'll see him will be at some family party in the White House. I wonder if he'll have seen any of the Boston shows.

"Oh, yeah. I did vote for him."

## SIGNIFICANT OTHERS

**Name: TIMBER**
**Age: 21**
**Job: Helicopter Pilot**

**TIMBER:** "The six months of *The Real World* were the hardest Jason and I have ever been through together. Some of the stuff we experienced would've been difficult on any relationship, but the cameras certainly added to the pressure. I'm an emotional person, but I thought I could shelve my feelings whenever the cameras were around. Well, I proved myself wrong again. I got so upset at Jason sometimes it didn't matter if the cameras were around. They were just *one more* thing to be angry at Jason for. I'd think, 'Jason, it's all your fault, and it's all your fault your faults are being filmed.'

"Jason has a tendency to downplay situations. I told him I don't want to discover something on television that he failed to tell me about. I don't want to be the last to learn. He and I put ourselves through a lot of serious things during those six months. Now, we've moved on with our lives, but those six months will be replayed over and over and over again. We'll be living in the present, but the viewers, and some of our friends, will be looking at us in the past.

"The future? Oh, boy! I think Jason and I are going to get past this. I know a lot of relationships have been destroyed by *The Real World.* But I think we're strong and we've overcome a lot together. This is just one more mountain to climb."

**JASON:** "I love Timber. I love her a lot. I hope the show doesn't destroy our relationship.

"We had some pretty nasty fights that weren't cool. We said some things to each other that were really mean, which I wish they hadn't filmed. One time, Timber and I were in the midst of a fight and I screamed at the cameraman to 'get that f**king camera out of my face!' He just shrugged his shoulders, as if to say, 'I'm just doing my job.' I was pissed off, but I understood where he was coming from. I felt sorry for him and he felt sorry for me. No hard feelings. After all, I signed up for this s**t.

"Listen, fights happen in every relationship when you're angry and hurt. Usually, you get to put them behind you and not have to relive those awful moments again and again. For that reason, I feel badly about dragging Timber into all of this. I guess she's what they'd call an 'unwilling accomplice.'"

# "I...told myself I wasn't going to

## Kameelah

**"When I first came into the house, I didn't like that people were in such a rush. Montana was like, 'I'm a feminist. Hear me roar!'; Elka was like, 'I'm a Catholic. Hear me roar!'; Sean was like, 'I'm an All-American white boy. Hear me roar!' Everyone rushed in with their issues the first day and was already drawing lines and forcing relationships.**

"As early as February, I had the realization I just didn't like these people. I had four more months to go and I didn't know how I was going to get through it. They just weren't like me and my friends back home. I didn't even think there was a potential for a single friendship with any person in the group.

"But things started to get better the more I talked to Jason and Genesis. Funny thing is the first day I met them, they were both drunk and that left a bad impression. Once I got to know them, I really started liking them a lot.

"The biggest hurdle was getting over Genesis' secret—why she insisted on rooming with the men.

# let six people transform me."

**"I'm better off being Kameelah first and if the black community comes out of that, so be it."**

**I figured Genesis was this whore who had to sleep with men. When I found out the real reason she'd roomed with Syrus and Jason, I really respected her. I admired her for taking our feelings into consideration. That's when I thought, 'Wow, she's really cool.'**

"Before I left for Boston, one of the black ladies in my church said to me, 'Hey, we're going to be watching you, so you represent us.' That stuck with me for a while and it was too much for me to bear. I had to say to myself, 'You know what? Forget this. I'm black. But I'm a female, too. And I live in a sorority.' In other words, I potentially have all these constituencies to represent. I'm better off being Kameelah first and if the black community comes out of that, so be it.

"I also told myself I wasn't going to let six people transform me. Yes, I was open to change. But I figured if I was corruptible, then I wasn't too stable. If there was positive change to be had, I was open to that. But I wasn't up for remolding all 19 years of my life, because I was already happy with who I am.

"Did I change? Not in any earth-shattering way. It takes someone who has really struggled, walked on water and flown to the moon to really change me. Jason, Genesis and Elka touched my heart in positive ways. But no one in the house got me to 'see the light,' so to speak.

**"Perhaps, the biggest influences on me were some of the negative traits I saw in a few of my roommates—like Montana's lying or Sean's annoying curiosity. I never want to be like that.** Those were overpowering influences. I thought, 'Wow! I hope I never turn into that!'

"As for my future plans, they're still a bit unclear. I was majoring in human biology prior to Boston, but I'm unsure if I'll continue to do so. Long term, I plan to pursue something in the sciences, possibly medicine. At least I know I won't be pursuing a career in television. Six months of *Real World* was really draining and taught me I'd never want to be in front of the camera again."

# THE LIST



"Most people ask me, 'Who thought of **The List?'** and 'How long did it take to put together?' Well, I got the original idea from my girlfriend at Stanford, Kim. I started my List about a year ago and I've been adding to it piecemeal ever since.

**"I know everyone thinks The List is set in stone. But the truth is, a lot of things are totally negotiable—things like, 'Sings to me.' You don't have to sing to me, but I like it.** Some things, however, are very serious—things like, 'Doesn't lie." Now, that's nonnegotiable.

"I don't show a guy The List, if I'm on a first date. It puts too much pressure on him. But I'll show it to him if things are getting serious, just to put my priorities out on the table and intimidate him a bit.

**"But the main reason I put together The List was so I could be clear in my own head about what I want. So many people aren't sure what they want. Or they get into a relationship and forget what's important to them. The List is a reminder. It's mine and it's for me."**

## A Good Man...

(excerpts from The List)

9. makes me use my mind.
11. never lies.
12. buys me flowers, but not too often.
13. is original.
21. knows how to buy fruit.
24. has an excellent relationship with his father and mother.
27. would wear pink if I bought it for him.
34. can take a joke.
35. can tell jokes.
37. can teach me.
45. respects every woman like his mother.
55. oils my scalp.
63. loves me without makeup.
66. doesn't mind if I become a BIG GIRL.
74. uses my hand to shift the gear in his car.
79. sucks my fingers.
90. kisses all 2,000 body parts.
100. can booty shake.
106. NEVER EVER HITS!
146. is extremely attractive.
148. works out but doesn't make me.
153. has a nice smile.
173. will never sport a flat-top

**(Total # of items on Kameelah's list: 204 & still growing)**

**What advice would you give to future *Real World*-ers?**

**"Think...really think about what it's going to be like before you send in your audition tape. Believe me, it's a lot more stressful than you ever imagine."**

24¢

**IF *REAL WORLD* WAS MADE INTO A MOVIE, WHO WOULD YOU WANT TO PLAY YOU?**

"Angela Bassett. She seems like a very powerful actress and person."

## SIGNIFICANT OTHERS

(Kameelah and Doug)

Name: DOUG
Age: 24
Job: Software Engineer

DOUG: "One word couldn't describe our relationship. I like Kameelah and care for her a lot. But from the very beginning, we knew there would be a likely end six months later—she'd go back to Stanford and I'd remain in Boston. So, we took it day by day and played it by ear. I think my place became an escape for her from the cameras and her roommates. She told me stories about her roommates that I couldn't even imagine. Things about talking behind people's backs and jeopardizing jobs. My housemates and I argue, but never to the same degree as her house did."

KAMEELAH: "How would I describe my relationship with Doug? I still don't know [laughter]. We were 'involved,' but he wasn't actually my boyfriend. He has so many things going on in his life and I don't like coming in second or third on anyone's list. So, I'd have to say Doug was simply 'my closest friend' in Boston. I like him a lot and I know we'll stay in touch the rest of our lives."

## DREAM TEAM

Name six people from the real world you'd wish to live with on *The Real World?*

1. LL COOL J. ("He makes good music and he's darn good lookin'.")
2. KIM ("She's my girl at Stanford.")
3. WILLY WONKA ("He'll supply the gumdrops.")
4. LOUIS FARRAKHAN ("He's really intelligent and tosses around a lot of ideas.")
5. MOM ("Only if she doesn't act like a mom.")
6. GRANDFATHER ("He's very, very, very important to me.")

**KAMEELAH AND JASON**

Did they or didn't they?

JASON: "I had a crush on Kameelah and I was told she had a crush on me. But we were never physically together. I was seeing Timber and Kameelah was seeing Doug. Now, if Timber hadn't been around and Kameelah wasn't dating Doug, well yeah, maybe something might've happened. But that's all hypothetical. Besides, I'd have been afraid of f**king up my friendship with Kameelah. That's a lot more important to me than hooking up."

KAMEELAH: "When I first arrived in the house, I ranked the guys in order of attractiveness–Sean...then Jason...and finally Syrus. But by the end, Jason had definitely moved up to first.

"Yeah, Jason and I flirted some. I definitely think he's a very attractive man with extraordinary qualities. But it *never* got beyond that. We never even kissed. Jason had Timber and I was dating Doug. But even if we hadn't been, I don't think it would've been a very good idea. As moody as the two of us are, it could've gotten really ugly."

SEAN: "There was some big-time sexual tension between Jason and Kameelah. So much so, I think Jason's better judgment was blinded by his like for her. I didn't like Kameelah and he definitely chose Kameelah over me."

MONTANA: "No question, Jason and Kameelah had an attraction for each other, much more than Sean and I did. Put it this way: Jason and Kameelah would definitely have sex long before Sean and I would."

# About Kameelah

**JASON: "Kameelah knows who she is. She knows what she wants. And she's willing to work for it. She is one of the strongest people I've ever met in my entire life. And nothing is going to sidetrack her."**

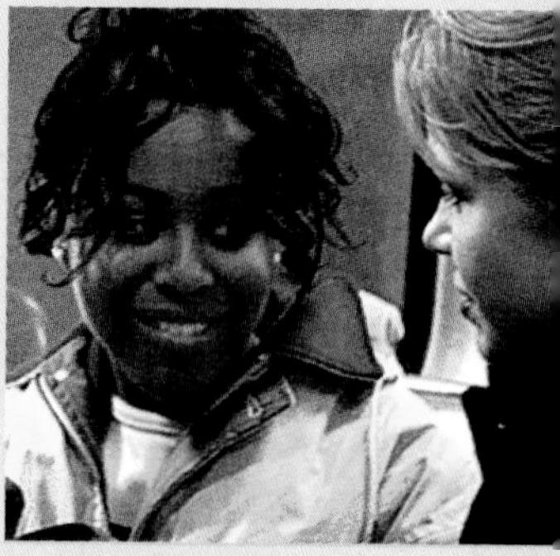

SYRUS: "I don't like Kameelah, but I don't hate her. It just took too much out of me hating her. So, I learned to deal with her. She did little sly things. When she came home late at night, like I did, some of the roommates sweated her. Instead of taking it, she responded, 'Well, Syrus did it all the time, blah, blah, blah, blah...' I'm thinking, 'You don't got to play hate, girl. You want to play with the big dogs, you got to be a big dog.'"

ELKA: "Kameelah is a very, very intelligent young woman. I admire and respect her, especially for being at Stanford. She helped point out my inconsistencies and hypocrisies, and I really tried to work on them. Kameelah feels she doesn't get the kind of respect that she deserves because she's black. Well, she ought to, 'cause she's very smart."

MONTANA: "I have more animosity for Kameelah than anyone else in the house. She's a hypocrite. She looks down on you if don't live your life according to some high moral standard. But she doesn't either. She behaves just as low and immorally as the rest of us."

SEAN: "Kameelah is at that time of her life where she thinks she knows everything. She thinks who Kameelah is right now is who Kameelah is going to be at 80. She felt she'd been true to herself because she left Boston exactly the way she came. Goddamn, I moved into the house and experienced six new people. Those experiences have broadened my horizons and changed me, at least some.

**"The purpose of this experience was to learn and grow. Obviously, Kameelah didn't think so. I hope when she gets older, she'll realize what she missed out on."**

# "She's a hypocrite."

GENESIS: "It was a privilege getting to live with Kameelah. She came in Day One, stated exactly how it was going to be and never wavered. She didn't change a bit. She's one of the most together people I've ever met in my entire life. I consider her a role model. She doesn't let anybody hold her down and the only place she's headed is straight up."

**WOULD YOU DO IT AGAIN?**

**"Oh yeah, I'd do it again. But please give me six new people. Otherwise, the same problems we had would continue on and on and on..."**

2¢

**What advice would you give to future *Real World*-ers?**

**"Remember these six people are just six people. They don't make up 100 percent of the population. At times, it seems that if half your roommates are against you, then 50 percent of the world is too. Keep in mind, they're just six dorky-ass people who are no more important than anyone else."**

# Montana

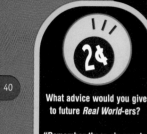

**"I'm a very open person. I'm like, 'This is me. Dig it!'**

"When I got to the house, I was very open with everybody. I think I was probably the most open person in the house. But I think I should've been a little more careful with whom I opened myself up to. When people know a lot about you, they can use it against you. **I should've been more careful with certain people in the house, like Kameelah.**

"Sure, there are things I wish I hadn't done. Vaj and I agreed to date other people. I don't wish that I hadn't dated Matt. But I wish I hadn't gotten so involved with him. I wish I could get the tape back from the big fight I had with Vaj—the one where he called me a whore 27 times. I'd like that back.

**“It’s really powerful having the cameras as your audience. It blows up little conflicts into major fights...Some people used the camera as a weapon. I’m not saying I didn’t, too, especially against a roommate. It’s a powerful way to retaliate.**

**“Going in, I knew I’d conflict with some in the house. I just didn’t know how exhausting the daily confrontations would become. Every day, I’d find myself against one, two or three people. It wore me down and weakened my confidence. I really didn’t expect to care what my roommates thought about me. But I did.**

“And yet, I was still really sad when the six months were over. I had this great sense of loss. I found it especially hard getting used to being alone again, as hard as it was getting used to having the cameras around all the time. In Boston, I always had the feeling somebody—usually the crew—cared where I was or what I was doing. But when I returned to New York, it was back to nobody cares. Nobody cares that I’m going to my friend’s house. Nobody cares that I’m going to work. Nobody cares, period!

“Saying good-bye to some cast and crew hurt—really hurt. I’d shared major parts of my life with them. But now, everyone is far away and staying in touch is not the same. But I guess it was finally time to go home again.

“I know I’ll keep in touch with Sean, Syrus and Elka. **The friendship I got from Sean and Syrus honestly touched me. It went way beyond what I’d expect from a friend.** I’ll probably talk to Jason again. I wouldn’t want to talk to Kameelah after this. **The best thing about the experience being over was not having to live with Kameelah any longer.** I don’t think I’ll call or write Genesis, but I’d probably be glad to see her if our paths crossed.

IF *REAL WORLD* WAS MADE INTO A MOVIE, WHO WOULD YOU WANT TO PLAY YOU?

**“Winona Ryder. I think we have similar features, except for the hair. She’s kind of quirky and unapologetic. I like that.”**

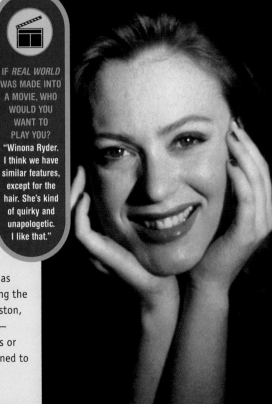

**"I learned two major things from this experience—one from Sean and the other from Syrus. From Sean, I realized that I may have missed out on some very important relationships in my past. Sean and I met on the train and I figured, he's nice but we'll never be good friends. Because we were *forced* to live together, I was *forced* to give him and our relationship a chance. Discovering how awesome he is taught me to never dismiss another person so quickly.**

**"And from Syrus, I learned that holding a grudge is not the way to go. I can hold a grudge like a motherf**ker. I still have grudges from sixth grade. Getting over my grudge with Syrus and developing such a close friendship with him, well, it questions all the other grudges I still hold.**

"I don't know what to say about my future, other than to say that my life has always taken a lot of unexpected turns. I plan to finish up my undergraduate degree and I'd like to go to graduate school, perhaps in archaeology or museum education and administration. But you never know where life is going to take you. At least, I don't."

## DREAM TEAM

**Name six people from the real world you'd wish to live with on *The Real World?***

1. **SEAN** ("His friendship truly touched me.")
2. **JOHN IRVING**, best-selling author ("He's one of my most favorite writers.")
3. **JOHNNY DEPP** ("Oh my God, he's so hot!")
4. **ANGELA DAVIS**, black activist ("She rocks.")
5. **STEPHEN HAWKING** ("We'd have some awesome conversations about physics. And he'd force them to install an elevator in the house.")
6. **BILLY RAINEY**, *RW* Director ("He helped see me through *The Real World.*")

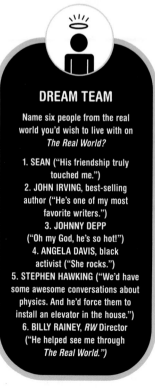

# First Impressions

SEAN: "When I first met Montana in the train station in New York, I thought she wasn't very attractive. She seemed kind of dirty. Vaj also seemed kind of dirty. They were both looking real grunge. And she had this sweater on with a pretty big-sized stain on it. I was thinking, 'This is probably the biggest experience of your life. You'd think you might want to look your best. Not show up with a big-ass stain.'

"On the ride up to Boston, she acted as if she was *the* s**t 'cause she's from New York and I'm some lumberjack from Wisconsin. I was, like, 'Who the f**k do you think you are?' But by the time we reached Boston, we were pretty cool with each other. After I met my other roommates and checked them all out, I was, like, 'Now, I *love* Montana. She and I are hanging out.' 'Cause after ten minutes, there wasn't any other person in the house that I thought I might like."

## "She seemed kind of dirty."

MONTANA'S RESPONSE: "The first thing I thought when I saw Sean in the train station was: 'Oh, my God. That is the straightest, straightest, whitest, whitest guy I've ever seen in my entire life.'

"I guess I can see now how he thought I was condescending to him on the trip up to Boston. I was just jabbing him, calling him a 'lumberjack and stuff.' I was just giving him a little grief [laughing]. He was telling me, 'This is the biggest day of your life and you have a big stain on your sweater.' And I'm like, 'So what. I like this cardigan. Big deal if I've got a stain. I don't care. Leave me alone.' But by the end of the five-hour train ride, we were definitely friends. Real friends!"

## "I thought... 'Oh, my God. That is the straightest, straight-est, whitest, whitest guy I've ever seen in my entire life.'"

**SIGNIFICANT OTHERS**
(Montana and Vaj)

Name: VAJ
Age: 26
Job: Filmmaker

VAJ: "My advice to the significant others of future *Real World*-ers:

1. Say, 'Yes, honey. I'm very happy for you.'
2. When he/she is not looking, knock him/her out.
3. Take him/her to the nearest psychiatric ward immediately.
4. Administer electroshock therapy until he/she is purged of any desire to ever go on *The Real World* again.
5. Don't blame me if you don't follow steps 1-4."

MONTANA: "I think the whole experience—the distance, the time and the cameras—put a lot of stress on my relationship with Vaj. Stronger couples have been broken up by less. But I still remain very optimistic for us."

# About Montana

## ELKA: "In ma ways, I'd s I felt the closes to Montana of a one in the hous

Perhaps, a large part of that was bec roomed together. The truth is we rea have that much in common. We don't the same lifestyle. She's very strongl opposed to Christianity and God. She in premarital sex, and all that kind o But we both learned to respect each and respect each other's lifestyles.

"I must say, I do not agree with t relationships she had with other guys she was supposedly in love with Vaj. I dream of seeing someone else while I 'in love' with another. Am I screwed u the head? I don't think so. In my opir you're in love with a person you don't yourself with anybody else. Gee whiz, other people agree with me."

JASON: "Montana and I got along when we were partying. But our friendship was never a very serious one. Talking to Montana was difficult because the conversation always seemed to work its way back to Montana. If you had real problems, she was *not* the one to go to. But if you just wanted to go out drinking and dancing, then she was great fun."

**WOULD YOU DO IT AGAIN?**
**"Nuh-uh. I'll never live with another roommate again, unless we are romantically involved. I have no more tolerance for roommates. But I'd seriously consider doing *Road Rules* to go on all those missions."**

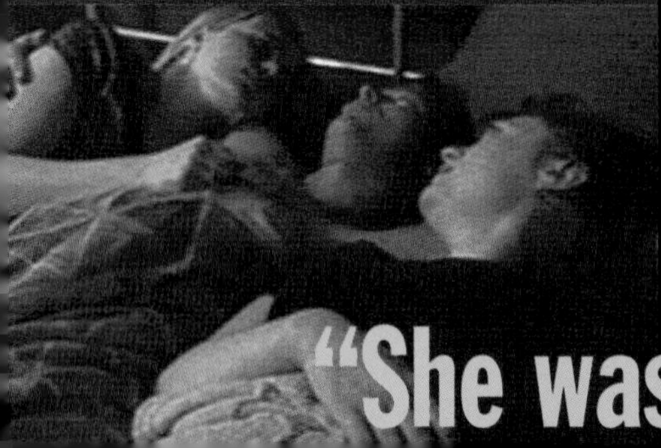

## "She was the funni

KAMEELAH: "I know Montana struggles with issues of child abuse and relationships with men, but at 22 years old, I think she should have gotten hold of those issues by now. They're still very much in control of her life.

"Montana announced early on, 'I'm a feminist. I don't shave my underarms.' I thought, 'Okay she's a feminist.' But I discovered that she can do little to nothing without a man by her side. For me, feminism has nothing to do with whether or not you shave your underarms. I don't care about that. I think it has to do with how you respect your body and how you handle yourself. What difference does it make if you shave, if you're sleeping with three guys at the same time?

"She's just so f**king manly to me. She drinks like a man. She talks like a man. She dresses like a man. Is that feminism? Or is that just trying to be one of the big boys? To me, feminism is about respecting your body and being body conscious, not walking around without a bra when you're a double D-cup, and letting your breasts fly.

"After Montana's Matt-Vaj scandal, I couldn't see myself having a friendship with somebody like her. The last straw was when she read the letter I wrote my friend. She had the nerve to throw it in *my* face and say, 'How dare you write this letter?' when she's the one who invaded *my* space. That sealed it for me."

**GENESIS: "I couldn't stand Montana and I'm sure the feeling was mutual.**

I thought she was immature, overly dramatic and blew things out of proportion. I caught her in many, many lies, adopting stories and taking them on as her own. I think she has a lot of problems. I just had to distance myself from her."

SYRUS: "My nickname for Montana was 'Lady Jeopardy.' You'd be walking down the street with her and she'd come upon an acorn. She'd be like, 'Oh, this is a *hotta tamopolis* acorn that only grows in the polar regions. There are only three of its kind.' She knows so much *Jeopardy* crap. I'd be like, 'Damn, girl. Go on with your bad self.' I got the biggest kick out of it every time. She was the funniest person in the house.

"I think we overcame some major problems. We became friends instead of holding on to our dislike. I respect her for realizing what she'd done to me and learning to deal with it. It takes a lot for someone to go through that kind of embarrassment and still face it the way she did."

**person in the house."**

# Sean

# "I realize now that everybody has something to offer."

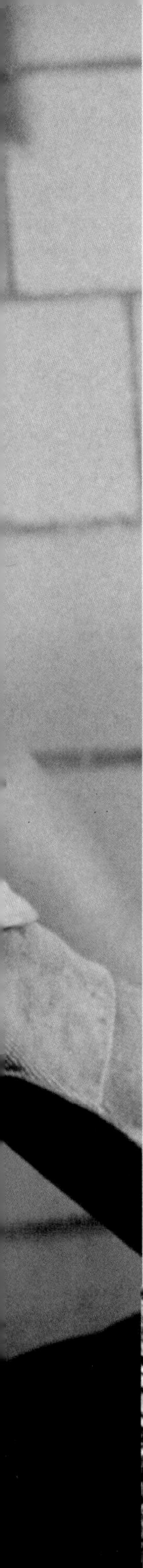

What advice would you give to future *Real World*-ers?

"Unless you have a significant other—and I mean real significant—cut off your relationship before you arrive. You just have to arrive fully prepared to say, 'What the f**k!'"

"Boy, had I over-glamorized this thing. I thought it was going to be an awesome time with awesome people. I thought there would be one or two attractive women with whom I might.... **But the moment I walked into the house and met the people, I thought, 'Damn! This is going to f**cking suck!'**

"I wasn't prepared for the loneliness, particularly during the first half of my stay. It was really hard being in Boston and not having anybody to turn to, either in the house or in the city. **When people say to me, 'That's not the *real* world,' I'm like, 'Kiss my ass!' The feelings I felt—like loneliness—were the most real and intense I've ever had.**

"I consider myself a pretty understanding guy. I figured I could be a mediator in the house. But there were people, like Kameelah and Genesis, who wouldn't even let you into their lives. I'd try to talk to them, but they wouldn't

listen. You can try so many times, but eventually you say to yourself, 'Screw this!'

"Even Syrus, whom I eventually became very tight with, had the attitude of 'Screw the house. I'm partying myself.' At the beginning, he had a major problem with all the girls in the house, including Montana. But since I got to be good friends with both Montana and Syrus, I always felt like I had to choose between them.

"While quitting never crossed my mind, I did wonder what the hell I'd gotten myself into. As time went on, though, I got to know my roommates better and do things with them. Those people who I didn't care for on first impression, turned out to be really cool, especially Syrus and Montana. And once Syrus and Montana started getting along, my time in Boston skyrocketed. The three of us had an awesome time together.

"The greatest thing about *The Real World* is that you're forced to interact with six people you'd ordinarily not be associated with. Ordinarily, I'd just piece people like Montana, Syrus and Genesis out of my life. Well, I can honestly say, I won't do that any more. That's the biggest thing I've learned out of this whole experience—to no longer look at the color of someone's skin, their sexual preference or their religion and dismiss them. I realize now that everybody has something to offer.

"Communication seemed to be the key to overcoming differences. The directors beat the piss out of us trying to get us to reveal our true feelings. Each week they'd interview us on camera for two hours about the week just passed. I've never analyzed relationships like that before. *The Real World* encouraged us to express those inner thoughts normally inappropriate in the real world. It's a really cool, therapeutic thing. In fact, I think everybody felt awesome after they'd done their interviews. You get to unload all this s**t from the previous week. It's liberating.

**"But that doesn't mean I left town a totally happy camper. I arrived in Boston with a lot of self-esteem. I left**

**"I arrived in Boston with a lot of self-esteem. I left with a lot less. I think we all kind of left battered and abused."**

**with a lot less. I think we all kind of left battered and abused. You leave the real world where you have family, your job and perhaps a boyfriend and girlfriend—in other words, a very secure environment. You enter *The Real World,* where people attack you for who you are and what you are. Hopefully, our self-esteems returned, once we returned home.**

"My future goals include graduating from law school in the winter of '98 and passing the Wisconsin bar after that. I'd like to practice law with my dad in Hayward, Wisconsin, where my whole family lives. Of course, I'll continue to do lumberjack contests and shows. And I'll certainly stay in touch with Syrus, Montana and Elka, too.

**"I got to experience a lot in *The Real World.* I got to travel quite a bit in all ways—physically and culturally. After all, I'd never experienced 'the hood' or drag queens before. It opened up a whole new, real world for me. And for that, I'm grateful."**

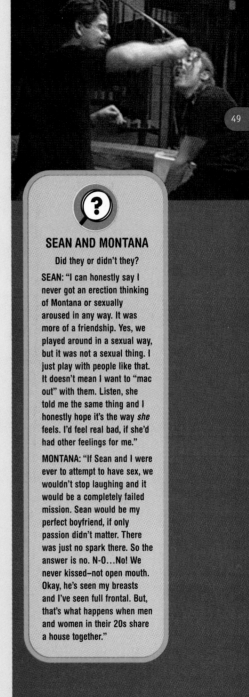

### SEAN AND MONTANA

**Did they or didn't they?**

**SEAN:** "I can honestly say I never got an erection thinking of Montana or sexually aroused in any way. It was more of a friendship. Yes, we played around in a sexual way, but it was not a sexual thing. I just play with people like that. It doesn't mean I want to "mac out" with them. Listen, she told me the same thing and I honestly hope it's the way *she* feels. I'd feel real bad, if she'd had other feelings for me."

**MONTANA:** "If Sean and I were ever to attempt to have sex, we wouldn't stop laughing and it would be a completely failed mission. Sean would be my perfect boyfriend, if only passion didn't matter. There was just no spark there. So the answer is no. N-O...No! We never kissed—not open mouth. Okay, he's seen my breasts and I've seen full frontal. But, that's what happens when men and women in their 20s share a house together."

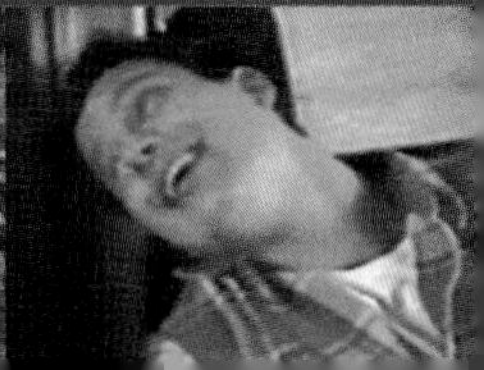

## DREAM TEAM

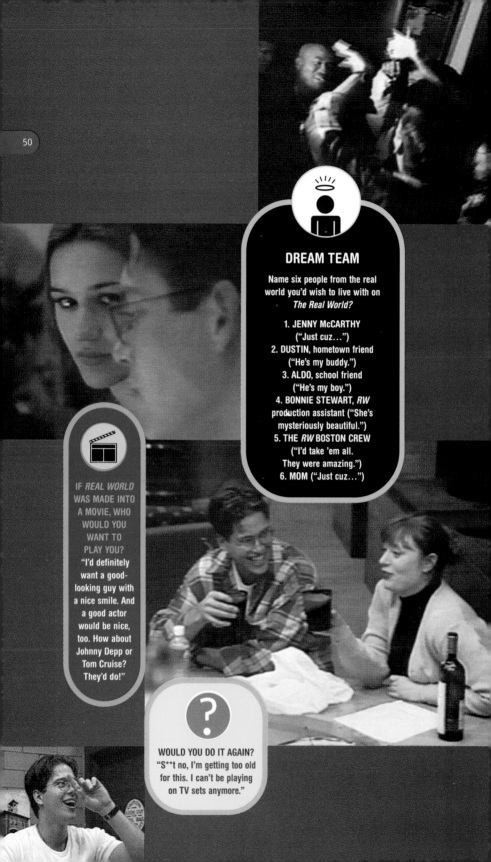

**Name six people from the real world you'd wish to live with on *The Real World?***

1. JENNY McCARTHY ("Just cuz…")
2. DUSTIN, hometown friend ("He's my buddy.")
3. ALDO, school friend ("He's my boy.")
4. BONNIE STEWART, *RW* production assistant ("She's mysteriously beautiful.")
5. THE *RW* BOSTON CREW ("I'd take 'em all. They were amazing.")
6. MOM ("Just cuz…")

IF *REAL WORLD* WAS MADE INTO A MOVIE, WHO WOULD YOU WANT TO PLAY YOU?
**"I'd definitely want a good-looking guy with a nice smile. And a good actor would be nice, too. How about Johnny Depp or Tom Cruise? They'd do!"**

**WOULD YOU DO IT AGAIN?**
**"S**t no, I'm getting too old for this. I can't be playing on TV sets anymore."**

# About Sean

## "He's got a heart of gold."

SYRUS: "I love Sean. I love him to death. He's my boy for life. He came to me with open arms, willing to take in all that I had to say. He learned from me and I learned from him. If you'd asked me what I thought of Wisconsin before I met Sean, being a black guy, I'd have probably said, 'A town of racist hicks.' Well, Sean and his friends taught me a different point of view. My boy, Sean, comes from a perfect world. It may not be a big city, like I'm used to. But his way of thinking is beautiful. Just beautiful!"

MONTANA: "Sean is one of the better friends I've had in my entire life. He's got a heart of gold. He and I liked doing the same things—dorky, dorky things—like singing really bad '80s duets together."

JASON: "Sean and I didn't like each other at first, but we developed a pretty tight friendship during the middle of the show. We talked about some important s**t. But then, he and Montana started hanging out real hard—going to bars and drinking a lot—and he and I sort of cooled off a bit. After our big fight in Martha's Vineyard, we spent a lot less time together. But I still respect him; I think he's got a really good heart."

**GENESIS: "Sean is a good guy, but he's definitely a politician.** He'll tell you exactly what he knows you want to hear. He reminds me of a five-year-old sometimes. He's always curious, asking questions. He's like a big sponge trying to absorb everything around him. He's never been around gay or black people, so he was constantly asking questions. It was nerve-wracking but admirable."

ELKA: "Sean is so dorky. He's such a dork! He's also a very sensitive person. I talked to him about some very personal things, including my mother. I told him about the night my mother died. How I held her hand on her deathbed and saw her breathe her last breath. After talking to him about my mother, I found it easy to talk to him about anything."

KAMEELAH: "Overall, I'm sure Sean is a nice person, but I didn't get along with him. I just got tired of answering all of his questions."

## "He's such a dork!"

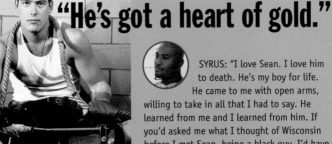

# Syrus

"I had two main reasons for doing *The Real World:*

"One, I have a few views about interracial dealings and relationships I'd like the world to know;

"Two, I needed to get away from home.

"I want people to understand racism. Racism is taught, bro. It's not something we're born with. Some people are fed a bunch of lines: 'The opposite of you is enemy, enemy, enemy'; 'You're the reason why I can't get a job'; 'You're the reason why I live in this neighborhood.'

## "If there are boundaries, you can look around and see me outside both of them."

Messages like that can go a long way, if you're taught them as a kid. If you learn to tie your shoes one way, it's hard for you to learn another.

"My purpose in life is to educate people about racial unity. I want to break out a big can of paint and paint the lines thick. I want everyone to hear what I have to say. I can't fault white people for what happened 400 years ago. If I'm angry at *all* white people, then I'd just be doing what white people did to my people.

**"As black as I am black, I'm as white as I am black. That sums it all up. At home, my black friends think I hang out in the white neighborhood, while the white dudes think I hang out in the black neighborhood. That's exactly where I want to be. Don't look at Sy' and say, 'That's one big, black dude.' I pride myself on being able to walk in between different situations—to feel comfortable and knowledgeable about different types of people.**

**"I've surfed for seven years; I've played basketball all my life. I can flip the script and hang out with the Yuppies; I can kick it in a Reggae spot with my dreadlock friends. You'll see me in a Sky spot doing stage dives; or at a cowboy bar Texas two-stepping. I'm out hip-hopping one night; cooling out at a beach bar the next. Man, me and my boys do it all.**

2¢

**What advice would you give to future *Real World*-ers?**

"Keep your head up the whole time. Take your time and try to soak it all in. Don't worry about getting down and out. You're going to cry, so don't even try and hold it in. And remember, the pot of gold at the end of the rainbow feels real good."

**IF *REAL WORLD* WAS MADE INTO A MOVIE, WHO WOULD YOU WANT TO PLAY YOU?**

"I couldn't pick one person to play me. I'd need someone as deep as Samuel Jackson, as hip and cool as Wesley Snipes, and as bald-headed and goateed—symbolizing strength—as Cuba Gooding."

"Secondly, my world back home started to beat me up a little bit. I was losing the mental battle. I'd been taught all my life to go to school, play ball, go to college, graduate and get a job. So, I'd gone to school, played ball, gone to college, graduated, and then...struggled like hell. I couldn't find anything but a ten-dollar-an-hour job. I was confused. Was it 'cause there were no jobs or 'cause I was black?

**"So, I thought I'd come to Boston and cool out. People who knew me said, 'Syrus, you get along with everybody. You'd be perfect for the show. You're going to be the one person who gets along with everybody in the house.' But, I turned out to be the most *controversial* outcast from the beginning. It was ridiculous!**

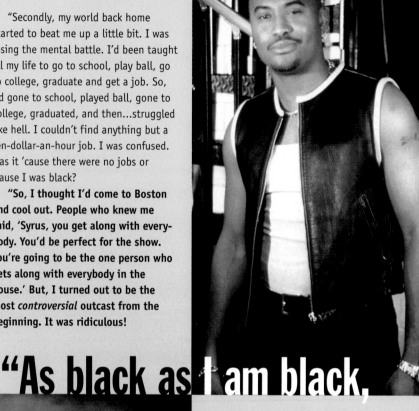

# "As black as I am black,

"The first few months, there was negative feedback from everyone–from the women, especially. When I arrived, I perceived the women of the house in the following way: **Genesis was the gay bitch; Elka was the snobby, prissy bitch; Montana was the educated, witty bitch, and Kameelah was the militant bitch.** I've never lived with people who didn't have my back. Only Sean and Jason would throw constructive criticisms my way.

"I, myself, am a social butterfly. I've got to spread my wings, show my colors and fly around. I live a very diverse social life. I love meeting and talking to people of *both* genders. That sent people for a tizzy. Just because I came home with a lot of girls, some girls in the house thought I was a "Big Mac-player-dude." Well, it ain't really like that. And if you think it was, I can assure you I was 102 times worse in high school.

**"I told my roommates at the beginning, 'I push everything to the limit.' That's the way I live. If there are boundaries, you can look around and see me outside both of them. If you're my friend, I'm going to jack with you 'til you want to kill me. Same thing when I'm playing ball. I'm going to push my body 'til I yak. I did that game after game.**

"I hope people see some of the controversy I created as raising important issues, not petty squabbling. Don't dwell on negative things you may perceive from me. Dwell on the diversity of my lifestyle. I had a lot to learn myself, like how to control my temper and not let my passions rule the moment. Sean helped me a lot on that score.

"As for my future plans, Jennifer and I hope to get married in a year's time. I

# I'm as white as I am black."

hope to work in an occupation that will allow my true colors to shine–dealing with people and communicating. I might be coaching basketball, teaching history or working in the entertainment field. Don't know yet. I know I'll be in touch with Montana, Sean and probably Elka, too. And I plan to enjoy this *Real World* stuff for a bit and just keep on 'painting the lines thick.'"

## DREAM TEAM

**Name six people from the real world you'd wish to live with on *The Real World?***

1. SEAN ("He and I got down!")
2. MIKE, college roommate ("We've shared our goals and our struggles.")
3. KEN, high school roommate ("He's family and always will be.")
4. JEFF SPICOLI, Sean Penn's character in *Fast Times at Ridgemont High* ("He partied hard.")
5. MICKEY, a friend's pit bull ("Strong outside, but a teddy bear inside—just like me.")
6. JENNIFER ("That's my girl.")

# About Syrus

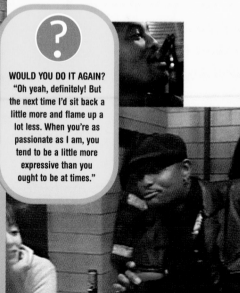

KAMEELAH: "Syrus is probably a very sweet man, but all I feel like I know about him is his name, his hometown, his drinking and smoking, his materialism and that his brother is in jail. Every time I made an effort to get to know Syrus he'd put me off. He was always 'Mr. Man' on the go. I tried to make time for him toward the beginning, especially when we were fighting, but he never made time for me. Eventually, I just shut off the relationship. Whatever."

SEAN: "Syrus and I started on the same wavelength. We wanted to drink some beer, make some money and meet some girls. But our relationship grew to a much deeper level.

## "He's my first black friend and I learned a lot about race from him."

For one, I didn't think racism existed the way it does today. I just thought it was a thing of the past. He'd tell me stories and I was like, 'Bulls**t, that doesn't happen anymore.' But we'd go out to bars and I saw how some gave him dirty looks just 'cause he's black. I was like, 'Holy s**t!' It opened my eyes. Given the way I feel about him, it was very hard to see."

**WOULD YOU DO IT AGAIN?**
**"Oh yeah, definitely! But the next time I'd sit back a little more and flame up a lot less. When you're as passionate as I am, you tend to be a little more expressive than you ought to be at times."**

JASON: "Syrus has the biggest heart of any man I've ever met in my entire life. I like him and respect him a lot. But he's not that much of a one-on-one person. He's much more of a hanging-around-in-a-group-and-talking-a-bunch-of-smack kind of person."

MONTANA: "Syrus talks the talk and walks the walk, but that's not really who he is inside. He's exactly the opposite of what he looks like on the outside. He's so much more insecure and vulnerable than he'll ever admit. I consider vulnerability a positive quality, but Syrus hates showing that side of himself.

"Listen, we certainly had our differences at the beginning.

**"Syrus came home with a different girl every night. Not that he was having sex with them, but I thought he didn't have respect for the house."**

Then, when he and I had a falling out over the rape issue, things got more estranged. I honestly believe Syrus when he says he was falsely accused of rape. I believe him even more, now that I know him so well. What offended me the most during our argument was his reaction after I told him I'd been sexually abused as a child. He was, like, 'Yeah, whatever,' showing little compassion for what I'd been through.

"It took many, many long conversations for us to turn around our relationship. We both had to swallow our pride. Sean was the biggest catalyst in bringing Syrus and me together. Sean would say, 'If you really knew Syrus like I do, you'd love him, too.' Well, Sean was right. I love that guy now."

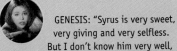

GENESIS: "Syrus is very sweet, very giving and very selfless. But I don't know him very well, even though we shared a room together. He was always out clubbing or at some girl's house. I assume he ate out a lot 'cause he never bought groceries. On average, I saw him one or two hours a day, usually when he was coming home to get dressed before going back out."

ELKA: "Syrus puts this shell around him that's very difficult to break through. I tried to get through it, but I got the sense that he's very sensitive about what's buried inside."

**SIGNIFICANT OTHERS**
(Syrus and Jennifer)

Name: JENNIFER
Age: 27
Job: Retail Manager

JENNIFER: "When Syrus left for *The Real World*, we were broken up. So, anything Syrus did in Boston is none of my business. Of course, it appears on the show and I have to witness it. But, I can't let myself be bothered by any of it or hold it against him. According to me, he did nothing wrong. Now, my father might see things a little differently, but then again I'm *his* little girl [laughing]."

SYRUS: "If Jennifer can deal with me on the show, we'll probably get married a year from now. I want to give myself enough time to get a job and become the kind of man that supports his woman, or should I say, supports our living habits. It takes a million pieces of a puzzle to become a man, but the final step is being able to support a household, both mentally and financially.

"The truth is I don't really worry about how *Jennifer* views me on the show. I worry about how the rest of *her* world sees it. I'm talking about her friends and family. Jennifer and I understand each other. But I don't know if her loved ones are going to perceive my actions any differently and try to influence her."

# Race Relations

SYRUS: "The very first hour we were in the house, Kameelah and I had differences over race.

"She said, 'You date white women?'

"I responded, 'Yeah, I've dated it all.'

"She said, 'Well a white man could never please me—physically or emotionally,' and added, 'A white guy couldn't grease my hair.'

"I'm thinking, 'What the hell!'

"From that point on, Kameelah interpreted 'I date everything' to mean 'I *don't* date black women.' Well, I'll be honest with you. I haven't dated a s**t load of black ladies, but I've dated my share. If a black woman approaches me in a club, I'll speak to her just like I'll speak to anybody else. My mother is black and I have such respect for my mom.

**"You gotta be smoke, if you're going to call *me* a 'sellout.' That's the worst thing you could call me. If you don't know me, don't judge me. And if you don't know, then you just haven't taken the time *to know!***

"You know what kills me? When people say I date white women 'cause it's a trendy thing for a black man to do. Let me tell you, if you think I'm in a trend...I *set* the trend! I've been doing this a long time. Some of it has to do with growing up and going to school in Santa Monica, which is largely white. But most importantly, it's cause the women I date are the women I'm attracted to—white, brown, green or yellow.

"I'd definitely say that Kameelah is a very book-smart black woman. I've got to give her *props* for going to Stanford. But outside of that, I'm not sure how smart she is. Sean would ask us a lot of questions about being black. She refused to answer him. She said she was 'sick of being lumped together with other blacks.' Well, I think she just doesn't want to identify herself with certain black individuals—someone like me, who wears baggy jeans and s**t. If you ask me, that's her being racist.

**"One major reason I did *Real World* was to educate people just like Sean about blackness. If you're interested in knowing about blackness, then I want to let you know."**

## WORDS TO LIVE BY (A Dictionary)

The words and expressions most frequently used by the Boston gang... and what they mean:

All up in that—Nosy (as Kameelah would say, "Don't be getting all up in that about my date with Doug.").

Babe—A boy/girlfriend (as in Elka and Walter).

Bee—A buddy (as in Sean and Syrus).

Blowin' up like nitro—1. A big vibrating sound (as in Syrus' beeper). 2. A big, bad smell (as in the guys' room after Tex-Mex).

Calling someone out—Putting someone on the spot (as in Kameelah "calling out" Montana on whether or not she read her letter).

Cheese—$$$$ (as in "making cheese").

Cyclops—The camera (as in "Look out...here comes cyclops").

Dang it—A substitute word for "Damn it!"

Don't sweat yourself—Humility (as in "Don't sweat yourself thinking you're so fine").

Drama Crib—A place where things get melodramatic (as in the Firehouse).

Dropping the kids off at the pool—Going to the bathroom (as in "I'm stopping at the 7-11 'cause I got to drop the kids off at the pool").

Grundy—A wedgie.

Hella—A helluva lot of something.

Hizzaaaayyyy—A house (as in "Check out that bitchin' hizzaaaaayyy").

Hot—1. Good. 2. Bad. (as in "That's hot!").

Humor—Very funny (as in "That s**t is humor").

I'll provide—To buy the drinks (as in "Would you like to come up and see my etchings....I'll provide").

Little something something—To get some (as in "Did ya' get a little something something last night?").

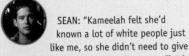

**KAMEELAH: "I wanted Syrus to be a lot like the people I hang out with back home. I wanted him to have the same pro-black opinions we all have.**

"But when I'd talk to him about race, he'd either have no opinion or some off-the-wall view. I had a very hard time relating to his perspective. It just struck me that Syrus doesn't spend a lot of time around black people."

SEAN: "Kameelah felt she'd known a lot of white people just like me, so she didn't need to give me a chance. I think that's so ignorant. That's like saying, 'I've met a couple of black people before, so I know everything there is to know about blacks.' Well, I'll bet she's never met a white guy before, who's a lumberjack from Wisconsin, attends law school and is from a family of eleven kids. She could've learned a lot from me, just as I could've learned a lot from her."

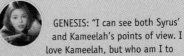

GENESIS: "I can see both Syrus' and Kameelah's points of view. I love Kameelah, but who am I to disagree with Syrus? After all, how can I have a problem with Syrus choosing to date white women, when I date lesbians and hang out with drag queens? If that's what Syrus wants, then I want it for him. But Kameelah never saw it that way."

JASON: "The way I saw it, Kameelah only dates black men and Syrus only dates white women. Those are pretty strong points of view and made for pretty interesting arguments."

ELKA: "As a minority, I think I'm conscious of the struggles that Kameelah, Syrus and even Genesis must go through. But I never personally experienced any sort of racial tension in the house directed at me."

MONTANA: "Personally, I tried to stay out of the race wars."

**Nathan**—To get none (as in "No, man. I got nathan").

**Piecing you out**—To cut a person out of your life (as in Kameelah and Syrus).

**Phat** (pronounced fat)—Very cool (as in that "s**t is phat!").

**Pinky swear**—To swear to tell the truth.

**Quee-ah**—A local term for gay people (must pronounce with a heavy East Boston accent).

**Raaaack 'em**—To set the pool table.

**Regulate**—To take control of a situation (as in "Don't make me come over there and have to regulate").

**Represent**—To state the truth (as in "Yo, man, represent where you're from").

**Skeeter**—A penis (as in the male sex organ).

**Swordfish**—The absolute truth. (as in "That s**t is swordfish").

**Tart**—Very smelly, ripe (as in smell Jason's sheets).

**The Bomb**—Absolutely awesome (as in "That movie is The Bomb!").

**Uppy**—Very good (as in "I'm not feeling uppy this morning." Must pronounce with an English accent).

**Vietnam**—Very, very ripe (as in smell Jason's sheets at close range).

**What up, dog?**—A greeting among buddies.

**Whatever**—The proper way to change the subject (must be accompanied by a hand flip).

**Whoopy**—Genesis' favorite blanket.

**Wooooorrd**—Woooorrddd is a substitute word for any other word in the English language (go figure!).

**Wubby**—A loved one (as in "Wub me tender, wub me tight....").

# "Cyclops"

**How did you feel about the cameras and what was your best plan of escape from them?**

**ELKA:** "The cameras became like flies on the wall. They got annoying when they buzzed in your ear and got too close. But most of the time, I didn't even notice they were around."

**BEST ESCAPE:** "I'd turn off my microphone and run. But the directors would usually page me within 15 minutes and chew me out."

**SEAN:** "It was kind of weird having them follow me around, especially from my bedroom to the shower when I was in a towel. But after a while, I got comfortable with the cameras because I got comfortable with the crew. It was like having my brothers and sisters seeing me in my underwear. You'd just forget that a million people were watching as well."

**BEST ESCAPE: "I'd just sit in the house and do nothing. When I wasn't doing anything, there was nothing to film. So, I'd make sure I was very, very boring."**

**JASON:** "Was it hard to be completely myself in front of the cameras? Did it make me a little more paranoid than I already am? Absolutely. I still sit in my room and think, 'F**k, can they still hear me? [laughing]' I expect a camera crew to come busting through my door at any moment."

**BEST ESCAPE:** "Beginning and ending each day, I'd take a 30-45 minute shower to process my thoughts. The shower was one of the only places off-limits. I'd just sit and cool out on the shower floor, which was probably the reason I got hives so often 'cause it was disgustingly dirty."

**MONTANA:** "After a while, I began to think of the cameras as squirt guns and the cameramen as roommates. Only after heated arguments or an embarrassing moment would I think, 'Oh, my God. I can't believe someone just filmed that.'"

**BEST ESCAPE:** "I'd sit in the sauna at the gym for a long time, knowing the cameras and sound equipment couldn't last inside as long as me [laughing]."

**"Only after heated arguments or embarrassing moment would I think, 'Oh, my God. I can't believe someone just filmed that.'"**

**GENESIS: "I didn't mind having my phone calls recorded. I didn't mind being taped. I didn't care if they saw me in my underwear. I didn't care that they could hear everything I said. None of that bothered me. I knew what I was getting into before I ever signed up. So, if I have any complaints I should only complain to me."**

**BEST ESCAPE:** "I'd shut myself inside the bathroom and sit on the floor for 10-15 minutes. Just long enough to collect myself. The directors didn't know what I was doing in there."

**KAMEELAH:** "As far I was concerned, the cameras were like furniture in the house. The only time I felt uncomfortable was on dates, when the camera seemed to make the guys nervous. I felt guilty about that. But unfortunately, there was nothing I could do about it."

**BEST ESCAPE:** "My friend, Doug—his place was my safe haven. He was real cool about letting me chill, especially because he stashed his kitchen with all my favorite snacks—raw cookie dough (chocolate chip with walnuts), cinnamon rolls and fruit punch."

**SYRUS:** "I got used to the cameras real quick. It's hard to say whether I would've been any different without them, maybe just a little wilder."

**BEST ESCAPE:** "Partying! The crew called me the Energizer Bunny because I never stopped going out. They just couldn't keep up."

## SEX IN THE HOUSE

**Where in the house did you have sex?**

**SEAN:** "I had sex only once in the house and it was in my bed. I knew the crew could probably hear us, but since I couldn't *see* them listening I put them out of my mind."

**KAMEELAH:** "What kind of question is that!"

**JASON:** "When I had sex in the house, I usually did it in the shower. One time, Timber and I hadn't seen each other for a while and we were 'taking a shower together.' Well, apparently we got pretty loud in there. Afterward, I heard that the crew had been outside the entire time filming the bathroom door and my roommates' reactions. I didn't care, but Timber was mortified 'cause she was the one making all the noise [laughing]."

**SYRUS:** "I never had sex in the house."

**MONTANA:** "Whenever Vaj came to visit, I'd ask the directors to turn off the lights in my bedroom and allow us some privacy. They were very understanding. And no, my roommate Elka wasn't in the room, too [laughing]."

**ELKA:** "I don't believe in premarital sex."

**GENESIS:** "I never had sex the entire time I was in Boston."

# A Tale of Two Cities

## About the Sides

KAMEELAH: "I'd say the best way of describing the two side was Bulls**t vs. Non-bulls**t!"

GENESIS: "Our idea of fun just wasn't the same as theirs. They were always in bars trying to pick up people. We've outgrown that phase...and, to think, we're younger than they are."

SYRUS: "The best way I can think of describing what separated the two sides is the name 'Kameelah.'"

MONTANA: "I think of Sean, Syrus, and myself as the Jedi rebels...and Kameelah and Genesis as the Empire. Jason preferred hanging out with the Empire, but he'd come over to the Jedi and cool out from time to time. Elka preferred playing for the Jedi, but she'd occasionally pinch-hit for the Empire."

SEAN: "Ours was the fun-loving, outgoing, up-for-a-good-time side and theirs was the introspective, homebody, dull side."

## About the Middle

JASON: "Our group was tight, but didn't need to talk about it all the time. Their group was always competing to see who could be the funniest, who went out more...They talked so much s**t it was like they were still in high school.

"I started in the middle, but got tired of all the constant s**t-talking Syrus, Sean and Montana did. It's okay some of the time, but not around the clock. Had we all lived together another month, I think Elka would've tired of it too and come over to our side."

ELKA: "Montana, Syrus and Sean were the party animals. They were out trying to find someone to drink and make out with. Jason, Genesis and Kameelah were the searchers. They were inside trying to find themselves.

"I was the floater. I genuinely liked and respected everyone in the house."

# FACTOIDS OF LIFE

**Everything you wanted to know about *Real World–Boston*, but didn't know whom to ask.**



The number of half-hour episodes 24

The number of minutes in a half hour 30

The number of people who applied to be on *Real World–Boston* 12,234

The number of people who were selected to be on *Real World–Boston* 7

The number of times Sean did his wash 18

The number of times Genesis changed her sheets 0

The number of months the roommates lived together in Boston 6

The number of days the cast was filmed each week 7

The number of hours the cast might be filmed each day 24

The number of times Jason and Timber had sex in the shower 10

The number of times Jason cleaned the shower 0

The number of minutes of videotape shot per week 7,000

The number of times the camera caught Kameelah in a state of undress 19

The number of hours of sleep Elka and Genesis averaged each night 12

The number of hours of sleep Syrus averaged each night 4.5

The number of girls' phone numbers Syrus accumulated one "lucky" night 20+

The number of security cameras that monitored the cast inside the house 8

The number of times Sean was monitored "making out" inside the house 3

The number of rolls of raw cookie dough eaten by Kameelah 34

The number of rolls of toilet paper used up by the roommates 500+

JASON: "We ran out of so much toilet paper it wasn't funny. Well, actually it was, sort of. I had to use newspaper a few times and someone's magazine once. We were all so broke, we'd bring home extra toilet paper from restaurants and bars whenever we went out."

# After School Program

## A Report Card

### Overall Summary

**ANTHONY (Supervisor):** "After the first week, the *Real World–Boston* cast looked like they were going to be a complete disaster for our After School Program.

"When the cast arrived, I decided to give everyone total autonomy. I allowed them to choose their activities and determine which kids they wanted to work with. Well, I gave them so much freedom they chose to do absolutely nothing.

**"Instead of interacting with the kids, they'd sit in the kitchen and complain about each other.**

Instead of helping out the other staff members, they tried to use the staff as allies against each other. They brought all the problems of their house into our center. On top of that, they were unmotivated and unfocused.

"I took a survey of the kids and asked them what they thought of the cast. Most said they had no relationship whatsoever with any of them. As far as the kids were concerned, they couldn't care less if the cast stayed or left!

**"But things changed with Philadelphia. I think the temporary suspensions of Syrus and Sean and the subsequent firing of Montana really shook up the cast. It forced each member to reevaluate why and what they were doing here. Suddenly, they started pulling themselves together and running with the ball.**

Syrus started really getting into basketball with the kids. Sean taught a dozen children how to logroll. Elka put together an ambitious play. It was like night and day. Most importantly, the cast began to have real and meaningful interactions with the kids.

"Halfway through *The Real World–Boston,* I'd have said not one kid would have benefited from having the cast here. But by the end, I can say a lot of them really did."

# Anthony's Individual Evaluations

**ELKA:** "Elka started off by isolating herself from the kids. She was always in the kitchen talking with Genesis and Kameelah. But by the end, she became focused and attentive to the kids' issues and concerns. She went all-out on her final project—the sound, the lights, the script, the rehearsals. She did a great job. Without a doubt, it was the best performance the After School Program has seen in the three years I've been here."
**Grade: B+**

**JASON:** "Jason is one to sit in a dark corner and ponder the question, 'Why?" Unfortunately, kids demand, 'Now!' If things got too chaotic, Jason would squirrel out the door without telling anybody. He's the king of secret-squirreling. But by the end, he learned to participate more fully in the kids' lives and got them to express themselves through their journaling."
**Grade: B**

**KAMEELAH:** "The other cast members accused me of making Kameelah my teacher's pet. They said I would always use her as an example of what they ought to be doing. Well, the truth is that Kameelah was *the most* motivated, *the most* goal-oriented and *the most* dependable in the cast. If she said she was going to do something, she did. You never had to ask twice. Kameelah is a doer, not a dreamer."
**Grade: A**

**SYRUS:** "He was all style and no substance at the beginning. All he could think of was what girl he'd be going out with later that night. In fact, he was so tired from all his late-night activities that he was spending most of his time at the center catching up on his sleep. But by the end, he really delivered. He bought a lower basketball hoop, so the kids could reach it. He brought in a Boston Celtic, Dana Barros, to talk with the children. He taught the kids the importance of discipline and teamwork. And his 'zero-tolerance/drug-free' message made quite an impact on all of the kids. He became a real role model."
**Grade: B+**

**GENESIS:** "She arrived in tears. She was afraid of everything—the parents, the children, the projects... She was paranoid of failing and about being accepted. I think she overcame a lot of those fears and I think she has great potential."
**Grade: B-**

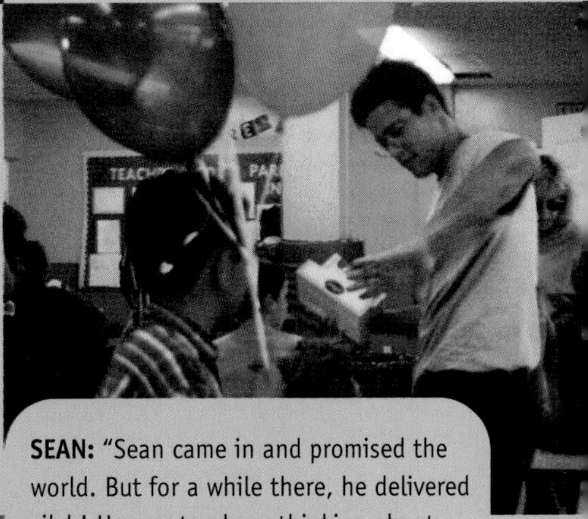

**MONTANA:** "She had so much potential. She's very bright and she had a lot of good ideas. But, for showing poor judgment...."
**Grade: F**

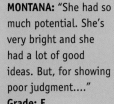

**SEAN:** "Sean came in and promised the world. But for a while there, he delivered zilch! He was too busy thinking about where he was going bar-hopping that night, than about bonding with the kids. But after his suspension, Sean did a 180-degree turn. He taught logrolling, model airplanes and bottle rockets. He became an inspiration to the kids. One child, in particular, went from being a kid with absolutely no self-confidence to the person who now teaches other kids how to logroll."
**Grade: A-**

# The Firing



**ANTHONY (Director):** "On the morning we left for the 'President's Summit' in Philadelphia, I gathered the entire cast together and told them, 'Each of you guys will be responsible for the safety and well-being of one child for four days—24 hours a day. That means, I don't want you drinking alcohol, period!' I knew some of the cast members were big partyers, so I told them, 'If you can't go without alcohol for four days and nights, then don't come.' Only Jason stayed behind, but he did so because of a bad leg. Elka stayed in Boston to be with her boyfriend, Walter, who had flown in from London.

"Well, off we went to Philadelphia and the trip was a big success for the kids. One night, we attended a special event called 'The Taste of Philadelphia,' which featured food prepared by the finest restaurants in town. It seemed like that went well, as well.

"But, on the train ride back to Boston, I began to hear rumors from the kids that three of the cast members—Sean, Syrus and Montana—had been drinking alcohol in front of them at the the Taste of Philadelphia event. So, after we got back to Boston, I spent the next few days trying to get all the facts straight. I spoke with the kids. I spoke with the cast. And I also felt it was necessary to suspend Sean, Syrus and Montana—with pay—pending my investigation.

"Here's what I learned:

1. That Syrus had done nothing wrong;
2. That both Sean and Montana had been drinking in front of the kids;
3. That Sean was holding a beer in his hand when he put one of the kids on top of his shoulders; and
4. That Montana, most alarmingly, had given two of the children—ten-year-olds—a sip of wine.

**"Drinking in front of the kids, I could tolerate—barely. But, giving alcohol to a minor... that just blew my mind.**

Not only was it completely against our Program's mission to provide an alcohol- and drug-free environment, but it's illegal. It could cost us our license. Needless to say, I was furious.

"I met with Sean and Montana to get their sides of the story. Sean admitted to drinking in front of the kids. And Montana did, too. But she denied giving any of the children alcohol, saying they'd taken it without her permission.

"I'm not calling Montana a liar, but I'm not saying I believe her, either.

"A number of people told me the opposite occurred, including one of her housemates. I also met individually with the two kids in question, and asked them to write down exactly what happened. Both of them wrote exactly the same thing—that Montana *gave them* the drinks.

"Listen, it's difficult firing anybody. All you have to do is put yourself in that person's shoes and ya realize just how painful it can be. I also blame myself for not staying more on top of the cast. Perhaps I put them in a situation that was too difficult for them. After all, none of them had extensive training working with kids before. But Montana's actions left me no choice. I think she knows that. I had no choice but to do what I did."

MONTANA: "Okay, here's what happened.

"At the food festival in Philadelphia, the restaurants were offering small samples of wine. I made the mistake of drinking one in front of the kids. Two of the kids asked me if they could have a sip. I said, 'No.' They asked me several more times. I said, 'No,' until finally, I said something like, 'Just don't let me see you doing it.'

"Well, the next time I looked up both kids had grabbed hold of wine samples. Each one took a sip, made a sour face and spat it out. The whole thing was kind of funny at the time. If anything, I thought the incident might've discouraged them from drinking 'cause they hated the wine so much. I really didn't think it was such a big deal. Not until, I got back to Boston.

"I don't know what the kids told their parents when we returned. Maybe, they exaggerated and said they got drunk. Or perhaps, they said I encouraged them to drink. But that certainly wasn't the case. If anything, I willingly and, now, regretfully turned a blind eye.

"When Anthony questioned me, I panicked. I thought I might not only be fired by the After School program, but by The Real World as well. I lied to Anthony. I told him the kids took the wine without my knowledge, because, frankly, I was scared.

**"I must say that getting fired from the After School Program was one of the hardest things I've ever gone through in my entire life. I've never been fired from a job, so for that to happen on *The Real World* was humiliating."**

"But what really upset me the most was hearing Anthony say to me, 'It's not safe for you to work with children.' It made me think back to my own childhood and how many times I'd felt unsafe. And now, Anthony was comparing me to those same people who had hurt me as a kid. Someone was telling *me* I was unfit to be with children. That was devastating.

**"Yes, I can understand why he asked me to leave, even if he doesn't believe my side of the story. Even if I didn't give the kids alcohol, they were still under my supervision. So no, I don't think I was unjustly fired. I'm not passing the buck. I messed up and take full responsibility for what happened. I messed up big time!**

"But I do question how well the After School Program prepared me for that situation in Philadelphia—caring for two children in an unfriendly environment where alcohol was present. I don't believe I was properly trained.

"As for being unfit for children, I don't agree. I know I'll be a good parent and I hope to work with children again.

## United We Stand

**SYRUS:** "I think I won Montana's loyalty when I said, 'If you get fired, maybe I should get fired, too.' I might not have done what she'd done in *front* of the children, but I certainly had done what she had done, in my life. I think I displayed loyalty to Montana in a way that she was completely unfamiliar with."

**MONTANA'S RESPONSE:** "Syrus' loyalty *does not* waver. He is the most loyal friend that anyone could ever ask for. At the time of my firing, I thought, 'I don't deserve that kind of loyalty I'm getting from Syrus, especially considering how rocky our relationship has been.' I still feel like I didn't deserve it from him, but I'm very grateful."

## SHELTER, INC.

**(Comments about Montana's work at the Homeless Shelter)**

**ANDREA (Day Manager): "I think Montana enjoyed working at the shelter, and we definitely enjoyed having her here. She was a big hit with both our staff and guests. She was responsible, easygoing and willing to help out whenever we needed. And thanks to Montana's orchestration, an accomplished stylist is now coming regularly to our shelter to do the women's hair and makeup—free of charge. I can't tell you how much that has meant to the women who stay here."**

**GRADE: A**

**MONTANA: "After I got fired from the After School Program, I decided to volunteer at a place in Cambridge called Shelter, Inc. At night, it sheltered homeless men and women. And during the day, it functioned as a drop-in center for women in need, serving them free meals and providing them a place to hang out.**

**"Shelter, Inc. was the best possible experience I could've hoped for, especially after the way I got fired from the After School Program. I never thought one month of working anywhere could affect me the way that shelter did. I've always considered myself an advocate of homeless people. But going into that homeless shelter, I realized I had so many stereotypes of my own. Those people challenged all my assumptions."**

## About the After School Progam

(Comments about working at the East Boston Social Centers)

ELKA: "Working at the After School Program was a very powerful experience. It was very difficult accepting that some of the kids were nine and couldn't read. That some kids had been abused and neglected. And that some of the kids needed to be given food to take home because their parents couldn't afford it. That broke my heart.

"I wanted to work with those children, who don't get much attention at home. I wanted to help them with their homework and help them learn. Nothing was more rewarding than having one of the kids come to me all excited 'cause he'd gotten a good grade on his spelling test the day after I'd helped him prepare.

"The play I directed was one of the biggest highlights for me. I cast kids, who are never in the limelight and never get to sing and dance in cute outfits. I wanted the best costumes and best backdrops. I called their parents to make sure they came to the show. I wanted those kids to finally get the chance to shine...and I think they did.

"Those kids at the center had a big impact on me, really big. I know I'll never forget them and I hope they'll never forget us."

SYRUS: "I didn't think the experience would be nearly as challenging as it was. I was hesitant to teach basketball 'cause that's what I'm always pushed into doing. But the children I'm used to working with back home are real serious about hoops. At the center, the kids' idea of basketball was getting the girls to chase them. They had me pulling my hair out...what little hair I've got left."

KAMEELAH: "The After School Program was awesome. I hope at least one of them remembers who I am. I hope a few years from now, a few of the kids remember I worked with them on their math or taught them how to cook. It's nice knowing they'll walk past our murals every time they pass through the center."

GENESIS: "I'd never been around kids like that before. I love children, but they made me nervous. I didn't know how I was going to act or react around them. But I feel a lot better about it now. The kids at the center were wonderful. They taught me so many things adults can't—about purity, innocence and having clean fun. I'm so happy we helped them some 'cause they certainly gave us more than we gave them!"

**SEAN: "I think we failed at the beginning. But by the end, we had succeeded. I only wish it had all started more smoothly at the Center, 'cause working with those kids was so gratifying."**

JASON: "I learned that I'd better take a good, long look at the people I'm working with before I ever take a job. If they ain't cool, then the job won't be. But I also learned how to work out my differences with my colleagues.

**"Most importantly, I learned that kids have got it on us. Kids are pure. Kids are beautiful. Kids are themselves. They're the realest human beings you'll ever come in contact with."**

# Vacation in Puerto Rico

ELKA: "I hoped we would get a trip to Europe, preferably London, so I could see Walter [laughing]. But after I got over that disappointment, I had a great time. Puerto Rico was just what I needed. And what I needed was a tan."

GENESIS: "Puerto Rico was spectacular. As good as other *Real World* vacations? Oh, yeah! I plan to go back."

JASON: "God, I was in such a terrible mood in Puerto Rico. My roommates were really bugging me. It just bugged me whenever I had to be around them 24/7, like in Puerto Rico. I really wanted to escape."

KAMEELAH: "I had a very good time, but it wasn't as relaxing as I hoped. Too many things to do and not enough time to chill. Boy, did we all need to chill."

MONTANA: "I loved Puerto Rico. The trip to Palomino Island in the speedboat was one of my favorite days of the entire show. It was heaven."

SEAN: "When I look at past *Real World* vacations, I think we got screwed. Puerto Rico wasn't anything like going to Hawaii or f**king Africa. Even the Miami cast got to go to the Bahamas. And we barely got any free time in Puerto Rico to boot. Although, on the other hand, we did get *more* trips than the other seasons—Philadelphia, skiing...."

SYRUS: "My memories of Puerto Rico are a gynecologist's stirrups, a big needle...and a doctor telling me he'd just given me the wrong shot. Not exactly a picture-postcard vacation. That hospital in Puerto Rico was nuts. I was scared s**tless."

### MONTANA'S PUERTO RICO FLING

**MONTANA: "Hey, you're on vacation. What else are you going to do? A little splishing...a little splashing. Just a couple of kisses, that's all. No big deal. A little fun for a night. I just love those Latin men. A nice little chest with no hair on it. Spanish-speaking. Che Guevara-like. Yum! Give me a little Colombian busboy any day over Sean. My God, yeah!"**

# *Road Rules* on *Real World*

## What did you think of the cast from *Real World?*

**JAKE:** "I liked all the guys. Syrus was really cool. Jason was cool, too. Sean was nice, but, I don't know, a little lonely...I thought Kameelah, Montana and Genesis were all bitches. I'm so glad they weren't on our squad. Elka was the nicest of all the girls. She was a little fluffy...a little airheaded. All I can say is I'm happy I was on *Road Rules* and not in the *Real World* house."

**KALLE:** "Before we actually met the cast of *The Real World,* we'd received dossiers on each one of them. So, I'd already prejudged them before we met.

"I figured Jason was going to be a total Puck-jerk. I thought he was going to be some normal kid, who was trying hard to be different. Well, I ended up next to him at lunch and we started talking. You know, I was totally surprised and shocked, because he's this normal guy.

"I thought Syrus was going to turn out to be some self-centered, high-on-himself creep. So, I was completely floored when I met him. He's a sweetheart—a big teddy bear.

"Sean was really nice, too. But it's weird 'cause he's, like, 25. I couldn't imagine living in a house with some guy who's 25. That just sounds so old to me.

"Montana was one of those people, who tries very, very hard to be something she's not. For whatever reason it comes off really raw and I don't like her.

"Kameelah was just a straight-out snot to me. She just threw me a big attitude, so I left her alone. I don't know what her problem was, but I just wanted to avoid her at all costs.

"The first second I met Genesis, I thought she was really high on herself. She made this big effort to act like she was better than everyone else around her.

"On the other hand, Elka was super, super nice. She really had a big thing about being Latino and I don't think she looks Latino at all, but whatever. She was probably the only female in that house that I could ever imagine living with.

"Basically, I thought the guys were really, really nice and super down-to-earth. I thought all the girls, except for Elka, were pretty much snots. I'm so lucky I ended up with my group and not stuck in some dungeon with all of those bitches."

**VINCE:** "Genesis was really snotty right off the bat. As for Kameelah, in all my life I've never met such a rare breed of bitch. It's like she took pleasure in being this ball-breaker. She's evil, seriously. Elka and Montana were the only nice women. And all three guys seemed really nice. I liked them a lot."

**ERIKA:** "The girls on *The Real World* were probably some of the rudest, most unfriendly women I've ever encountered in all my life. The three guys, however, were really, really nice."

**OSCAR:** "Syrus is my man. Syrus is my boy. We were like meant to meet each other. He's like the outcast of *The Real World* with a lot of s**t built up for a whole bunch of his housemates. And in many ways, I've felt like the outcast of my group.

"Sean was funny 'cause he was so proud of being a logroller. He'd tell you about climbing up a tree with so much enthusiasm, you'd get involved in this mental trip about logrolling. You actually feel like you were logrolling with him.

"When I first got Jason's dossier, I was like, 'Look at this guy. Who the f**k does he think he is?' He was, like 'I'm so cool.' But when I actually met him, he was this bohemian poet from some very deep place. And he was nice, too.

"Elka was the nicest of all the girls. In fact, the rest of them sucked—a whole bunch of weird mental cases right there. Kameelah had this big attitude problem. I felt like saying, 'Kameelah, your finger is not going to fall off if you're nice to me.' I'd have to say that Genesis was the cutest one, but when she arrived, the first thing she said was, 'Ah, we're gonna kick your ass!' I was like, 'All right, hold it right there...take it calmly.' She had a serious attitude.

"As for Montana, she has no guts. The whole mud fight we had, I was like, 'Yo, what's wrong with her? What kind of attitude is that? What kind of human being is this?' I mean, I don't like her at all.

"I'm just glad I didn't live in that house."

## *REAL WORLD* ON *ROAD RULES*

What did you think of the cast from *Road Rules?*

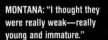

MONTANA: "I thought they were really weak—really young and immature."

GENESIS: "I thought a couple of the girls were sweet, but I thought the guys left a lot to be desired. They seemed very immature. They didn't impress me at all!"

JASON: "Oh, I liked Kalle. She's got the nicest ass. But the Puerto Rican guy was a jerk. And the other two guys were young and arrogant. I'm so f**king glad I didn't have to live with any of them."

ELKA: "I'm just glad I didn't get picked for that show and have to live with *them.*"

SYRUS: "Beating *Road Rules* was probably the best moment our house experienced as a group. We all came together to beat them. Maybe, we should've had *Road Rules* around all the time just to unify us."

KAMEELAH: "It would've been more fun beating *Road Rules,* if they hadn't started pouting afterward."

## SEAN AND ERIKA OF *ROAD RULES*

What really happened in Puerto Rico?

SEAN: "Erika and I were hanging out in the bar and, at some point, we both went off to the bathroom. As soon as she came out, I grabbed her and we started making out against the wall. While I was kissing her, I kept looking around for a camera.

"Well, at one point, Erika and I flipped positions and I found myself facing the wall. As soon as I spun back around, I saw one of the cameramen filming us. So, I took Erika's hand and walked her back to the bar. Whenever the camera stopped rolling on us, I'd grab Erika and kiss her again. When the cameras started shooting again, I'd stop. Back and forth we went.

"Erika and I hung out together the rest of the night, but nothing serious happened, intimacy-wise. There were always cameras or other people milling around. We just kissed a bit. That's all that happened. I promise! Of course, now, I wish I had just said, 'What the f**k,' and totally made out with her.

"No, I haven't seen or spoken to Erika since. I don't even have her number. I just kissed the girl. I wouldn't call it love [laughing]."

ERIKA: "All I know was that I talked to Syrus and Sean 'til five o'clock in the morning. And Sean tried to give me sixty bucks to take a cab ride home later that morning. And I was like, 'You're high, buddy.' I'm sorry, but that was exactly how I felt.

"Listen, Sean was just a really, really nice person. He was very outgoing and easy to talk to. He really seemed interested in our trip and how the five of us on *Road Rules* were getting along. Sean knew what it was like to be on a show like this, where cameras follow you all the time. So, there was a certain understanding and empathy between the two of us."

# Farewell, My Lovelies

## (The Departure)

**JASON:** "It was a full day of torture. I hate saying good-bye, so I usually don't. If I'd had my druthers, I'd have split in less than thirty minutes. Instead, I had to be the last one to go."

**GENESIS:** "Saying good-bye was the hardest thing I've ever had to do in my entire life!"

**SYRUS:** "I just sprinted down the runway. I bawled enough in my interview a few weeks before, so I didn't want to go through that again."

**ELKA:** "I wanted to be the first to leave, so I didn't have to say good-bye to everybody. I felt really attached to some of those people. I definitely shed a few tears, that's for sure. But it was time for me to go home."

**MONTANA:** "Ugh! It was really hard seeing everybody go. Whether we got along or not, we'd certainly been through quite an experience together."

**SEAN:** "Saying good-bye was as hard as s**t, especially because we weren't allowed to hug the crew."

**KAMEELAH:** "I was really, really sad. I got very close to some people and I knew I was going to miss them a lot."

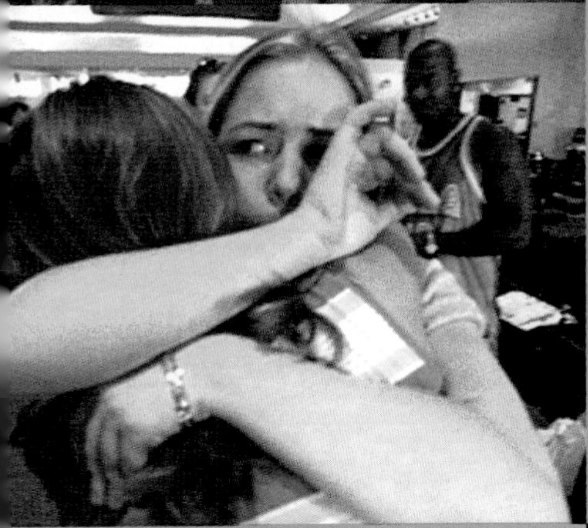

**JIM JOHNSTON (producer):**
**"Everyone was sobbing. And I mean everyone! The cameramen were having trouble seeing through their viewfinders because they were crying so much. They had to tie bandannas to their lenses to wipe away their tears between shots."**

**BILLY RAINEY (director):**
**"I've worked on *Real World* since San Francisco and I've never witnessed a scene like that. The entire cast and crew were a wreck."**

# Quiz BOSTON

## MULTIPLE CHOICE

1. **What did Genesis consider hiding from her female roommates?**
   a. That she's gay
   b. That she's named after a band led by Phil Collins
   c. That she's the first book of the Bible

2. **What did Elka attempt to hide from the cameras and her roommates?**
   a. Her Spice Girls CD
   b. Her smoking
   c. Her cold medicine

3. **What "house rule" did Kameelah and Montana institute with Syrus in mind?**
   a. No basketball in the house
   b. No guests upstairs
   c. No guests in bed unless you know their names

4. **What did Montana "rat" to the head of the After School Program about Syrus?**
   a. That Syrus was dating one of the kids' mothers
   b. That Syrus was dating one of the kids' fathers
   c. That Syrus was dating one of the kids

5. **What did Kameelah say she did when ever she wanted to "dismiss" someone?**
   a. Roll her pierced tongue
   b. Roll her eyes
   c. Roll cookie dough

6. **What activity didn't Sean teach to the kids in the After School Program?**
   a. Logrolling
   b. Model airplane-ing
   c. Sky diving

7. **What did Jason teach to his kids at the After School Program?**
   a. Journaling
   b. Mime
   c. Cousin Bill's "State of the Union Address"

8. **What religious icon was featured on Montana's nightlight?**
   a. The Virgin Mary
   b. The Bloody Mary
   c. Peter, Paul & Mary

9. **What was one of the primary purposes for the cast's trip to Puerto Rico?**
   a. To attend a Masai tribal wedding
   b. To meet men and sleep with a crew member
   c. To set up "CU See Me" at a local after-school program

10. **What pair did not kiss on the trip to Puerto Rico?**
    a. Montana and Raphael from the hotel
    b. Sean and Erika from *Road Rules*
    c. Elka and Puck from *Real World–San Francisco*

## DID THEY REALLY SAY THAT?

**Which lines were really said by cast members on *The Real World–Boston* and which lines are fake?**

11. ELKA: "Is anybody Catholic here?"

12. GENESIS: "Almost every girl I've ever encountered thinks that I like her when they find out that I'm a lesbian."

13. JASON: "Timberrrrrrrrrrrr..."

14. KAMEELAH:"I think people need to ease into me."

15. MONTANA: "If I kiss some guy in a bar one night, I don't want it to ruin my relationship."

16. SEAN: "Does anyone mind if I climb this tree?"

17. SYRUS: "Show me the honey!"

## MATCH GAME

**Match the member of the British Invasion mock band, *ScotchTape,* with his or her alias:**

| | |
|---|---|
| 18. ELKA | a. Cheeky Simon |
| 19. JASON | b. April Christ |
| 20. MONTANA | c. Charlotte BloodyJaw |

## MULTIPLE ROMANCES

**21. Where did Elka meet her boyfriend, Walter?**

a. Traveling in Greece

b. Attending a *Babe* convention

c. On the set of the *CBS Evening News*



**22. What agreement did Vaj and Montana make before she left for Boston?**

a. To date other people

b. Not to date other people

c. Not to kiss on the first date

**23. How did Jason "retaliate" against Timber for kissing another guy?**

a. He kissed another guy

b. He kissed another girl

c. He kissed off Timber

**24. What does *not* appear in Kameelah's list of "Things I Require in a Man"?**

a. Sings to me

b. Cooks for me

c. Dresses like me

**25. What is it about Kameelah's friend, Doug, that conflicts with her infamous list?**

a. His name is Doug

b. He has a child

c. He will not eat green eggs and ham

## SCORING GUIDE

20–25: As the cast would say, The Bomb! As in, hella score. Ring the Firehouse alarms. Jason wants to write about you in his journal. And Kameelah wants to add you to her "List."

15–19: Phat! The gang wants to take you on the town, while Genesis wants to take you on-line.

10–14: Cheers! Sean and Syrus want to pour you a drink at a place where everyone knows your name.

5–9: Okay, so you still deserve a little something something. Perhaps, Elka will remember to share a swig of her cold medicine.

0–4: The Bomb! As in, you really bombed.

ANSWER KEY: 1.a 2.b 3.b 4.a 5.b 6.c 7.a 8.a 9.c 10.c 11.did 12.did 13.did not 14.did 15.did 16.did not 17.did not 18.b 19.a 20.c 21.a 22.a 23.b 24.c 25.b

# Casting the Big Show

## (How they cast *The Real World—Boston*)

**In the beginning, Bunim/Murray said, "Let there be applicants."**
**And there were applicants—12,234 of them.**
**Here's how the casting directors pared them down to 7.**

**STAGE 1: Videotape/Open Casting Call 12,234 people**
All *Real World–Boston* hopefuls applied in one of two ways:
1) Interviewed at open casting calls in several major cities.
2) Sent in ten-minute videotape responses to the question:
Why would you be a good cast member for *The Real World–Boston?*

**STAGE 2: Written Application 1,500 people left**
A fraction of the original pool received written applications to fill out. If you made it this far, you were in the top 88th percentile of *The Real World–Boston* Class of '97.
Only 12% remaining.

**STAGE 3: Phone Interview 450 people left**
The remaining applicants were asked to aim a video camera at their telephone and record their answers to questions asked by a casting director over the phone.
Only 4% remaining.

**STAGE 4: Semifinal Round Interviews (Regional) 90 people left**
The casting directors and producers flew to several regions of the country and conducted a series of in-person interviews with the semifinalists.
Only .7% remaining.

**STAGE 5: Follows 35 people left**
A camera crew followed the chosen few around for several hours, much the way they do on the show. Most hopefuls were placed in unfamiliar environments to see how they would react.
Only .3% remaining.

**STAGE 6: Final Round Interviews (L.A.) 25 people left**
The finalists were brought to Los Angeles for a half day of interviews with the producers. They were put up in different hotels, so they wouldn't meet any of their potential roommates before the show began.
Only .2% remaining.

**STAGE 7: Winners Notified 7 people left**
The winners were hand-delivered invitations to join the cast of *The Real World–Boston.*

**Only .06% remained.**

## (An Interview with Andrew Hoegl)

# The Casting Director



***What do you look for when you're casting the show?***

"We look for people with strong personalities. The kind of personalities and presence that would project across a room. That's often a good indicator if someone is going to have real screen presence.

"We look for people with interesting histories. Those people tend to have interesting things to draw upon and reveal.

"And we look for people who are at a crossroads in their lives, either personally or professionally. That can mean they've just graduated from high school and are about to go out on their own. Or they could be questioning their career paths and what they're doing with their lives. We want to catch someone on the cusp of some big change, so we can watch it emerge over the ensuing six months."

***Is previous theater or film experience desirable?***

"Absolutely not. It's a liability. When someone is casting for an actor, they're asking them to play someone else. We want our cast members to be *themselves*. People that tend to be theatrical tend not to work so well on our show. People who are more natural and have very strong personalities tend to work the best for us."

***What about movie-star types?***

"The people who tend to work best on this show are the ones who are the most relatable to the audience. We want our viewers to go, 'Wow, I go through that too.' We're not looking for James Dean matinee idols, who have no flaws. You can watch *Melrose Place* and *Beverly Hills 90210* for that."

***Is there a formula or a certain type you're looking for?***

"Casting is very much a puzzle. That puzzle changes depending on the candidates that emerge. We don't say beforehand that we need a basketball player from L.A. and a southern lesbian from Gulfport. That would be futile, anyway. People just fall into our laps and then we try to figure out the best possible group. We want each member of the group to relate to each other enough, so they'll have mutual interests. But we want there to be plenty of differences to generate enough conflict and drama for this show to work."

***In other words, you cast them to fight?***

"A lot of people ask us that. No, it is not our primary goal. However, when you cast people with strong personalities and differences of opinion and put them in the same house together for six months, it's inevitable that they will generate story and drama."

**The Casting Directors' top four ways not to begin your *Real World* application:**

1. **"I want to be an actor or a model…"**
2. **"Get me out of this small town…"**
3. **"I've seen every episode of your show and I'm your biggest fan…"**
4. **"I think the people on your show are real interesting and if I were picked I could be real interesting too…"**

# A Day in the Life of *The Real World–Boston*

## (Monday, June 9, 1997, Day 149)

**8:02 A.M. (Eastern Time)** While no creature is stirring inside (not even a mouse), a production assistant quietly opens a green door, along the side of a turn-of-the-century firehouse, before slipping inside. She crosses a narrow hallway, down one flight through a darkened stairwell, under coiling cables, and, finally, into the "BAT CAVE"—the basement bunker serving as *The Real World–Boston*'s Command Center.

Directly beneath the *RW* Cast's bedrooms, pool room and fish tanks, are converted gas and boiler rooms storing the latest in state-of-the-art camera and sound equipment. The area—no bigger than three side-by-side bowling lanes—is part home-base, part surveillance station for the *RW–Boston* production team. ("This is where the CIA meets C-Span," quips one crew member—only half-jokingly.)

While the seven inhabitants of *RW–Boston* sleep soundly upstairs, BONNIE STEWART—the first of the more than 50-member *RW* Crew—prepares for another day of eavesdropping, videotaping and "hurry-up-and-waiting."

**8:33 A.M.** "Let's see what our heroes are up to," exclaims Segment Director CRAIG BORDERS, as he settles inside the basement bunker. ("Heroes" are what the Crew affectionately calls the *RW* Cast.) Borders carefully examines two items—the "ABOUT LAST NIGHT" and the "HOT SHEET."

The "About Last Night" discloses the Cast's exploits during the previous night:

## ABOUT LAST NIGHT

| | |
|---|---|
| ELKA | "Home all night thinking about Walter." |
| GENESIS | "Home all night on-line." |
| KAMEELAH | "Went to Doug's and watched a movie." |
| JASON | "Did spoken word at the Lizard's Lounge." |
| MONTANA | "Hung out with Sean at B.B. Brewing Company." |
| SEAN | "Hung out with Montana. In bed by midnight." |
| SYRUS | "Hung out all night." |

The "Hot Sheet" lists the Cast's scheduled activities for the upcoming day.

## HOT SHEET

| | |
|---|---|
| ELKA | "No Plans" |
| GENESIS | "No Plans" |
| KAMEELAH | "After School Program all day to finish mural." |
| JASON | "No Plans" |
| MONTANA | "Working at Shelter in A.M." |
| SEAN | "Cardioboxing in A.M. Model Airplanes in P.M." |
| SYRUS | "No Plans" |

ALL CAST (except MONTANA)—
"PARENTS NIGHT @ A.S.P – 6:30 P.M."

**8:42 A.M.** "Is that DOUG?" BORDERS calls out, spotting the first sign of movement upstairs. He eyeballs one of twelve monitors lining the wall in front of him—monitors linked to security cameras strategically placed throughout the Firehouse.

(Security-type cameras are placed in every room in the Firehouse, except the bed and bathrooms, allowing some degree of privacy.)

**8:43 A.M.** "That's definitely DOUG!" confirms BORDERS. "And he's leaving. Quick. Get up there."

**8:44 A.M.** LILLA FIUMI and MARTIN TALTY dash through a heavy metal door separating the Crew's base-of-operations downstairs from the seven residents upstairs.

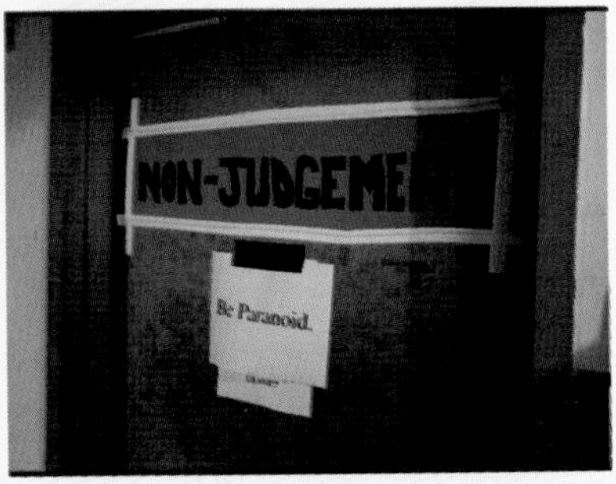


**(The dividing door bears the hand-written sign, "NON-JUDGEMENT," a gentle, self-reminder to the Crew not to "judge" the members of the Cast.)**

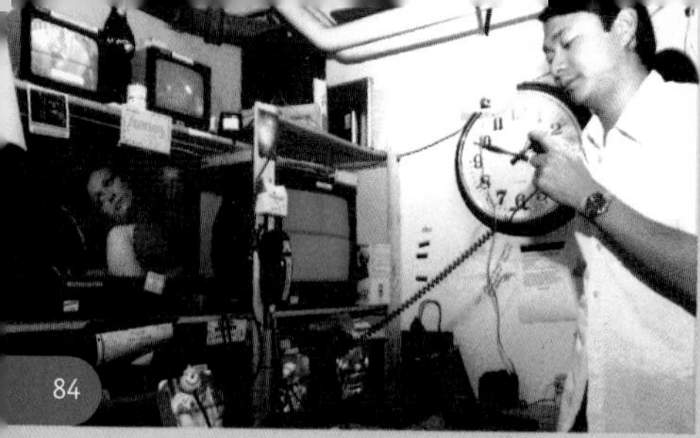



Camera Operator and Sound Mixer race up a narrow staircase leading straight into the Cast's ground floor living room. Just as the pair reach the scene, KAMEELAH is waving good-bye to her close friend, DOUG, who drives off in his car.

Observing the entire scene on his "Bat Cave" monitors downstairs, BORDERS radios into his Camera Operator's ear-piece, "Stay on Kameelah."

**9:08 A.M.** Ten blocks away, Producer JIM JOHNSTON is telephoning the Boston Mayor's office. He's sitting inside the second floor of an ordinary red-brick building, which once housed the Eye Research Institute and now houses a *RW–Boston* production office. An elevated "T" train (the name for Boston's mass transit system) thunders by the window.

Johnston is organizing an end-of-filming wrap party/fund-raiser for the Boston After School Program, an extravaganza that will feature special musical performances by NEIL (of *RW–London*) and his band, Unilever, and MOHAMMED (of *RW–San Francisco*) with his band, Midnight Voices. One thousand spectators are expected and Johnston hopes the Mayor of Boston will be among them.

**9:37 A.M.** Back in the Basement Bunker, the "BAT PHONE" is ringing. (The "Bat Phone" is the only means of direct contact between the Cast and Crew inside the Firehouse. The Cast is asked to check in on the "Bat Phone" whenever they leave the house, or if they have information to share)

"Quiet please," calls out Director BILLY RAINEY, as all talking immediately ceases around him. (The Crew is silent so the Cast gets no hint of the size of the surveillance operation underneath them. "They know we're below them," says Rainey. "They just don't know so many of us are here.")

The caller is JASON. "I'm picking up Timber tonight," he informs Rainey. "But I don't remember the flight number or the arrival time."

**9:41 A.M.** Production Coordinator DWAYNE RAYMOND hands Rainey a note with Timber's flight number and arrival time, after having sleuthed the information from the airline. ("We know their schedules better than they do," Raymond laughs.)

**10:18 A.M.** GENESIS is on the telephone. (The Firehouse has only one outside line—and no Call Waiting.) Genesis is notifying the head of the After School Program that she will not be coming in to work today. "I've got terrible cramps," she exclaims. "I'm just not up to it."

Meanwhile, Director RAINEY is eavesdropping on Genesis' conversation down in the "Bat Cave." (Not only are the telephones tapped, but tiny "lipstick'

**"As far as we're concerned, if something great happens and we're not there to film it...it never happened."**

cameras are placed directly across from the phones.) As soon as Genesis hangs up, the Crew is busy speculating if there's another reason for Genesis' cancellation. The most popular theory—Genesis is terrified of interacting with the parents at Parents Night this evening. ("After doing this show, we all deserve master's degrees in psychology," posits Producer JIM JOHNSTON.)

**11:02 A.M.** The second half of the DAY CREW arrives for work.

(Crews are brought in throughout the day and night on a staggered schedule. Each crew consists of four members—a Director, Camera Operator, Sound Mixer and Camera Assistant.
Each crew works approximately 10-hour shifts, six days a week. Two Crews cover the Cast's daytime activities and two shoot the Cast's nighttime exploits. Generally speaking, more nighttime action gets used on the show than daytime events.)

(With only two Camera Crews at a time to follow seven Cast members, the Directors must continuously choose which "Hero" to film. That explains why the Directors have to stay on top of the Cast's movements."As far as we're concerned, if something great happens and we're not there to film it...it never happened," sighs Director BILLY RAINEY.)

(Most Crew members are under the age of 30—many have worked on several prior seasons of *RW*. "You get sucked in by this show," says Rainey, a veteran *RW*-er since San Francisco. "I thought I'd do it two seasons, tops—not four. Like a friend of mine once said, I'm drawn to it, the same way I need to look inside my tissue every time I blow my nose.")

**11:37 A.M.** A beeper is going off in the middle of the men's section at a Boston department store—a beeper belonging to SYRUS.

"I'm blowing up like nitro," he exclaims with a smile. Syrus doesn't even bother checking the indicator, because he already knows who's paging him—the "Bat Cave." He heads straight for the nearest pay phone and checks in. (Each cast member is given a beeper, so the directors can check on his or her whereabouts at all times. The Cast is "strongly advised" to return all *RW*-related pages within fifteen minutes.)



**11:43 A.M.** Back inside the "Bat Cave," Production Assistant DAMON KARYS is updating a big board on the wall:

| HEROES | IN/OUT | LOCATION |
|---|---|---|
| ELKA | In | Asleep |
| GENESIS | In | Asleep |
| JASON | Out | On Front Stoop |
| KAMEELAH | Out | After School Program |
| MONTANA | Out | Shelter |
| SEAN | Out | Gym |
| SYRUS | Out | Shopping |

"Genesis and Elka are our committed sleepers," Producer JIM JOHNSTON says, glancing up at the top two names on the board.

**12:16 P.M.** SEAN returns home from the gym, looking as if he has something on his mind. He immediately dials up a local sporting-goods store and inquires about climbing gear. He says he'll drop by tomorrow night, then hangs up with a suspicious smirk.

Producer JIM JOHNSTON is monitoring the conversation down in the "Bat Cave." "I think he's planning to scale the Firehouse," Johnston says to Associate Producer STEVE LONGO. "Tomorrow, I want a camera following him to the store."

**12:18 P.M.** Longo immediately calls back the sporting goods store and asks permission to film inside their premises, which they grant.

("Whenever possible, we try to call ahead," Longo says. "We tell people, 'You'll hardly notice we're there.' Most places give us permission.")

**12:54 P.M.** JASON is now making his way up historic Charles Street with a Camera Crew in tow. For most of the ten blocks, the Camera Crew must walk backwards to film Jason. (Camera Crews get very adept at walking backwards.)

**1:09 P.M.** Back at the *RW* production office, Release Coordinators STEPHANIE RICHMOND and TODD SHAPIRO are seated in front of two VCRs, poring over hours and hours of footage. Their job is to connect the releases to the individuals, who have spoken on camera (2,104 releases will be signed during the course of filming *RW–Boston*).

**2:13 P.M.** After more than one hour, three train transfers, five signed release forms and twenty-two minutes worth of raw footage, JASON finally arrives at the East Boston Social Center—home to the After School Program.

## 2,104 releases will be signed during

Most passersby stop and stare. A few yell, "Hi, Mom," into the camera. And one savvy pedestrian shouts, "Yo, Puck."

(The Crews do not identify themselves as working on *RW*, but the show's reputation often precedes them. "We tell everyone that we're working on a documentary," notes Producer Johnston, "Unfortunately, someone usually figures it out.")

**1:07 P.M.** JASON has just boarded a crowded "T" train and is standing beside a woman in her mid-30s. With the camera fixed on Jason, all eyes in the train are also fixed on him—as if to say, "Who the heck are you?" Jason strikes up a brief conversation with the woman until he spots an open seat and plops himself down.

No sooner has Jason turned away from her, then Camera Assistant TRACY CHAPLIN is handing the woman a release form to sign.

**2:13 P.M.** At the same time, but 3,000 miles away, 37 members of the *RW* POST PRODUCTION CREW are already well into their own workday—developing and editing the season's 22 episodes.

The setting is Van Nuys, California—a combination industrial/residential community twenty minutes drive from the famed "Hollywood" sign and twenty-five minutes in the opposite direction to the *RW–Los Angeles* house in Venice.

The place is a two-story building that looks more like a bank than a production company. On the second floor, a brightly colored mural of fish serves as the first indication you've entered the world of *Real World*—it's the very same mural that hung in the vestibule of the *RW–Miami* house.

The atmosphere is commercial-meets-kitsch. The humdrum of white walls, gray carpeting and office dividers is offset by the hip-hop of *RW* mementos. Colorful *RW* applications from the past, such as a letter sent in on a roll of toilet paper and another written on a red-sequined high-heel shoe, are prominently displayed.

The scene is remarkably calm, especially considering that all of *Road Rules* and *Real World* are put together here. Like parents careful to avoid favoring either child, Executive Producers MARY-ELLIS BUNIM and JON MURRAY have divided the work space equally between *RR* on one side and *RW* on the other.

## the course of filming *RW—Boston*

**3:07 P.M.** At one end of the hallway, Day Dubber LUIGI PORCO stands in front of a rack of videotape machines, which are blinking and blipping. Porco is dubbing video shot the previous day in Boston. (An average of 7,000 minutes of video is shot each week.)

**3:33 P.M.** In an adjacent suite, Transcriber STEVE OAKLEY is hunched over his computer, typing a verbatim transcript of every *RW* Cast interview and confessional. (Oakley types eighty words per minute.)

**4:19 P.M** Across from Oakley, four Day Loggers are arranged in a semicircle logging the footage shot in Philadelphia during the "President's Summit on America's Future," which will be featured in Episodes 18 and 19.

(The Loggers note important action and dialogue for the Story Editors, while also marking special visual cues for the Video Editors. During the course of the season, *RW* Loggers will watch every single second of video shot in Boston—more than 11 million seconds of footage overall.)

**4:42 P.M.** Nearby, the four-member Story Department is meeting to discuss the Cast's trip to Puerto Rico, which will be featured in Episode 12.

Story Editors ANDREW HOEGL and JEFF LERNER are exploring a subplot involving MONTANA and RAPHAEL, a handsome Puerto Rican man working at the hotel where the Cast is staying. Hoegl glances at the Directors' notes from that trip, while Lerner pops in a tape of Montana and Raphael's moonlit walk on the beach; Associate Story Editor ROBIN SAMUELS reviews a lengthy transcript of the Montana interview, in which she discusses the date; Story Assistant CANDICE FRANCISCO is fast-forwarding through the footage of Montana and Raphael's farewell.

(Ultimately, the Story Editors will write a brief proposal for the episode, which they'll submit for comment to the *RW* Producers and Directors. Then they'll draft a more detailed treatment, roughly fifteen pages long, and resubmit it for approval. Once the requisite changes have been made, this so-called "paper-edit" will be passed on to the video editors, who'll begin cutting Episode 12.)

("In general, we look for the hot-button moments in a day," notes Story Editor Andrew Hoegl. "Like, do I kiss this guy or don't I?")

**5:17 P.M.** A hop, skip, and jump away from the story meeting, Editor SARAH GARTNER is holed up inside her editing bay just beginning to make the first cuts

on Episode 11—the one where WALTER tells ELKA he's coming to visit. On either side of Gartner, other editors are cutting different episodes of *RW–Boston*.

(During the summer months, a total of ten *RW* episodes are being cut simultaneously. Each half-hour show—approximately twenty-two minutes without commercials—takes roughly ten weeks to edit, requires an average of four "cuts," or versions, and contains an average of 300 separate edits.)

**6:32 P.M.** In North Hollywood, Postproducer RUSS HELDT, Editorial Director OSKAR DEKTYAR, Postproduction Supervisor SANDRA SOCZKA, and Rerecording Mixer PETER ERATA are putting the finishing touches on Episode 2. The group is using a highly sophisticated on-line editing system to minimize less sophisticated sounds, like bird noises and car horns, which make it difficult to hear important dialogue.

After this stage is completed, a nearby editing suite will be used to blur images that can't be shown on TV. ("Generally speaking," Soczka explains, "we blur out no-no images—like naked breasts or butts.")

**7:18 P.M.** Back in East Boston a baby cries, creating exactly the kind of sound that makes it difficult to hear important dialogue. It's Parents Night at the After School Program. ELKA's kids are in the middle of performing The City Mouse and the Country Mouse in front of a room full of parents and children. Unfortunately, the baby is wailing loudly through the entire second act.

The entire Cast (except for MONTANA) is present. And so is Executive Producer MARY-ELLIS BUNIM, who has flown in from California for the evening's festivities.

As Elka paces nervously in the back of the room, two Camera Crews roam through the crowd, filming the kids on-stage and in the audience. Remarkably, the children seem to ignore the cameras. ("Our kids stopped caring about the cameras the second day they were here," recalls ANTHONY, the head of the East Boston After School Program. "I was far more uncomfortable being filmed than they were.")

**8:14 P.M.** "Let's take this show on the road," bellows Director DAVID PARK, as the Cast begins to depart en masse from the East Boston Social Centers.

Park quickly dispatches one Crew to follow KAMEELAH and GENESIS on the "T" train, while another jumps inside a van to follow SYRUS, SEAN and ELKA. No one follows JASON, as he heads to the airport to pick up TIMBER.

**8:14 P.M** At the same time, Director of Photography STEPHEN McCARTHY is back at the Firehouse, adjusting the lighting before everyone returns.

**(Four times a day, the Crew resets the lighting in the house to reflect the time of day—morning, noon, afternoon and night. Aside from the assorted desk and standing lamps, the Cast has no control over the lighting inside their house. In fact, they're dependent on the Crew to switch off the lights in their own bedrooms whenever they wish to go to sleep.)**

(Before the Cast arrived in Boston, 10,000 feet of cable and 50 movie lights were rigged throughout the Firehouse by Lighting Designer VICTOR NELLI JR. In past *RW* seasons, the bright movie lights often heated the house interiors—sometimes more than 20 degrees above the outside temperature. New movie lamps called "Kino Flows" were brought in for the Miami and Boston seasons and the comfort level for Cast and Crew has increased considerably.)

**9:17 P.M.** Back in considerably more comfortable Santa Monica, California, MTV Executives JOHN MILLER and CLAIRE McCABE have just finished viewing the premiere episode of *RW–Boston*. McCabe and Miller phone Executive Producer JON MURRAY to give him MTV's blessing to "lock picture," meaning that no further edits are required.



(In addition to helping develop each episode of *RW*, MTV has the authority to reject any content appearing in the show; it seldom does. "No one knows *The Real World* like its creators—Mary-Ellis Bunim and Jon Murray," says Miller, Vice President for Original Programming and Series Development at MTV, who oversees both *Road Rules* and *Real World*.)

**9:24 P.M.** On the other side of the Santa Monica Mountains, Executive Producer JON MURRAY hangs up with MTV and immediately turns his attention to the *RW–Casting Special*—airing the week before the Boston premiere.

(In any given day, Murray and Mary-Ellis Bunim will review as many as a dozen different episodes of *RW* in their various stages of completion. And that doesn't include the episodes of *Road Rules*, which they must keep on top of as well.)

**10:18 P.M.** No further than Puck-can-shoot-a-snot-rocket away, Manager of Development SCOTT FREEMAN is evaluating potential application questions for next season's *RW–Hawaii*. (The casting process begins in late August and continues until Christmas. More than 10,000 people are expected to apply for *RW–Hawaii*—meaning it's a lot easier to get into Harvard University than onto this show.)

(Incidentally, inside Freeman's top desk drawer is the actual "8" ball that was stolen from the *RW–Miami* house by *Road Rules.)*

**10:34 P.M.** A transcontinental flight away, ELKA is sorting through her belongings back at the Firehouse. She's beginning to prepare for the end of the Cast's stay—now just a week away. Elka grabs her frequently played Spice Girls cassette, examines it a moment, then tosses it in the trash.

**10:38 P.M.** ELKA grabs her Spice Girls cassette out of the trash, walks over to Kameelah's room, and presents it to KAMEELAH as a gift. Kameelah squeals with delight, as she playfully kisses the cassette.

Downstairs in the "Bat Cave," Director DAVID PARK, who's been watching the entire sequence on his security monitor—from Elka's trash to Kameelah's lips—exclaims with resignation, "Damn, I wish we'd been rolling on that."

**11:17 P.M. KAMEELAH exits the Firehouse and jumps inside DOUG's car. But Doug and Kameelah are not alone—Camera Apprentice JORGE ALVES is already tucked into the backseat, ready to film the ride to Doug's house;** a microphone is propped up in the seat beside him to record any dialogue; and a Crew van is trailing two car-lengths behind, loaded with Segment Director DAVE ALBRECHT, Sound Mixer FRANK DEANGELIS and Camera Assistant DAMON KARYS.

(A receiver inside the van—mounted on the dashboard—enables the director to eavesdrop on Doug and Kameelah's conversation. The dialogue is actually transmitted through the van's stereo, so it seems like the director is listening to talk radio—and the hosts are Doug and Kameelah.)

**11:43 P.M.** The Camera Crew arrives in front of Doug's house and jumps out of the van like a *RW* S.W.A.T. team. Several neighbors in this quiet, residential suburb of Boston watch the scene with a combined look of befuddlement and horror.

**11:47 P.M.** Back at the Firehouse, Director DAVID PARK and his Crew are preparing to leave for the Back Bay Brewing Company, where SEAN and SYRUS tend bar. But just as they're about to drive off, Camera Operator GLENN TAYLOR spots TIMBER crying alone on a stoop across the street. But where is JASON? Rather than meet up with Sean and Syrus, Park and company decide to stay here and stake out Timber, sensing a potential confrontation.

**12:08 A.M.** Segment Director ALBRECHT, who is driving back from Doug's house, receives a call on his cellular phone from Director PARK. Park explains what's happening back at the Firehouse and dispatches Albrecht to film SYRUS and SEAN.

**12:16 A.M.** Camera Operator GLENN TAYLOR spots JASON approaching a block away. But Jason spots Taylor, too, and tries an alternate route to avoid the camera.

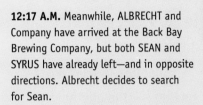

**12:17 A.M.** Meanwhile, ALBRECHT and Company have arrived at the Back Bay Brewing Company, but both SEAN and SYRUS have already left—and in opposite directions. Albrecht decides to search for Sean.

**12:19 A.M.** JASON loses his game of cat and mouse with the camera, as Camera Operator TAYLOR is already in place when Jason arrives in front of the Firehouse.

**12:21 A.M.** Meanwhile, ALBRECHT and Company continue their search for SEAN.

**12:24 A.M. JASON breaks the news to TIMBER that he kissed another girl—a climactic moment in their relationship. Timber sobs uncontrollably, as TAYLOR films from just a few paces away. At one point, Taylor moves even closer. But at no point, do either Jason or Timber ask him to stop filming or try to hide from his lens.**

**12:31 A.M.** Back in downtown Boston, ALBRECHT and Company continue their seemingly futile search for SEAN.

Sound Mixer FRANK DEANGELIS is seated in the back of the van and all eyes are on him. With a wireless microphone receiver cradled in his arms, Deangelis listens intently for any sign of Sean. (Sean's wireless microphone, which all cast members must wear, is so powerful it can transmit a signal from the penthouse of a 25-story building all the way down to the street. So, even if Sean were whispering inside a bar, Deangelis could hear him from two blocks away.)

Suddenly, Deangelis begins shouting, "I've got a hit. I've got a hit...he's around here somewhere." So, Albrecht slows the van to a crawl, as he drives past several packed bars.

"Wait a second...wait a second" Deangelis yells frantically. "He's not in there, he's over there...follow that car. Follow that car!" At precisely that moment, Sean drives across the intersection in a two-door—completely unaware of the passengers and the commotion inside the nearby van.

Director Albrecht takes a quick left and races after Sean. Albrecht pulls up two cars behind Sean and begins tailing him, as though he'd seen too many cop shows in his life. This is Albrecht playing his own version of cat and mouse. The director waits now for an unsuspecting Sean to lead him to some late-night rendezvous.

**12:44 A.M.** Instead, SEAN leads him to...the Firehouse.

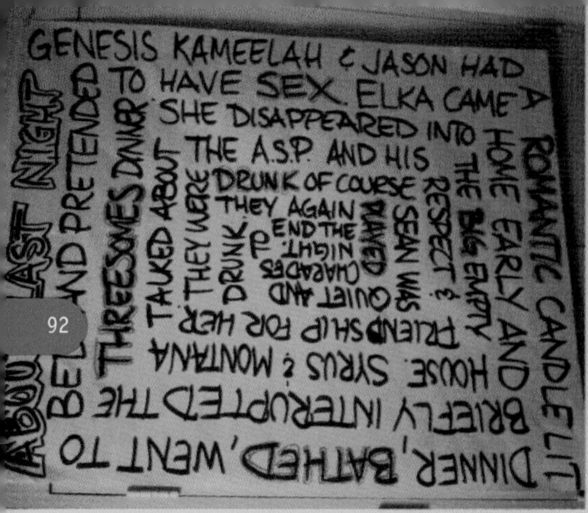




1:47 A.M. The evening begins to wind down for both Cast and Crew. JASON and TIMBER have retired to Jason's bedroom. SEAN is brushing his teeth. KAMEELAH is spending the night at DOUG's place. MONTANA is asleep. SYRUS is out partying. GENESIS is on-line with cyberpal JOE. And ELKA is on her way to bed.

While down in the "Bat Cave," Director PARK teases Director ALBRECHT (he has been doing so for nearly an hour) about their respective contributions on this particular night. "I guess one of us earned his paycheck," Park tells Albrecht, referring to his raw footage of Jason and Timber, which is guaranteed to make one of the *RW–Boston* episodes; Albrecht's misadventures with Sean are sure to make the cutting-room floor.

2:09 A.M. The "Bat Phone" rings. It's GENESIS calling to ask the Directors to switch off the lights in her bedroom, so she can go to sleep.

**2:16 A.M. As a precautionary measure, PARK says to ALBRECHT, "We ought to check on JASON and TIMBER to see if they've started arguing again."**

**Expecting to hear angry screams—the pair hear amorous moans, instead. The Directors decide to give the coital couple a little privacy.**

**("We're voyeurs for work, not for sport," Albrecht explains. "We allow them some privacy, especially when something doesn't relate to the show.")**

2:47 A.M. Production Assistant DAMON KARYS carries out the "Bat Cave" trash, certain that all "vital documents" have been shredded. (During the winter, a major Boston newspaper ran a feature story based largely upon material it "scooped" out of the *RW–Boston* trash. Paper shredders were immediately brought in to avoid future instances of trashy journalism.

**3:19 A.M. As the evening winds to a close, Director ALBRECHT does a quick check of the house to make certain nothing "relevant" is being missed. He hears MONTANA and ELKA whispering to each other. Immediately, he dispatches a Crew upstairs.**

3:20 A.M. The Crew knocks on the wall outside the girls' room. (There are no actual bedroom doors, only curtains. But the Crews knock before entering the bedrooms for the sake of courtesy.) On this occasion, ELKA and MONTANA stop their conversation as soon as the Crew announces itself.

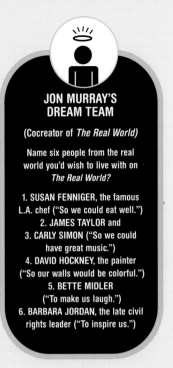

**JON MURRAY'S DREAM TEAM**

**(Cocreator of *The Real World*)**

**Name six people from the real world you'd wish to live with on *The Real World?***

1. **SUSAN FENNIGER, the famous L.A. chef ("So we could eat well.")**
2. **JAMES TAYLOR and**
3. **CARLY SIMON ("So we could have great music.")**
4. **DAVID HOCKNEY, the painter ("So our walls would be colorful.")**
5. **BETTE MIDLER ("To make us laugh.")**
6. **BARBARA JORDAN, the late civil rights leader ("To inspire us.")**

3:43 A.M. Director ALBRECHT finishes typing up his notes and the evening's "About Last Night," which he posts on the wall for the MORNING CREW.

## ABOUT LAST NIGHT

| | |
|---|---|
| ELKA | "Home all night thinking about Walter." |
| GENESIS | "Home all night on-line." |
| KAMEELAH | "Went to Doug's and watched a movie." |
| JASON | "Told Timber he cheated on her." |
| MONTANA | "Quiet night." |
| SEAN | "Quiet night." |
| SYRUS | "Out all night." |

4:02 A.M. ALBRECHT exits the Firehouse into the darkness. Nineteen hours after the first arrival, he is the last departure among the more than fifty members of the *RW–Boston* family, scattered from coast to coast. Many have never met, but all have played a part in transporting you to *The Real World*.

As Albrecht locks the door behind him, he says with a smile, "They have four hours of peace...and so do we."

# Miami

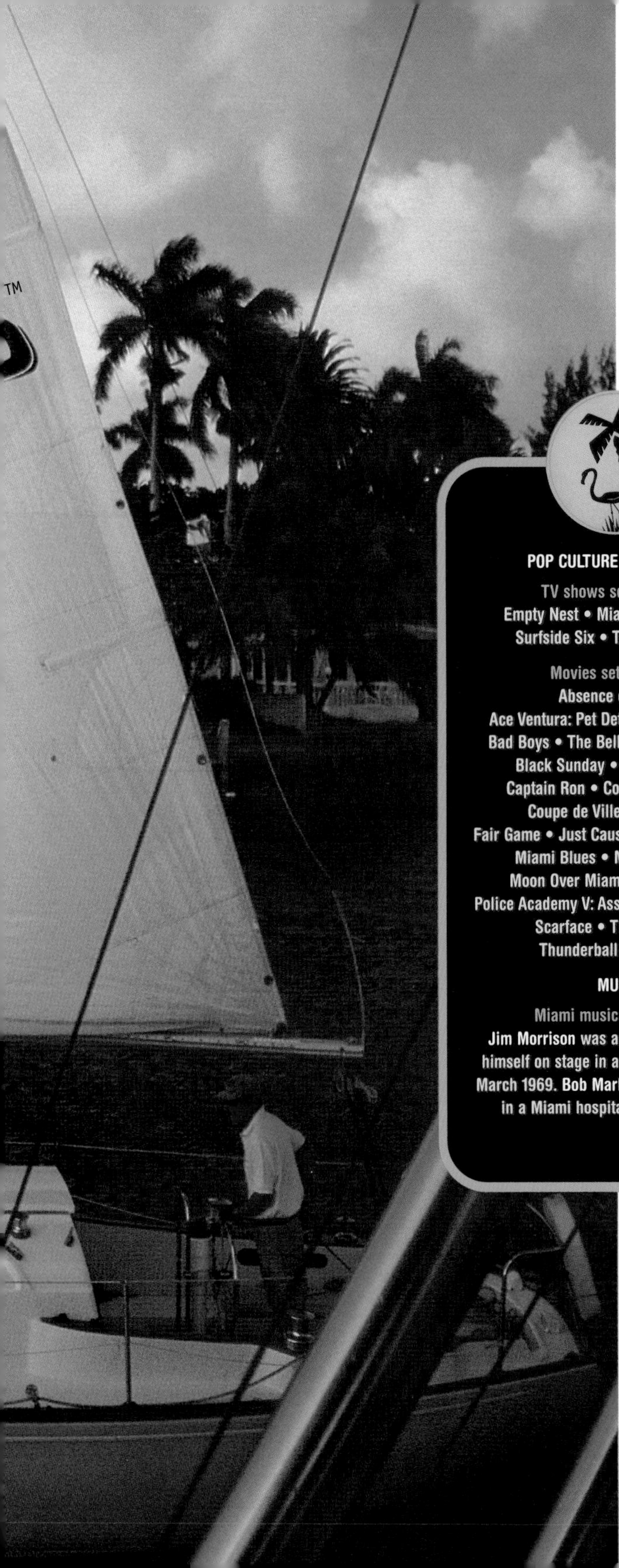

**POP CULTURE LANDMARKS**

TV shows set in Miami:
**Empty Nest • Miami Vice • Nurses**
**Surfside Six • The Golden Girls**

Movies set in Miami:
**Absence of Malice**
**Ace Ventura: Pet Detective • Airport '77**
**Bad Boys • The Bellboy • The Birdcage**
**Black Sunday • The Bodyguard**
**Captain Ron • Cocoon: The Return**
**Coupe de Ville • Dead Bang**
**Fair Game • Just Cause • The Mean Season**
**Miami Blues • Miami Rhapsody**
**Moon Over Miami • Perez Family**
**Police Academy V: Assignment Miami Beach**
**Scarface • The Specialist**
**Thunderball • Too Much**

**MUSIC**

Miami musical highlights:
**Jim Morrison was arrested for exposing himself on stage in a Miami auditorium in March 1969. Bob Marley, 36, died of cancer in a Miami hospital on May 11, 1981.**

# Class of '96
## The Miami Cast

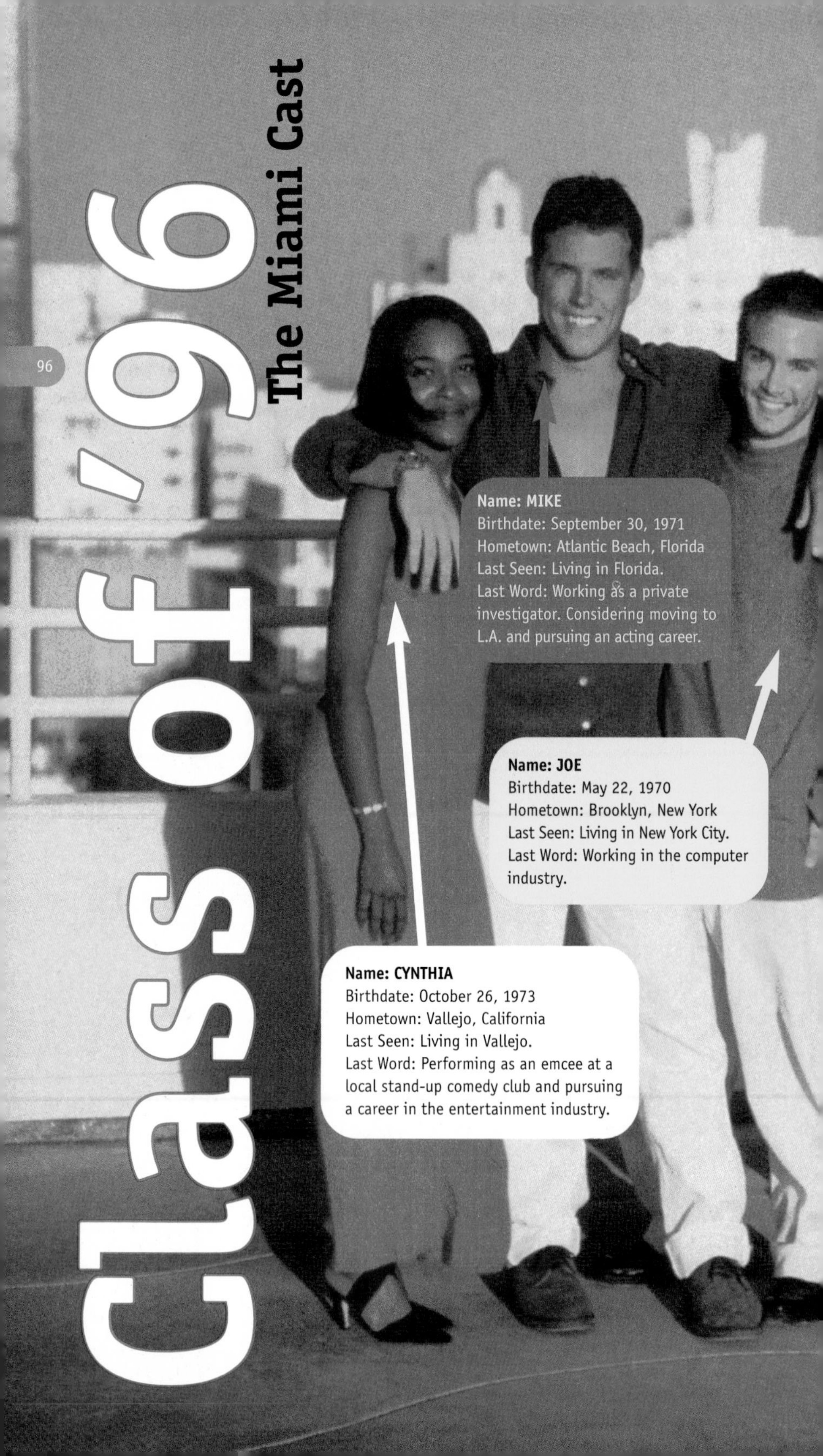

**Name: MIKE**
Birthdate: September 30, 1971
Hometown: Atlantic Beach, Florida
Last Seen: Living in Florida.
Last Word: Working as a private investigator. Considering moving to L.A. and pursuing an acting career.

**Name: JOE**
Birthdate: May 22, 1970
Hometown: Brooklyn, New York
Last Seen: Living in New York City.
Last Word: Working in the computer industry.

**Name: CYNTHIA**
Birthdate: October 26, 1973
Hometown: Vallejo, California
Last Seen: Living in Vallejo.
Last Word: Performing as an emcee at a local stand-up comedy club and pursuing a career in the entertainment industry.

Name: DAN
Birthdate: July 2, 1974
Hometown: Overland Park, Kansas
Last Seen: Living in New Jersey.
Last Word: Graduated from Rutgers University in June 1997. Continuing to model and act. Considering pursuing a career in economic policy.
Name: SARAH
Birthdate: November 3, 1970
Hometown: Zion, Illinois
Last Seen: Living in Los Angeles, California.
Last Word: Working at the Disney Channel and still skating up a storm.
Name: FLORA
Birthdate: September 18, 1971
Hometown: (born) Odessa, U.S.S.R. (raised) Brookline, Massachusetts
Last Seen: Living in Miami Beach (with Mitchell).
Last Word: Working in commercials and bartending. She and Neil (from *Real World-London*) cohosted the MTV home video, *The Real World You Never Saw*.
Name: LEROY
Name: MELISSA
Birthdate: June 2, 1973
Hometown: Miami, Florida
Last Seen: Living in Miami.
Last Word: Graduated magna cum laude from the University of Miami in May 1997. Planning to pursue a career in broadcast journalism.

# the house

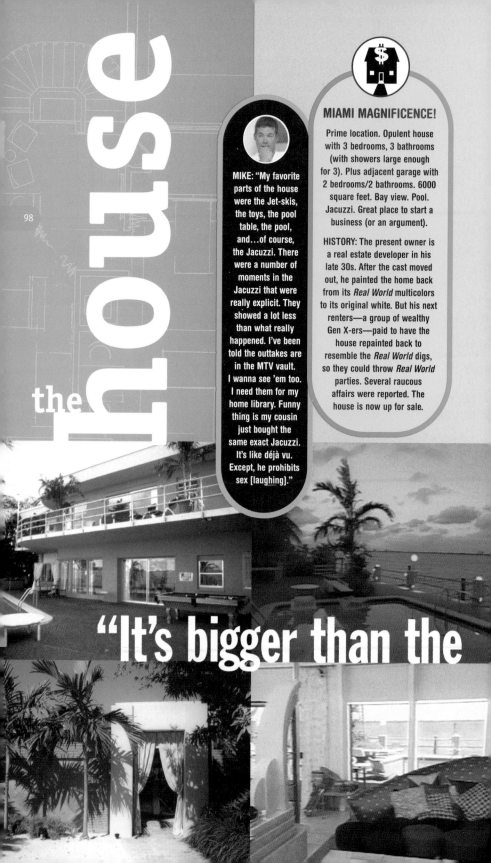

MIKE: "My favorite parts of the house were the Jet-skis, the toys, the pool table, the pool, and...of course, the Jacuzzi. There were a number of moments in the Jacuzzi that were really explicit. They showed a lot less than what really happened. I've been told the outtakes are in the MTV vault. I wanna see 'em too. I need them for my home library. Funny thing is my cousin just bought the same exact Jacuzzi. It's like déjà vu. Except, he prohibits sex [laughing]."

## MIAMI MAGNIFICENCE!

Prime location. Opulent house with 3 bedrooms, 3 bathrooms (with showers large enough for 3). Plus adjacent garage with 2 bedrooms/2 bathrooms. 6000 square feet. Bay view. Pool. Jacuzzi. Great place to start a business (or an argument).

HISTORY: The present owner is a real estate developer in his late 30s. After the cast moved out, he painted the home back from its *Real World* multicolors to its original white. But his next renters—a group of wealthy Gen X-ers—paid to have the house repainted back to resemble the *Real World* digs, so they could throw *Real World* parties. Several raucous affairs were reported. The house is now up for sale.

"It's bigger than the

DAN: "My favorite part of the house was the front door...when I was walking away from it. That's the truth! It was a beautiful house, but who gives a s**t. It was pretty, but it wasn't very comfortable. It was all for show. Not for comfort."



CYNTHIA: "I was cool with the Jacuzzi. But I didn't want none of that funny s**t floating on me. That pissed me off. Hell, yeah! Drain it before I get my little ass in there."

## design tip

from J. MARK HARRINGTON (Designer, *RW-Miami* and *RW-Boston):* "Fabric! It's cheaper than paint. Use it in ways you normally wouldn't—on walls, floors....Fabric and paint is all you need."

# Playboy Mansion!"

—SARAH

SARAH: "I liked sitting on the kitchen counter, playing with Leroy. He would always grab my feet when I sat there. I hated the couches. They were uncomfortable, except for the yellow one. That was totally comfortable. And I loved the pool. I used it every day."

## FOUL OR FINICKY

CYNTHIA: "I was the neat person and Dan was the slob. You'd think a model would be cleaner. He was a clean-cut-looking guy. But he's a damn slob. I cleaned all the time."

SARAH: "I was the neat one. The slobs? A toss-up between Dan's dishes and Melissa's newspapers."

MELISSA: "That's amazing that Sarah would say I was a slob. Everyone kept saying how anal and neat I was and needed to get over myself!"

FLORA: "My side of the room was always messy. My bed was never made. My clothes were all over. But Dan was really slobby and dirty. And Cynthia and Melissa were neat freaks."

MIKE: "I'm generally a slob, but in Miami I was pretty neat. But then again, anyone was neat compared to Dan. His bed was never made. He also had this rotten toe with fungus. Joe and I would go into the bathroom and he'd be putting foot spray on it. He was just dirty. And he'd admit it, too."

DAN: "I can't help it. I'm a slob. But I'm not dirty. I'm just a slob. I am perfectly hygienic. There's a difference between unhygienic and messy. When I'm done with something, I just drop it on the floor until I need it again. Some people in the house were anal. Cynthia is so anal. And Melissa has an obsessive-compulsive disorder. But enough of that; I'm trying to temper my criticisms of everyone."

MELISSA: "I loved the couch. But I hated the front driveway. Whose idea was it to make it out of sand? Every time we went outside our shoes filled with sand."

FLORA: "The only cozy place in the entire house was inside my car. Not one room was cozy. And there was only one place I could go with my boyfriend—the shower—'cause the microphones weren't waterproof. If they had been, I'm sure Mike would've had to wear one on his privates."

**MITCHELL**
Flora's Boston cream pie.

## CYNTHIA

Arrived with fingernails from California; Jacuzzi-ed with Joe; Wanted to drown Nic; Gushed about Trevor; Got over Trevor; Shed tears visiting family in Atlanta; Shed roommates and moved out.

## FLORA

Arrived from a bar in Boston; Dating Mitchell; Dated Louis; Flipped over toe bite; Booted kids out of the house; Fought Dan and Hank; Fought through window to see Mike and Melissa and Melody the Waitress.

**TREVOR**
Cynthia's California guy.

**LOUIS**
Flora's Miami meal plan.

## DAN

Arrived from New Jersey; Out-ed Arnie; In-ed with Johnny; Flashed red bikini briefs; Flushed red when letter was stolen; Tested negative for HIV; Tested positive for modeling.

**ARNIE**
Dan's closeted lawyer.

**JOHNNY**
Dan's out-of-the-closet newspaperman.

**LEROY BOW KNOW JACKSON**
Sarah's wonderdog.

## THE BUSINESS

Dream: Coffee Shop #1; Café; Sportswear; Swimwear; Delicious Deliveries; Coffee Shop #2. Reality: Nothing.

## NIC
Joe's New York high-rise.

## MIKE
Arrived at Melissa's; Thought her hot; Hot-tubbed with Joe and Cynthia; Hot and cold on marriage to Heather; Heated up with Melody the Waitress and Melissa; Cooled down on the business.

## JOE
Arrived in heat from New York City; Dreamed of porn; Encountered scorn; Proposed dumping Nic; Proposed marriage, instead; Abandoned business; Business school nearly abandoned him.

## HEATHER
Mike's old ex-girlfriend.

## MELISSA
Arrived with Mike; Fought with Flora; Made up with Flora; Made out with Mike and Melody?; Dated Cesar; E-mailed Hank; Attacked; Packed; Moved out.

## HANK
Sarah's bud; Melissa's on-line tease; And everyone else's most (or least) favorite home-video maker.

## CESAR
Conquered Rome, but couldn't conquer Melissa.

## SARAH
(a.k.a. Snow Leopard)
Arrived with toys; Swam with clothes; Bladed about town; Boasted about superheroes; Hosted friends; Toasted Melissa; Took in Leroy; Took off for San Diego.

# Cynthia

IF *REAL WORLD* WAS MADE INTO A MOVIE, WHO WOULD YOU WANT TO PLAY YOU?
**"Nia Long or Jada Pinkett."**

**MIKE: "I think Cynthia learned the most out of any of us. Considering where she came from and what she accomplished, she showed us all she had huge *cajones*. For one, she'd barely gone swimming in a pool, but there she was snorkeling in the middle of the ocean off the Bahamas. And not only was she incredibly courageous, she was also an extremely good friend. She was the kind of person you wanted to talk to about your issues, because she's such a good listener. And even when things weren't going well in her life, she still tried to see the good in everything and everyone."**

"I didn't give a damn about being on *The Real World*. I applied 'cause I needed a job. Truth is, I wanted to be on the other damn show—*Road Rules*. I never expected to get on *Real World*, especially 'cause so many people were trying out. I couldn't believe it when they picked me. I still don't believe it. When I see reruns, it's like it was someone else. Weird!

"I'm happy with the way I came out. I wished they'd put more emphasis on my family, but I have no complaints. Lots of people said I had them crying. That tripped me out. I think they appreciated how hard it was for me to be the only African-American, living in a house with a lot of people unlike me.

"But the hardest thing for me was waking up every day to filming. **The cameras were always in my damn face. You never forgot they were there. That was my first time in front of cameras. Occasionally I'd do booger-checks to make sure nothing was hanging out of my nose.**

"What came out was how I felt. There's no way I could've been acting. I'm no actress! I'd have been exactly the same way with or without the cameras. I was tripping that I was so normal. I was so regular. I didn't care about my hair. My mother was like, 'Cynthia, that scarf. Did you ever comb your damn hair?' I said, 'Mom, just be glad I didn't have a booger hanging...'

"I couldn't be bothered with what people thought of me. I didn't have a clue what was going on. I didn't know what I was going to do, where I was going to be. Just do whatever Cyn felt. **My only rule was that the audience wasn't gonna see anybody in my bed. Not on TV. I had enough of my business on camera already. I knew my Mama was going to be watching this show and if they filmed someone in my bed I'd have to hear about it from now until eternity. My**

**roommates, to each their own, but I was cool.**

"I met some awesome people. I keep in touch with Sarah more than anybody else. I don't know anyone in the world like her. My family has never met Sarah, but they like her a lot. She's so genuine. I talk with the boys and I'm cool with Flora and Melissa, too. I just don't think I'll be talking to them until we meet up again at a reunion or something.

"Every day I get stopped. Every time I leave my house people yell, 'Hey, Miss Movie Star!' They always ask me the same question: 'What are you doing now?' Simple answer: Making money and paying bills. And they also ask, 'Do you plan to stay in TV?'

**"Do I plan to stay in TV? Hell yes! You bet your ass I will. I don't want to work the rest of my life.**

"My only rule was that you weren't gonna see anybody in my bed."

**WOULD YOU DO IT AGAIN?**
**"Definitely, Yup! I was pretty much a virgin to cameras. So, the next time I'd be sure to be less of myself and act more."**

Right now, I'm the emcee at a comedy club, but I have an acting manager and I'm doing videos, too. I'm in and out of everything. Getting myself out there. Keeping myself going. I never intended to be in the entertainment field, but people just want to give me a chance."

**"The last day of taping, I was, like, 'F**k this! I'm gone. I'm moving. I've got a new job.' I took pots and pans. I took the statues. I took some candles, candle holders and picture frames. Hell yes! I was going to get my money's worth! The crew was rolling with laughter, like, 'Cynthia is being such a fool!'"**

**DID CYNTHIA REALLY SEE JOE NAKED IN THE JACUZZI?**
**"Not all the way naked. But I did see his little thangy-thang down there. I said it was big 'cause I didn't want to embarrass him. But it's not like it was hanging and swinging."**

# Dan

## "Fame is nothing.

"I've had two days—two days—since I did *The Real World* where people didn't stop me and ask about the show. Just two!

**"I went out with this one guy—a casual thing—at a trendy place in New York City. At one point, he puts his fork down and says, 'I need to ask you something. Why is everyone in the restaurant looking at you? I mean, you look good, but not that good.' I said, 'Do you ever watch TV?' When I told him I'd been on *Real World*, he said, 'Is that the show where they put people in a house together and try to make them fight?' 'That's the one,' I told him.**

"I've been critical of the show before, but I wish I could take a lot of it back. I cared way too much what my roommates were thinking. And that was *my* problem. In the end, it doesn't matter. A lot of people talked about me behind my back, so I figured, two can play at this game. Everyone said I gossiped. We all did it to each other. And by the end, it just got nasty.

"But I only started two fights. Once, I lost control with Melissa, which I would do again, and another time I snapped at Joe, because he made some rude comment to me. He even apologized afterward, but it wasn't on-camera. So, in truth, I was hardly a provocateur. But apparently, I got on a lot of peoples' nerves—a lot!

**MELISSA: "If Dan saw a camera, he'd make sure to get his face in front of it. He even did his own lighting."**

**WOULD YOU DO IT AGAIN?**

**"Oh, gosh, I don't know. It took me so long to regroup, put myself back together again and be happy. I know that sounds cheesy New Age. But I was so messed up by the whole experience. It wasn't at all what I expected. It was so intense and all-consuming. I would hope the next time I'd have a lot more perspective and wouldn't get sucked up by it. I'd definitely want to have a better time."**

**MIKE: "When you're one-on-one with Dan, he's one of the greatest guys in the world. But get him in front of people and a camera and he thinks he has to impress.**

**"One day he was on the deck, yelling, 'Oh, my God. Dolphins!' He's jumping up and down. Well, there were no cameras around at the time. So he kept looking over his shoulder, hoping the cameras would arrive. When they finally did, Dan stripped down to his tighty-whiteys, jumped into the damn bay and swam out to the dolphins. The camera and sound guys looked at each other, like, 'What are we doing here?' and walked back into the house. When Dan noticed they'd left, he had the dumbest, disappointed expression on his face. It was hilarious.**

**"He was always talking about himself. One night, Sarah and I heard him say 'I' about sixty times in two minutes."**

# TV is nothing!"

"*The Real World* is always looking for a bad guy, and I came dangerously close to being that person. But thank God I was living with Flora. I could've been portrayed as the really shallow and villainous one, if not for her. I'll tell you, though, I wasn't very happy in the Miami house. I was happy when I was on my own or with my friends. But inside the house, I was always being criticized. I felt like I wasn't given a chance or any credit. After all, I was the one who went out and got a job. I put myself out there. Just about everyone else sat inside and hung out.

**"Take the incident where I appeared in my red underwear. I thought I looked hideous. But I was willing to expose a flaw, and the others jumped all over me. I'd even thought of stuffing my crotch beforehand, but I decided, 'F**k it!'** I really think the others looked bad laughing at me, instead of *with* me. When people take criticism too far, it's so low class. So much of what the others did on the show was really low class.

"I am an attention hog, though. I admit that.

"How did *The Real World* change me? I definitely got more perspective. And I'm more relaxed. The experience helped me to focus on the more important things in life, like my schooling. **I learned that in the end, fame is nothing. TV is nothing! Fame is only glamorous to people who don't have it.**

"Since *The Real World*, I've graduated from Rutgers University with a degree in environmental policy. My goal is to work on economic policy for the government. And, no, I don't plan to run for office. I could never win—Flora would petition against me."

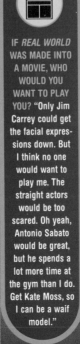

**IF *REAL WORLD* WAS MADE INTO A MOVIE, WHO WOULD YOU WANT TO PLAY YOU? "Only Jim Carrey could get the facial expressions down. But I think no one would want to play me. The straight actors would be too scared. Oh yeah, Antonio Sabato would be great, but he spends a lot more time at the gym than I do. Get Kate Moss, so I can be a waif model."**

SARAH: "Flora was probably the hardest to live with. She would bring home all these weirdoes. But I find her amusing. I don't hate her, even though she's crazy and whack. She's fun! One-on-one she's great. She'd say some hysterical stuff. She's a show pony."

DAN: "Flora should have her own talk show. She was far more interesting than the other six of us combined."

# Flora

## "'Are you really a bitch?'

CYNTHIA: "Flora was a bitch the first day she walked in. She pre-warned us, too. So, we knew she'd be unbearable and she was going to be a nightmare. I respect her for that.

"I think they made her look a lot better on TV. She was much worse in person. Most of the things she did or said you couldn't put on TV. She was so uninhibited. The girl is truly that way. How can she stand herself? Flora has nerve. She has balls. She doesn't care what anybody thinks. I don't know anyone who would've said the stuff about the black s**t to me [laughing]. I was thinking, 'This bitch has some balls.' Everyone sees me and asks why I didn't whip that bitch's ass. 'Cause I love Flora."

"I took 'Charlie the Puppet'—the one flushed down the toilet. He scared everyone, but I liked him. Fact is, there wasn't much left after Cynthia got through with the place. She looted the house. She took boxes of stuff. I had to ask her for one of the picture frames 'cause she took six. She had no shame."

# "Of course, everybody's favorite question is: 'Are you really a bitch?' You know what? I am.

Everyone has one in them. Certain people can bring it out in me. Most of the people on the show brought it out.

"I knew right from the start—just by the way I was chosen—that they wanted a bitch for the show. They found me bartending and I was yelling at people, screaming 'Who wants another drink?' So they didn't choose me to play the preacher's daughter, you know. But I love my character. I get the most publicity. I love it!

**"A lot of kids follow me, like, in the mall. They'll scream out my name and run. I don't bite. But people know not to f**k with me. Forgive my French. They know if they step on me, I'll turn into a monster. As long as people are nice to me, I'm a nice person.**

"I'm that Flora on *The Real World*, but not 100 percent of the time. There is about 10 percent of that person in me. They made her into a whole character. That's fine. I can be a bitchy person. **Screw with me. And I'll screw you right back.** If you're nice to me, though, I'll be more than happy to give you my life and my blood. So, it's part of me. But only a part.

"I'm also fun to hang out with. I'm very carefree. I do what pleases me. If someone doesn't like it, I suggest they turn the other way.

"Like when Mitchell stayed with me. I could care less if the others liked it or not. But he and I never had sex when we were in the house, strange as that may seem. I wouldn't have sex with six other people in the house. I wouldn't disrespect my roommates that way. I'm also noisy [laughing]. I wouldn't do it 'cause I'd be embarrassed. Unlike Mike, who had no shame. I'm a wild person, but I respect people.

"But those three kids that Sarah brought to the house, well they had no respect for anyone. The viewers didn't see what actually went on. They were grabbing Cynthia's boobs, Melissa's ass. To me, kids or no kids, you don't *disrespect* people. You don't do s**t like that. I'd baby-sat them all day. No one made a point of saying that. I watched them in the pool. I fed them. They were out of control. And if they had gotten hurt, we'd have been in big trouble. **If I had a choice (and it was legal), I'd have spanked those kids.**

"As for our business, I think the producers set us up to fail. Pool. Beach. Jet-skis. Jacuzzi. Think about it. All that fun stuff. Seven people, who don't know each other, and fifty grand...which, by the way, is absolutely nothing. You couldn't start a business with your own mother or father with fifty grand. It was all for show.

"Everyone asks me about my toe. 'Was that fake?' Absolutely not! But it was funny. I think the whole incident was even funnier in person. I *am* absolutely petrified of needles. I was

You know what? I am."

on crutches and the doctors gave me Percoset painkillers. The whole thing was hilarious.

"As for Mitchell, we're still together. We're living down here in Miami. **It was always Mitchell. Louis was just a job. I needed a job, you know. He was a good guy, but I don't like to be used. So once I found out I was being used, I said, 'Hey, I'll use you right back. And when I'm done... see ya' later buddy.'**

"What do I miss most about the show? Absolutely nothing [laughing]. I live in a wonderful, big, huge apartment now with Mitchell. I have access to a boat and Jet-skis. I have lots of friends around me, but they're not in my house. I don't miss anything. I'm enjoying the leisure life now. I didn't do *The Real World* to become an actress. I'm basically doing nothing right now, just some commercials and independent projects. But mostly leisure. Hey, I live on the beach.

"I still see Melissa. In fact, one of the best things about the whole experience was Melissa. But I don't want to have anything to do with the others, although Sarah was also fabulous. She was great. She showed her real colors by the end. I wouldn't have wanted to room with anyone else, which is funny 'cause I'm so close to Melissa. But I had good times with Sarah.

**MIKE: "Granted, Flora can be a bitch. She can be. But Flora and I were, and still are, great friends. We don't see each other all that much now, but when we do, we have a good time."**

**"Do I have any regrets? No. None. If I'd known more about what was involved, I might have done a few things differently. But I didn't, so all I could be was myself. I wasn't acting. I'm not ashamed of anything. I can be fun to hang out with. And I can be a big grouch, too."**

**IF *REAL WORLD* WAS MADE INTO A MOVIE, WHO WOULD YOU WANT TO PLAY YOU? "Sharon Stone, baby! That chick is me."**

**WOULD YOU DO IT AGAIN? "With six people? Never again! I'd never live with more than one. Too much interference."**

# Joe

## "Thank God it's over. Honest."

**CYNTHIA: "A lot of people ask me if I had a crush on Joe. He's cute...for a white guy [laughing]. No, he's okay. He's got a nice set of teeth and his breath never stinks, 'cause he's always chewing gum. I like that. But Joe's not my type. We were like brother-sister. And I was *never* jealous of Nic. Why would I be jealous of her? I look a lot better than her. I don't give a f**k what anybody says. She looks like a man."**

**What did you feel like at the end of doing *The Real World*?** "Thank God it's over. Honest. This was one hell of a learning experience for me—learning about what I do and don't want." **What did you get out of the experience?** "I got the two things I wanted to get out of it, when I applied to the show—I gained personal growth and I gained the best relationship of my entire life, my relationship with Nic." **Who do you think was the real-est of your *Real World* cast?** "Leroy, the dog, was the only real one in Miami Beach. That's a sad commentary on our group of seven, but at the same time it's one hell of a thumbs-up for animals and Leroy." **What do you predict your fellow cast members will be doing in five years?** "**Cynthia** will most likely be a broker of buildings and apartments. She'll have some knowledge about the housing industry and will be our connection into getting a roof over our heads. **Dan** will finally get the modeling thing out of his system by year 5, return to school and focus on what is deep in his heart—writing and giving back to the community and the earth. **Flora**, well, honestly I don't know. I just don't know. **Mike** will be wealthy in five years, isn't that when he receives all his money? Ah, Mike will be golfing a lot in five years. Mike will be relaxing in some kind of green, blue, watery area in five years...entertaining people and making them laugh. **Melissa** will be in the minds of some young men's dreams and on the covers of tabloid magazines everywhere, loving every minute of it. **Sarah** will probably be exactly where she is now—a comic book editor—doing what she absolutely loves. While at the same time, she'll be managing her own publishing dynasty of skateboarding magazines and paraphernalia." **What about yourself?** "In five years, I'm gonna have myself completely immersed in technology one way or another. Probably somehow connected to the entertainment industry, because I got a taste of it on the show and thought it was awesome."

**MIKE: "It appeared like I was jealous of Joe. I wasn't. It's just that everyplace we went, girls instantly had a crush on him. I didn't care. I really didn't. I got my share."**

# "We're a bunch of horny, crazy people having a good time in a big house!"



# Melissa

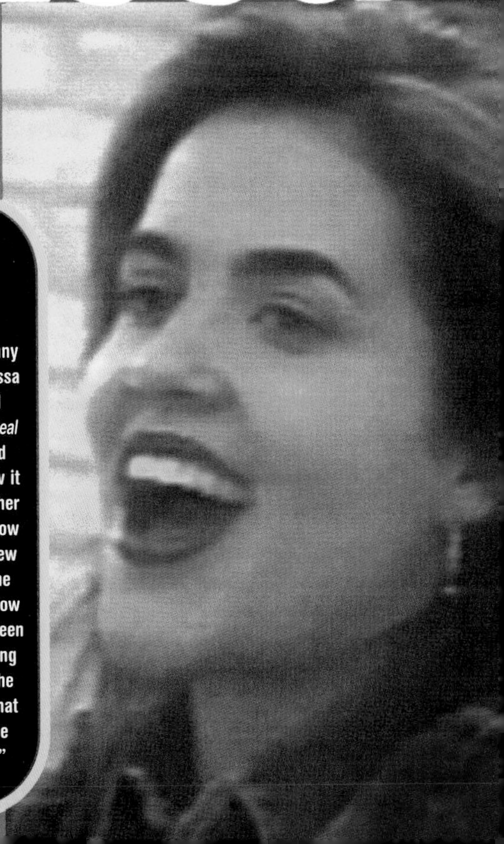

**How would you describe *The Real World* to the uninformed?**
"*The Real World* is entertainment. It's fun to watch. It's a soap. **We're a bunch of horny, crazy people having a good time in a big house!** I don't think it teaches anyone anything about tolerance. In a way, it reinforces stereotypes. Latin people come up and support me. In their eyes, I could do no wrong. They all disliked Sarah. All my African-American friends say, 'Cynthia is *the* s**t. She can do no wrong. She's the best.' All my gay friends beg me to put them in touch with Dan.

**SARAH: "The funny thing about Melissa was that she'd studied all the *Real World* books and shows. She knew it like the back of her hand. I didn't know s**t. But she knew exactly what she was doing. So, how could she have been unhappy revealing herself, when she knew exactly what was going to be put out there?"**

'Oh, my God. He's so fine. You have to introduce me to him.' Each of us project what we want on people."

**Was the experience what you expected?**
"When you go in to interview, they tell you a million times it's going to be stressful and emotionally draining. You get every warning in the book. But when I watched the show, everyone seemed to be having such a good time. Well, our group got so sick of each other. We were so tense and stressed, and it showed. You can't create episodes like ours unless the cast is crazy and off-balance."

**Why was it so "stressed"?**
"A lot of the problem resulted from people hogging the camera. Actually, for me, it was a relief when they weren't filming. It was like freedom! One time, Flora and I tried to make a getaway without the cameras. We began to drive off

IF *REAL WORLD* WAS MADE INTO A MOVIE, WHO WOULD YOU WANT TO PLAY YOU? **"I'd love to say Salma Hayek but she's Mexican, not Cuban. And she has a wayyyy better physical appearance than I do. So, I'll have to play myself."**

in her Jeep. One of the cameramen got in the way and she ran over his foot."

**Did you feel like your true self came out?**
"As the weeks went on, I got so disillusioned. The director would say to me, 'You're not giving of yourself. You're very protective.' I think there was a competition among the seven of us. There was always talk, like, 'Do you think you'll get a job with MTV when this is over?' That was not what we were supposed to be thinking. As the years go on, it must be harder and harder for the producers to make a show that's real. People watch the show now and know how they're supposed to act."

"I took a vase. Now I look at it and go, 'Free!' Flora swiped everything else I wanted. I heard Cynthia took the rest."

**Do you regret having done the show?**
"I have no regrets. None! Well, I think I would have hung out with my roommates less and kept more to myself. But I had to work with them on the business and that caused chaos between us. I wanted to dedicate myself to them. Get to know them. And I think it ended up backfiring. We just got sick of each other. I was one of the most blunt people in the house. I mean, I'd just say stuff and people would freak, especially Cynthia 'cause she's so anti-sex."

**WOULD YOU DO IT AGAIN?**
"No, I wouldn't. Not with six people. I have always lived alone and I will for the rest of my life, except for family."

**Any fond memories?**
"I have certain memories of the show that are great, like, when my mom cooked dinner for everyone. The first week was the best. There was no competition, no bitterness, no 'why are you taking the microphone off of me and putting it on him.' We went clubbing every day. That was great."

**Have you watched your episodes?**
"I watch them and laugh. Sometimes, I watch the show and hate myself. I'm so obnoxious. I'm thinking, 'I even hate me!' In the beginning, I was, like, 'They're going to hate me. They're going to think I'm this year's Rachel.' When the Dan episode aired, I thought for sure the honeymoon was over. But when I went out, the opposite happened. I was mobbed. People loved that stuff. They eat it up. I've told Flora, 'You were the smart one. You were such a bitch, and that's why everyone loves you.' I should've been worse!"

**What else do you hear from fans?**
"'You're soooo nice. You're not a bitch. Not at all like TV. What happened?'"

**What are you up to these days?**
"I finished school in May and not a moment too soon. I'm so excited. I was studying broadcast journalism, theater and political science. I want to do entertainment news out in L.A. I want to be on *Entertainment Tonight* or *Access Hollywood*. I know it's a cutthroat business and there's no loyalty, but I plan to pursue it anyway."

**CYNTHIA:** "I love Melissa to death, but she was, like, this big-ass phony. She tried to keep up this facade, but it's bound to come out. I'm, like, 'Just be yourself.' She acted differently when the cameras were off. She'd talk about everything. I think the directors were very easy on her."

**MIKE:** "It's true, Melissa and I did have a slight attraction to each other. But it got to the point where no one liked her. She got to be such a bitch. Toward the end, I got to like her again. But there was no more attraction."

**FLORA:** "I don't know why everyone had a problem with Melissa. She never did anything but be good to them. At worst, she was neutral. I think they were jealous of her. She's wealthy. She's good-looking. She dresses well. She's very well-mannered. Comes from a good family. It's sad they'd hold that against her. If anything, the others should be pissed at me 'cause I was the one that caused fights."

# "I'd describe *The Real World* as seven people with cameras in their faces, trying to get along, seeing who will have sex with them, who's going to hit them, and who will steal their food."

"I never did anything specifically because I thought the cameras would want to film it. I was, quote-unquote, myself. I think so were Joe, Sarah and Cynthia, at times. But Melissa was full of it, Dan was the master of being an idiot, and Flora hammed it up for the cameras. She tried to act smart, certainly smarter than she is. It was a pain in the ass to me that all these people were trying to prove points. I'd just sit back and have a beer.

"I'm glad they didn't show a lot of me. There was no chance for me to come across as the assh**e I can be sometimes [laughing]. You could tell from the shower scene, I was definitely the biggest partyer in the house. I kept people laughing and I think I contributed more than they showed. I was definitely a lot more active than it seemed on TV. They made me look like some dork who only hung out.

**DAN: "I liked Mike, but I never had a crush on him. Yeah, he's good-looking and nice. But around the third week, the producers were trying to get me to say I had a crush on him. I told them, 'If you want to create intrigue, use someone else. Not me.' I was too smart to play that game. I knew what they were doing. I'd watched the other seasons."**

"At the end of *Real World*'s first season, all the cast was hugging, saying 'We're going to miss you.' **By the end of our show, I just wanted to get the hell out of there. I wanted nothing to do with it. Let's split up the money and go our own ways. Every single thing was so repetitious. Talk...talk...talk. People were moving out early, just to get the hell away from each other.**

"All of us had extremely strong personalities. The business was their way of creating

conflict. I know the producers didn't want a repeat of London. They didn't want another bum season.

"We all had our little tricks to escape the house. Sarah and I went Rollerblading. We kept each other sane, and Joe as well.

"It's an unreal world. There's nothing real about it. Without the cameras it would have been completely different. It was impossible to ignore the cameras, although I got used to them after a few weeks.

**"About the shower incident, all the guys want to know: 'Hey, what happened?'; all the girls: 'You just think you're so cool.' Like, I'm some guy with a huge head on his shoulders**

# Mike

**just trying to get laid. Well, okay... I am. Just kidding.** I've grown out of that phase, you know, where you just want to screw everybody. But I still walk around naked. I have no problem with my body, not that it's a great body. And when I get drunk, I like to have a little fun. Make people go, 'Whoa!'

"I'm now a private investigator working for my uncle's agency. All I need now is a Ferrari and a boss named Higgins. I'm staying with a buddy of mine, looking to buy a condo on the ocean down here. It's still my passion to get back into acting, which I did a while back when I lived in L.A. Anyone that knows me, knows I'm happiest when I'm entertaining people."

**"I got the stuffed piranha and the life preserver. But the producer promised the preserver to Joe, so I had to send it to him."**

**?**

**WOULD YOU DO IT AGAIN? "I would, but mainly 'cause I know now what I didn't know then. I'd do some things differently, especially during confrontations. I'd just sit back and say, 'I don't give a f**k.'"**

**IF *REAL WORLD* WAS MADE INTO A MOVIE, WHO WOULD YOU WANT TO PLAY YOU? "Cindy Crawford...just kidding. I'd have to say, Val Kilmer. Yeah, Val Kilmer. Just to get Cindy Crawford to work with me."**

# Sarah

## "Our only common ground was that

"I didn't do it for the money. I didn't do it 'cause it was on TV. I did it because when an opportunity knocks, you can't ignore it. I thought, 'What do I have to lose?' I wasn't worried about impressing my family. I didn't have to be true to some boyfriend. I didn't have to worry about any of that s**t.

"I took the approach that I was just going to kick back, have fun and explore Miami. That's why I got a job driving a pickup truck. I didn't have a car down there, so it gave me a set of wheels to ride around town.

"I came away from the experience pretty satisfied with who I am. I tried to avoid all the pettiness. I don't deal well with that stuff. I don't know if I changed all that much. Melissa accused me of not liking people who were unlike me. I like everyone. But I just let criticism like that bounce off me. People will always have their own perception. I'm just staying true to myself.

"I'm still a tomboy. Can't seem to outgrow it. Tried the eye shadow and pumps thing, but I'm back to wearing baggy jeans and a T-shirt. Just can't

**MIKE: "Sarah is one of the main reasons I'm glad I did *The Real World.* She's awesome! I talk to her just about every day, and we talk about whatever. We both like to f**k around, play around and be ourselves. Most of the others in the house took themselves *way* too seriously. But Sarah and I just liked goofing on each other—slapping each other's heads or farting on each other.**

**"One of the unique things about Sarah is that she believes in the good in everyone and tries to overlook the bad. She cares about everyone else before herself. Take the kids she brought over to the house. That pissed off some of us, but Sarah was simply trying to make it better for those kids—if just for a short while."**

IF *REAL WORLD* WAS MADE INTO A MOVIE, WHO WOULD YOU WANT TO PLAY YOU?

**"I don't know anyone who has my personality. But, I've always liked Kelly Lynch."**

some people were girls and others were guys.”

“I barely took anything. One of the production guys gave me the 5-ball, which said ‘Real World 5’ on it. Oh yeah, I took all the koosh balls. Definitely!”

get into makeup. Flora and I got into a big fight about how I got my job, which really offended me. She's under the impression a girl needs to dress a certain way to get a job. I thought about hitting her, but why lower yourself?

“I have no regrets about doing *Real World*. None! Only about forty people can say they've done it. I wish I'd seen more of Florida. Yeah, and I wish we'd started the business. Or, at least, called it off right away. The business made everything and everybody so tense. Maybe, if the business had died earlier, we could've hung out more and gotten along. But the tension lasted to the end and we all left on a sour note.

“Truth is, I'm not at all surprised we didn't get along. We had nothing in common. **Our only common ground was that some people were girls and others were guys.** That's about it! We were all so totally different—education, background and experience.

“I still keep in touch with Cynthia and Joe. It's not that I don't want to speak to the others, we just don't. But I don't hold a grudge, not against anyone. I miss the city of Miami the most. God, Miami was awesome. I miss all the friends I met outside the house. I met a lot of great people down there.

“I'm editing comic books now, which I was doing before I did the show. **People point at me just about every day. Every day! Mostly 15-year-old girls. I think they got a kick out of seeing someone just like them, especially the tomboys. I guess that's how they pick us. When young people see someone with the same flaws and problems, they think to themselves, ‘Hey, I'm not so weird after all.’”**

# (an essay) by MIKE

"It's funny, you know. The irony of how a shower is supposed to make you feel clean and refreshed. Yet one time, I got out of the shower and felt just the opposite. Since the airing of the so-called 'shower episode,' I've been asked one question over and over: **"What the hell happened?**

"To be totally honest, I don't remember much. I know that answer pisses off a lot of people, especially the guys who want to hear all the juicy details. Most girls think I'm a disgusting pig. There's no gray area when it comes to people's reactions. They either love what happened or they're totally sickened by it.

"It was definitely a night—a night some of us call 'Ménage Night'—where the alcohol was mightier than the morals. A few of us were invited to the Comedy Zone for an innocent night of comedy and laughter...or so I thought.

"This is where things start to get a little hazy for me. Our waitress, Melody, seemed to really enjoy having the cameras around. She was real inquisitive about us and the project in general. Since she was a nice person with a great smile, I figured, 'Why not invite her back to see the house firsthand?' I don't remember how—or when—we all got home.

"What I do remember is the waitress took an instant liking to Melissa. By that point, Melissa and I really didn't care too much for each other. I can honestly say that I don't recall much of what happened in the Jacuzzi or the shower. But I know that Melissa and I never touched.

## The

"When I woke up the next night, I was informed of all the insane activities that went on the night before. I was told I ran around the house naked; that there'd been some mild forms of fornication in the Jacuzzi; and that Flora nearly killed herself climbing through the bathroom window just to get a peek. To make matters worse, I was dating Heather at the time. I knew I'd done something horrible, and it was on videotape and I could never take it back...or lie about it. To top it all off, Joe told me I owed him money for my share of the drinks. I must've forgotten my wallet, too.

"Do I regret it? Yes! Do I wish I could take it all back? YES! Do I wish it was Cindy Crawford and Elle MacPherson instead? What do you think? And yes, I did use protection.

"Oh, and if I ever get the entire uncut version of the "shower episode" from MTV, I promise to share it with everybody. Except for maybe Heather."

# (a rebuttal) by MELISSA

"Oh, God. I can't believe him. He 'doesn't remember.' He's such a liar. I've been piss-ass drunk and, although I'd like to forget things, I remember everything. What a liar! He knows nothing happened. All the crew guys were, like, 'Nothing happened.'

"So what really did happen? Finally, my chance to tell the true story.

"Mike was passed out in the shower. The girl was freaking out. And Flora broke the window. That's all that happened in that damn shower. The end.

"I've seen the episode. I laugh. But you all can hear is an Arkansas accent. A lot of fans heard it. She said something in between the moaning. Thank God for that. It wasn't me groaning. There's no way in hell Mike could ever get me to moan like that.

"People who know me said I might've done it. In a heartbeat! But not with those two. Perhaps, if it were anyone else but someone from Arkansas and Mike. But them? Noooooo way!

# Shower

"I didn't have sex with Mike in the shower, or in the Jacuzzi, or the ocean, or the entire state of Florida. He's not my kind of guy. Cesar is dark and Latin. I like Latin-looking guys. Dark hair. Hair on their chest, and legs, and butt, and body. Guys with real passion. Mike just sat around all day and drank beer. That's all he did.

"The whole incident was really hard for Cesar and my family. I regret the impact it had on him. Luckily, he and I are still totally together. As for me, I know what really happened. Some of you will believe and some won't.

"So from now on, when people ask, 'What happened in the shower?' I'll just say, 'What do you think?' Whatever they imagine, well then, that's exactly what happened."

**SARAH: "I think the true Melissa came out when she got in the hot tub with Mike and that girl. We would've loved it if she'd just said, 'Hey, this is who I am. I'm a voyeur. I like to get together with girls.' If it were me, I wouldn't have denied it. I was, like, 'Hey, Melissa. Be real.' I think she was afraid of her mom and Cesar finding out."**

**FLORA: "I never made it through the window 'cause my boobs got in the way. So I couldn't really see anything. It was too dark. That is, I didn't see anything with my own eyes. But I did hear Melissa banging on the door. I don't know what she was doing. All I know is that my Mom said it was her favorite episode. And my Dad, too."**

**Name: LANDON**
**Age:** 54
**Occupation:** Entrepreneur
**Income:** "Mid six figures"
**Career Highlight:** "Building a management team of all types to operate 25 Blockbuster stores in eight states."
**Business Philosophy:** "The best way to get good business experience is to seek good mentors, then roll up your sleeves and get to work."
**Secret Ambition:** "To become a novelist and produce feature films."

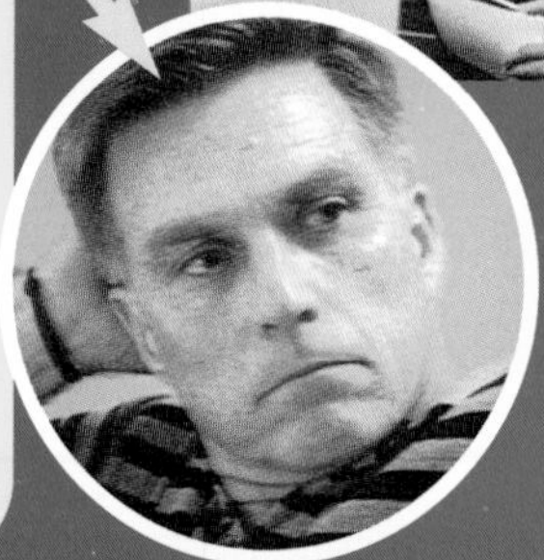

# the Business

**LANDON (The Business Adviser):** "I know some people think we 'blew it.' Many told me that if they'd been given fifty grand, they 'could've made it work.' But I don't think we failed—I think we showed how incredibly hard it is to build a business. If anything, we demonstrated what actually happens in the real, real world—that humans have conflicts that make it difficult to work together.

"If you ask me, I think the likelihood of the business succeeding on the show wasn't that great to begin with. We had seven people—all with powerful personalities and opposing agendas—who were not only working together, but living together as well. So, whatever personal conflicts they had were also being dragged into the business. On top of that, just a few cast members had any prior business experience, so everything we discussed was completely new to them. And I haven't even mentioned the pressure of the cameras, yet.

"You know, I honestly believe the cast should be proud of what they accomplished. Why? Because after all their arguments and missteps, they actually came up with a very solid business idea—Delicious Deliveries. I'm not saying a cake delivery company was destined to become the next McDonald's, but their venture had great potential.

"So what went wrong? Well, as I said before, it's not easy getting any group to agree, especially one with as many distractions and pressures. I think the only way Delicious Deliveries could've worked is if the entire cast had agreed to let Mark run the business. But that would've required making Mark a 50 percent partner, which would've forced the cast to accept a diminished role as silent partners. And few members of the cast were willing to remain silent—in any way, shape or form.

"As for me, I didn't apply for this job—my name was proposed to the show's producers by a colleague, unbeknownst to me. I have five sons—ages 7, 10, 15, 16 and 22—and the three oldest are avid *Real World* watchers, so I knew of the show. But, of course, you never really know what it's going to be like, until you're actually on it.

"Failed or not, the *Real World* business venture—or adventure—only increased my admiration for the cast. Thankfully, my kids feel the same way about me, too. I've gone from being a geek dad to a major-league cool dad, just for being on *The Real World*."

## LANDON'S INDIVIDUAL CAREER ADVICE

CYNTHIA "Cynthia is an exceptionally creative and nurturing person. She's especially terrific with children. My kids just adored her. She's the kind of person who would be great developing and managing youth programs. But, of course, you can never forget those fantastic fingernails of hers. So, she really ought to do something that combines the two." Recommended Career: Become the Dr. Seuss of fingernails.

DAN "Dan has a lot more to offer than he often allows people to see. He is an extremely good writer and very clever. Whatever he ends up doing, he'll undoubtedly excel. But based on his modeling book, I really think he ought to model to the max. And once he becomes a supermodel, he can become Dan Inc." Recommended Career: Become the male Cindy Crawford.

FLORA "Flora is a life force. She needs to be—and is very good at being—the center of attraction. What she ought to do is pursue her dream and open a trendy restaurant. More people would come to watch *her* than eat the food. All the customers would be on pins and needles wondering, 'What's Flora going to do tonight?' And all the staff would be pulling out their hair saying, 'God, she's *in* tonight.'" Recommended Career: Open the hottest restaurant in Miami and call it "Flora's."

JOE "Poor Joe had so many things on his plate in Miami—his studies, his girlfriend, his libido—I'm astounded he got through the show. But he's a very intelligent guy, who's already got excellent business savvy. He ought to do something that combines his love of writing and computers, something for non-propeller heads." Recommended Career: Internet guides for dunces called, Cyberspace for Airheads.

MIKE "Mike has a great sense of humor and was the calming influence in the group. He strikes me as someone capable of doing great things, but happier to live the good life. He should open sporting-goods stores at all his favorite vacation spots, so he wouldn't have to lug his gear around. But whatever he does, my advice to him is... Recommended Career: Make a lot of money quick and retire early."

MELISSA "Melissa *talked* about how much she wanted to be a TV *reporter.* But I think she has too much charisma to report on other people's exploits. We need to hear about hers. Instead of becoming a TV reporter, she ought to become a TV personality. Recommended Career: The Latin Oprah.

SARAH "Sarah has this wonderful childlike innocence and enthusiasm, which is so refreshing. She has such a vivid imagination and so many good ideas. In fact, Sarah was largely responsible for Delicious Deliveries coming as far as it did. My advice to her is quite simple and, I believe, quite possible for her... Recommended Career: Become 'Snow Leopard'"

# Quiz

## MIAMI

## MULTIPLE CHOICE

1. **What did the *Road Rules* cast steal from the Miami house?**
   a. Gas
   b. $
   c. "8" ball

2. **What lie did Flora accuse Dan of spreading?**
   a. That her boyfriend, Mitchell, beat her
   b. That she shared a shower with Mike and Melissa
   c. That she really liked Dan



3. **Who joined Mike and Melissa in the shower?**
   a. Melody the Waitress
   b. Missy the Masseuse
   c. Michelle the Plumber

4. **What was the name of Sarah's superhero?**
   a. Moon Zappa
   b. River Phoenix
   c. Snow Leopard

5. **What is the only feat Sarah does *not* claim her superhero can do?**
   a. Freeze the ocean with her finger
   b. Shoot ice cubes out her butt
   c. Leap tall buildings in a single bound

6. **What is the only thing Cynthia did *not* do on the show?**
   a. Paint her fingernails
   b. Peek at Joe's private parts
   c. Pee in the Jacuzzi

7. **What kind of degree did Joe earn while on the show?**
   a. MRS
   b. MBA
   c. NBA

8. **What was the name of the magazine where Dan and Mike worked?**
   a. *Miami Man*
   b. *Playgirl*
   c. *Ocean Drive*

9. **What were the roommates *not* given to help them launch their business?**
   a. $50,000
   b. A business adviser
   c. Diplomatic skills

10. **According to Sarah-speak, what did "get the Jackson" mean?**
    a. When something terrible happened to you
    b. When something terrible happened to your voice
    c. When something terrible happened to your skin color

## DID THEY REALLY SAY THAT?

**Which lines were really said by cast members on *The Real World-Miami* and which lines are fake?**

11. CYNTHIA: "Stuff like this doesn't happen to people like me—you know, people from Oakland."

12. DAN: "The truth is like a virus."

13. FLORA: "My dream is that someday there will be peace and harmony on the planet Earth. Why can't we all just get along?"

14. JOE: "I wanted to be a porn star all my life, so I practiced and did everything I could to learn."

15. MELISSA: "I like taking showers, that's all! I just needed someone to scrub my back."

16. MIKE: "I had this nightmare, this crazy nightmare, that all the good-looking girls in Miami got sent off to California for a photo shoot for six months. Man, that's scary."

17. SARAH: "Can someone give me a hand with these ice cubes? My 'gun' is stuck."

## MULTIPLE HISTORY

**18. What sporting event did Dan help organize?**
a. Ménage-à-trois-athon '96
b. Volleypalooza
c. The Tanning Olympics

**19. On what television program did Flora complain about *The Real World?***
a. *Nightline*
b. *Road Rules*
c. *Extra*

**20. What was historically significant about the final episode of the Miami season?**
a. Flora and Dan got along
b. President Clinton delivered a pizza
c. It was the 100th episode of *The Real World*

## TRUE or FALSE

21. *The Real World-Miami* house was located on Rivo Alto.

22. The hospital that treated Flora's toe bite was located on Hypo Chondriaco.

23. The Miami cast vacationed in the Bahamas.

24. The Miami cast visited Twin Key island.

25. The Miami cast defected to Cuba.

### SCORING GUIDE

**20-25: Awesome!** Take a dip in the Jacuzzi. Soak yourself in the shower. Melody the waitress will be right in to take your order.

**15-19: Good stuff.** Pour yourself a drink. Snow Leopard will shoot some ice cubes your way in just a moment.

**10-14: Better than average.** In fact, better than Joe's average in Professor Stoner's class his last semester at grad school.

**5-9: Reruns or else!** You don't want to end up on Flora's s**t list, do you?

**0-4: You've been watching way too much A&E and not enough MTV.**

ANSWER KEY: 1.c 2.a 3.a 4.c 5.c 6.c 7.b 8.c
9.c 10.a 11.did 12.did not 13.did not 14.did
15.did not 16.did 17.did not 18.b 19.c 20.c
21.true 22.false 23.true 24.true 25.false

## POP CULTURE LANDMARKS

**BIG BEN** is neither a clock nor a tower. He is a 14-ton bell that rings hourly at the Houses of Parliament. Ben was most likely named after Sir Benjamin Hall, who was the Commissioner of Works when the bell was first rung in 1858.

**Popular London-based TV shows imported to the United States:**
Absolutely Fabulous
Are You Being Served?
Benny Hill • Dr. Who
East Enders • Fawlty Towers
Masterpiece Theatre
Men Behaving Badly (the original)
Monty Python's Flying Circus
Politician's Wife • Prime Suspect
Red Dwarf • Rough Guide
Upstairs, Downstairs
Wallace & Gromit • Yes, Minister

**Movies set in London:**
Absolute Beginners
An American Werewolf in London
Austin Powers, International Man of Mystery • Betrayal • Black Beauty
Blow Up (original)
Bram Stoker's Dracula • Damage
84 Charing Cross Road
Elephant Man • A Fish Called Wanda
Frenzy • A Hard Day's Night
Hope and Glory • Howard's End
101 Dalmatians • Jekyll & Hyde
The Krays • Mary Poppins
Moll Flanders • Mona Lisa
My Beautiful Laundrette
My Fair Lady • Naked
Object of Beauty • Oliver
Phantom of the Opera
Prick Up Your Ears • Restoration
Sammy and Rosie Get Laid
Scandal • The Secret Agent
Secrets and Lies • Strapless
To Sir, With Love
Young Sherlock Holmes

# London

# Class of '95

## The London Cast

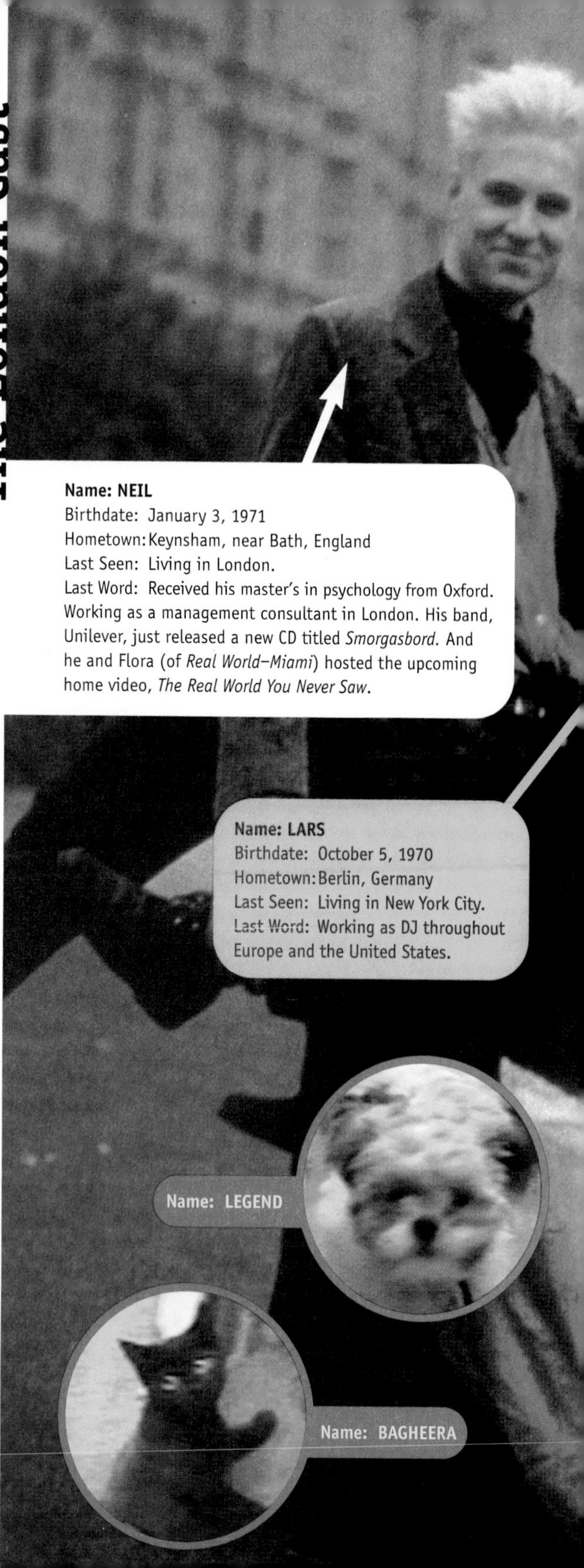

**Name: NEIL**
Birthdate: January 3, 1971
Hometown: Keynsham, near Bath, England
Last Seen: Living in London.
Last Word: Received his master's in psychology from Oxford. Working as a management consultant in London. His band, Unilever, just released a new CD titled *Smorgasbord.* And he and Flora (of *Real World–Miami*) hosted the upcoming home video, *The Real World You Never Saw*.

**Name: LARS**
Birthdate: October 5, 1970
Hometown: Berlin, Germany
Last Seen: Living in New York City.
Last Word: Working as DJ throughout Europe and the United States.

**Name: LEGEND**

**Name: BAGHEERA**

Name: JAY
Birthdate: December 7, 1975
Hometown: Portland, Oregon
Last Seen: Living in Portland.
Last Word: Working toward an undergraduate degree and still pursuing writing.
Name: SHARON
Birthdate: November 5, 1974
Hometown: Collier Row, Essex, England
Last Seen: Living in New York City.
Last Word: Singing and performing at various clubs in New York. Starting her own music publishing and production company.
Name: MIKE
Birthdate: July 17, 1973
Hometown: St. Louis, Missouri
Last Seen: Living in Orlando.
Last Word: Racing for Team Duke in the Formula 4200 pro auto series.
Name: KAT
Birthdate: June 13, 1975
Hometown: Yelm, Washington
Last Seen: Living in Seattle.
Last Word: Graduated from New York University in May 1997. Working for a Seattle company that stages live multimedia events.
Name: JACINDA
Birthdate: August 2, 1972
Hometown: Brisbane, Australia
Last Seen: Living in Los Angeles (with boyfriend, Chris Hardwick, host of MTV's *Singled Out*).
Last Word: Modeling and studying acting. Named one of the "50 Most Beautiful People" in 1997 by *People* magazine.

## LONDON JEWEL!

3-story flat in Notting Hill Gate, one of London's most happening areas. 4 bedrooms, 2 bathrooms, 5000 square feet. Roof terrace. Skylight. Fireplace. Old World charm. Horse carriage entrance. Gothic windows. Ranch dressing. Ideal place for mixing salads or cultures.

HISTORY: Built in the 1800s, *The Real World–London* townhouse was part residence, part catering company before the cast moved in. Extensive renovations were required beforehand, particularly in the living room and kitchen areas. The flat now serves as a private residence. None of the furnishings remain.



# the flat

**MIKE: "My favorite spot was the couch in front of the TV. Like, where else does one ever go?"**

## design tip

from AMANDA BERNSTEIN (Designer, *RW–London*): "Paint! Paint is very important. You can change the whole look of a room just with paint."



SHARON: "No one ever saw my bedroom on the show, but it was gorgeous. It had these thirteen-foot doors that opened onto this great terrace. I felt like a movie star from the '40s out there."

## FOUL OR FINICKY

MIKE: "I was the neat one, by far. I not only cleaned up after myself, but everyone else. I did most of the dishes. I vacuumed. I swept the floors. Picked up the trash. I was the man!"

SHARON: "I was the neatest. Mike might want to contest, but I was. He was Mr. Mom, though. Out of the boys, he was the clean one. Who was the slob? It depends on your definition. There wasn't a house slob, per se. But it didn't matter to Kat, whether or not her clothes were on the floor. It didn't faze Jacinda that Legend's dog s**t was laying around on the carpet for days. She thought covering it with a tissue was satisfactory. And I walked around my bedroom in bare feet!'

JAY: "When I first moved into my room with Mike, I told him, 'I'll keep all my stuff on my side of the room, but that's as far I'll go.' My area was definitely the biggest mess of all, though Neil definitely gave me a run for the crown of biggest slob."

JAY: "My favorite part of the house was the landing outside Sharon's room. It was one of the few places in the house that you could feel the sun—those few times in London you could actually see the sun."

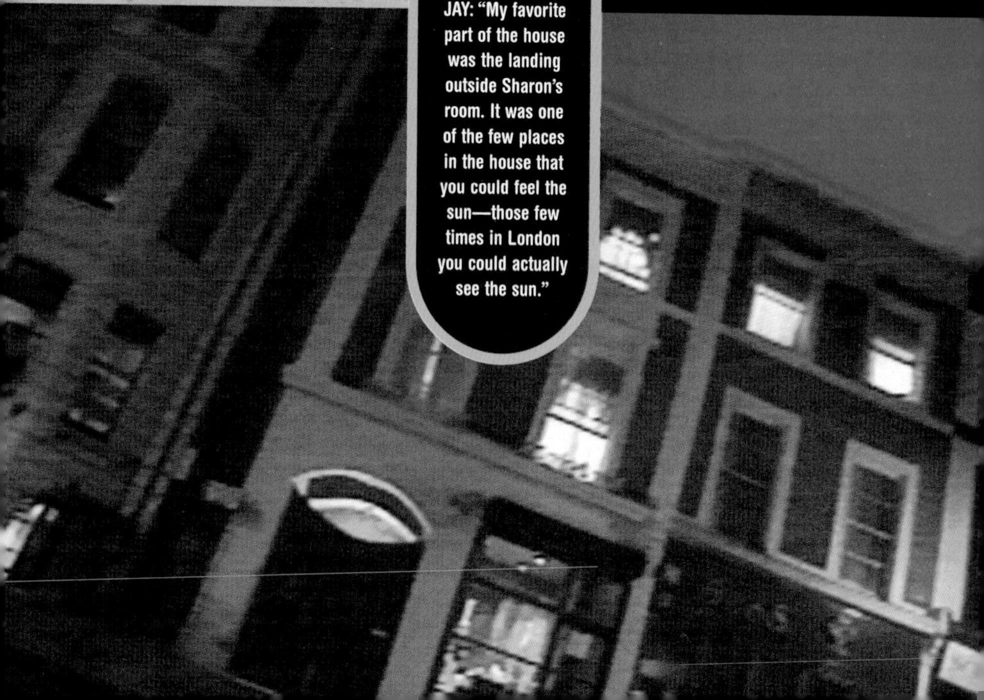

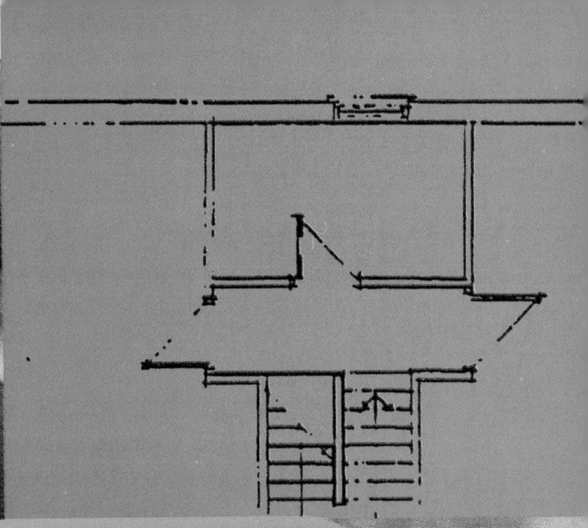

**NEIL: "I liked the big bath upstairs. My least favorite thing was the oppressive heat of the studio lighting. Oh yeah, and the dog s**t on the carpet."**

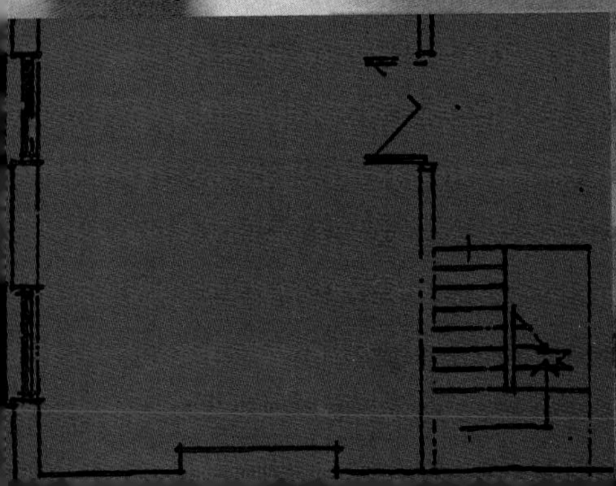

**PAUL**
Jacinda's "model" boyfriend.

# KAT

Arrived as fencer; Foiled with Neil; Competed at Junior Olympics; Defeated, but determined; Studied acting; Acted emotional; Dropped Lee; Held Leopard; Went with Spencer; Left with fond memories.

# JACINDA

Arrived as the model from Down Under; Posed; Pierced; Flew; Streaked; Dissed; Danced; Pranced; Paul-ed.



**SPENCER**
Kat's mild man.

**BAGHEERA**
Kat's kitty.

**LEGEND**
Pup; Peed; Pooped.

# MIKE

Arrived as racing driver; Drove for Kat; Detoured by Neil; Ranched dressing; Undressed Hannah; Boasted about Nina; Toasted a Redgrave; Joked with Hannah; Smoked race track.

**NINA**
Ignited Mike's engine.

**HANNAH**
Tested Mike's shocks.

## CHRYS
Neil's Valentine.

## SHARON
Arrived as a fast talker; Silenced by throat surgery; Quit waitressing; Split band; Teased (not pleased) during Outward Bound; Voided throat nodules; Avoided Masai sacrifice; Lost fears; Gained respect.

## NEIL
Arrived from Oxford; Researched Kat; Received pig's heart from Chrys; Jammed with Unilever; French-kissed a heckler; Bloodied his tongue; Tasted goat's blood.

## LARS
Arrived as DJ; Reverbed over stolen bike; Fought with Jacinda; Fell for Jeanette; Ballooned in Kenya; Swooned on safari.

## ALICIA
Jay's hometown girl.

## JEANETTE
Lars' greatest hit.

## JAY
Arrived as acclaimed playwright; Awarded "Slacker of the Week"; Dined Marisa; Pined for Alicia; Staged *Bedroom;* Shopped for lingerie; Sad to leave roomies; Glad to see Alicia.

**"I guess I never bought into *The Real World*, the way you're supposed to buy into it. I felt like I was married to someone, who wouldn't stop hounding me, but who still demanded I act completely natural at all times."**



# Jay

"I had a pretty rough time of it on *The Real World*. I'd never lived outside of my parents' home, so doing that for the first time in a foreign country was stressful enough. On top of that, I had passport and visa problems that prevented me from working or studying in London, which, in turn, prevented me from establishing a normal routine outside of the house.

"But unquestionably, the most stressful part of the experience was the cameras. It took me three weeks to relax in front of them. And even then, they still influenced my behavior. I couldn't help but censure myself—consciously and subconsciously. I think I was terrified of revealing something terrible in front of a million people.

"The producer, George Verschoor, sensed I was having a really tough time. At one point, he said, 'No one is forcing you to stay.' Perhaps, he was hoping to stir up a little drama. After all, we were

IF *REAL WORLD* WAS MADE INTO A MOVIE, WHO WOULD YOU WANT TO PLAY YOU? **"I want Fred Astaire to play me. I want him for the scene where I learn how to tap-dance, so I don't look like such a goof."**

the first cast in three seasons that didn't lose a cast member. But I never really considered quitting.

"However, as soon as I got back from London, I wanted to get as far away from *The Real World* as possible. I wanted to get my old life back and enjoy being spontaneous again. I was so happy to see Alicia, not to mention my family and friends.

**"Perhaps, that explains why I haven't kept in close contact with anyone from my cast. Of the entire group, I've only seen Jacinda and Sharon—at the MTV Movie Awards in Los Angeles—and I traded a few calls with Mike. But that's it! Ironically, I've kept in closer contact with John Popper of Blues Traveler, whom I met while I was on the show, than any of my housemates. I've even gotten to hang out with the band backstage at their concerts in Portland. That's definitely been one of my *Real World*-related highlights.**

"But probably, my biggest highlight on *Real World* was performing my play, *Bedroom*. Thanks to MTV's visibility, I have been invited since then to present the play on college campuses throughout the country. I've performed it everywhere from an 800-seat theater in Indianapolis to the lobby of an activity hall outside of Chicago. After each performance, I answer questions from the audience—of course, most are about the show.

**"A lot of people tell me they enjoyed our cast because we didn't bicker very much. Of course, a lot of people tell me our cast was *boring* because we didn't bicker very much. I guess those people prefer the Miami house, instead [laughing]. As for me, I get too nervous watching any of the other seasons—it makes me feel too much like a voyeur. I just feel like shouting, 'Mr. Cameraman, give those people some privacy, so they can sort out their differences.'**

"A lot of people ask me if I'm still going out with Alicia—the girl I started dating three years ago when she was 16. The short and sweet of it is that we broke up in June. She decided to go off to college in Southern California...and decided she needed to do that on her *own*. I'm not ashamed to say that I want her back. Unfortunately, she doesn't share my sentiment. You bet it's been hard!

"These days, I'm taking classes at the local community college toward a liberal arts degree. I'm still writing plenty; in fact, I just finished writing a musical about tap dancing. Speaking of tap dancing, you might recall my misadventures in London learning how to tap. Well, you'll be amused to learn I recently *taught* ballroom dancing here in Portland. My rumba and cha-cha, though, isn't a whole lot better than my tap [laughing].

**"It amazes me how many people still recognize me from the show. And I have to admit, I think it's a kick being a bit of a celebrity. The only downside is that I can't afford to go to the cool places celebrities go. Getting recognized on line at Taco Bell is not exactly like being spotted at a major celebrity hangout [laughing]."**

**NEIL: "Jay seems to get a lot of stick for being a slacker, but the guy was just a kid. People fail to realize just how strange it was being on *The Real World.* Beyond the surface level of 'seven strangers,' there's a whole lot of other baggage that comes along with being filmed intensively. Perhaps, Jay was more intimidated by that than it may have appeared on TV. I'm just glad I was 24 when I did the show, rather than 19 like him."**

**SHARON: "I saw Jay a while back in Los Angeles. He was, as always, a perfect pleasure. But I definitely get the feeling he wants to retreat from the whole *Real World* thing. Unfortunately, that means he's cut himself off from the old group as well. But if that's what he wants, then I respect that."**

# The Glamorous Life of a Model

**SHARON:** "Jacinda and I are very different women. We can be fire and water. But we still get on well. We lived together for six months in Los Angeles after the show was over and had a great time."

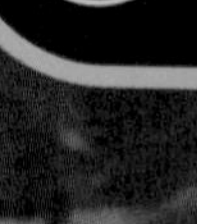

**NEIL:** "I still see Jacinda every now and then. I laughed long and hard when I heard she was considered one of the '50 Most Beautiful People' in the world by *People* magazine. Obviously, they've never seen her first thing in the morning..."

# Jacinda

JAY: "Jacinda was always really nice to me. She was the first person to make me feel comfortable in the house. I heard others complaining about Jacinda, but I had no complaints of my own."



LARS: "The only person I had problems with in the group was Jacinda. For the first two weeks we got along great. But after that, she got on my nerves. We avoided each other. We didn't talk. We didn't communicate. No nasty looks. We'd pass each other and be pleasant. We'd say, 'Good morning' and 'Good night.' But that was it.

"She'd do anything to be the center of attention. I didn't appreciate that. She also made fun of people. Like when Mike and Jacinda went for a walk, she'd ask Mike, 'So, what do you think of Neil's girlfriend, Chrys?' He'd say, 'She isn't my type, but she's cool.' Then, in front of Neil when the cameras were rolling, she'd say, 'Mike doesn't like your girlfriend.' Real evil s**t like that. She loved being noticed that way. She didn't think that was wrong, either. I thought it was cruel. Perhaps, she never had to be nice to people 'cause she was never in one place long enough because of modeling.

"But since *The Real World,* I think Jacinda has gotten a lot more relaxed and mature. She's very different off-camera, than on. Now, I really enjoy getting together with her. In fact, I see her for lunch or dinner whenever I'm out in L.A.

"By the way, Legend is huge now. He's five times the size he was in London."

MIKE: "Kat and I hit it off right away. We were good friends and she was the only one I talked to at first. I wasn't jealous that she had the hots for Neil. Kat can tell you, I've never been attracted to her. She's not my type. If you've seen any of the girls I've dated, Kat doesn't look like any of them. The only thing that bothered me was I felt like I was losing a friend. The directors sat me down and said, 'We know who Kat likes. It's Neil.' And they were, like, 'You thought it was you.' And I was, like, 'No. Why?' I mean, look at Nina. She and Kat are totally different. But when they aired the episode, they played that stupid, f**king jealousy song in the background. They do a lot of s**t like that. They won't just say Mike is jealous. Instead, they play that song."

JAY: "If you were around Kat, you just wanted to protect her."

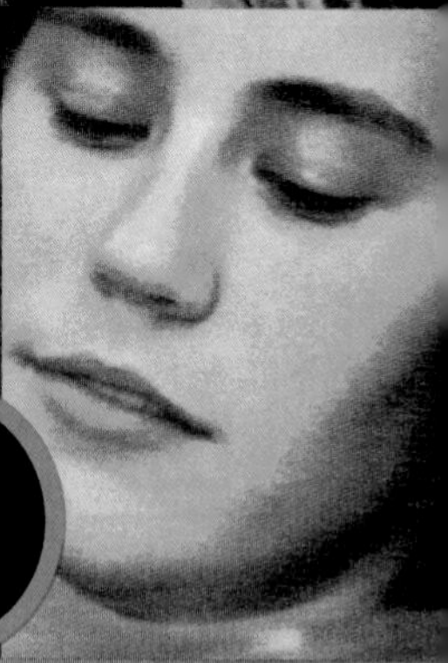

SHARON: "Kat has gone from strength to strength. She's definitely more outgoing than she was portrayed in the London house. And I think a lot happier, too."

# The Nine Lives of Kat

**NEIL: "I haven't really seen Kat since the show aired. I'd like to meet up and see how she's getting on."**

**LARS: "Since London, Kat and I have spent quite a lot of time together, especially when she was living in New York. The one thing that really surprised me about her was how little I actually knew about her when we'd lived together on *The Real World*. Obviously, I'd made very little effort to get to know her. She's a much more complex and interesting person, than I had previously thought."**

IF *REAL WORLD* WAS MADE INTO A MOVIE, WHO WOULD YOU WANT TO PLAY YOU?

"If I got to pick, I'd choose Nicolas Cage. But *Entertainment Weekly* said I looked like Tom Cruise in *Interview with a Vampire,* which I didn't exactly appreciate. People always come up and say I'm so much darker and beefier than I looked on TV. I don't know why I looked so pale on *Real World.* All my friends thought I looked horrible."

"I must say, after doing the show

**"Of** all the people who have ever done the show, I probably hated the constant attention the most. **I wanted to quit after three months. I spoke to the producers and said, 'I want out.' They said they'd never had someone come to them so quickly. They said it usually happens at the five-month period, but I wanted out after three. Obviously, they talked me out of it.**

"I hated having to report every single move I made. They gave us these cellular phones and you had to answer all these pages. It was a nightmare. I was just so frustrated with the show. I fell in love with Jeanette and she'd become my girlfriend on the show. Officially, we were not allowed to spend nights out of the house. We did anyway. We cut deals with the directors. They let me spend one night a week out of the house with my girlfriend. But it got to be, like, 'F**k off! I'm too old for this s**t.' My girlfriend and I used to hook up during the day and stuff, but it was hard.



**"It was worse than living with my parents. My parents always trusted me. They never asked where I was going. When I was 16, I could hang out 'til four in the**

# Lars

## it's incredibly easy to get laid."

**morning. All of a sudden, I couldn't go anywhere (even to the deli) without calling to let the directors know beforehand. I'd want to get a quart of milk and they'd say, 'Oh, can you wait? We want to film you.' I'm not kidding. We had this waiting bench in the hallway. You'd sit there until the camera crew got ready. Then, the phone would ring and they'd say, 'Okay, we're ready. You can go get your milk.' It made no sense to us what they filmed and what they didn't.**

**NEIL: "'DJ Fantastic,' I like to call him. He was a difficult character to capture on film, mainly because his primary social activity revolved around nightclubs where it's too dark and noisy to film. If there was a real 'cultural difference' issue in the London season, it was undoubtedly that the American producers had no idea about the nature of European club culture."**

"Even when I was prepared for all the cameras they were still a nightmare. The night of my most important gig they filmed me for three hours beforehand, putting on my shoes and my shirt. They filmed me with two cameras at the club

JAY: "Lars was the one person in the house who really said what he felt. If we needed someone to speak up in a situation, Lars was the one we turned to."

while I was doing my thing. I was sweating and everyone was looking at me like I'm some kind of superstar DJ. It was one of my most uncomfortable moments on the show.

"After the show first aired I arrived in America for the MTV Video Music Awards. Wow! Kat and I took a car to Radio City Music Hall. There were like, 200 girls screaming my name. It was pretty cool.

"It was weird, definitely weird, after the shows aired. I still couldn't afford a lot of things, like $15 cab rides home. **I was living in Brooklyn and I'd take the subway. People would say to me, 'Uh, what are *you* doing down here?' Like we all should be millionaires.** It's cool to be recognized at a fancy club when you're DJ-ing, or at the MTV Movie Awards. But not when you're on the L train going back to Brooklyn after midnight. Most people with equivalent exposure on TV are much richer than us.

**"I must say, after doing the show it's incredibly easy to get laid. I'm having a lot of sex. Not that I had a really hard time with that anyway [laughing], but things have improved. I mean, I'm a DJ. I'm in a different city every weekend, and I do sleep around. I admit it. But that doesn't mean I'm not capable of having a serious relationship. After *Real World*, I was with one girl for six months and I never cheated on her or nothing. I mean, it's just hard to find the right one.**

"Just about every day, especially when I'm on the road, I hear, 'Hey, aren't you that guy from *The Real World*?' New Yorkers, however, just stare at me, but don't say anything. They're not that excited 'cause they run into TV people all the time.

LARS: "I'm sure I took more than anyone else. After all the others left, I stuck around in London and lived with my girlfriend. I took tapes. Books. Cups. A friend called from Germany and said he'd heard we had huge cutlery in the house. He was right. We did. They were huge! So, I took some of those for him. It would've been really nice to have some of the bigger furnishings. But they were like 'No. We're giving it to charity.' The only large piece I have is the table on the balcony. I drove all the way back from Berlin to London just to get that table and those chairs. The table may have only been worth $40, but I figured, 'Why not. It's a beautiful table.'"

"I think *Real World* educates viewers more than a regular TV show. I know from Norm that he's gotten a lot of mail from young boys, who don't know how to deal with their sexuality. For them, he was the first gay person they'd ever seen on TV. I've had unique experiences, too. I was in the back of the store and a guy says to me, 'When you played Jungle on *The Real World*, that's when I started getting into Jungle. Those thirty seconds made me a Jungle DJ and producer.' And this guy had already produced four records.

"I've based myself in New York 'cause that's where the music business is largely situated. DJ work pays well. I know some that make thirty grand a month, but I'm not there...yet. I eventually want to get into producing and remixing music as well. I live with a girl, but she's just a roommate. I'm not into white girls, so it makes it very easy for me. She's a pretty girl, but she's not my type."

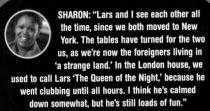

**SHARON: "Lars and I see each other all the time, since we both moved to New York. The tables have turned for the two us, as we're now the foreigners living in 'a strange land.' In the London house, we used to call Lars 'The Queen of the Night,' because he went clubbing until all hours. I think he's calmed down somewhat, but he's still loads of fun."**

## LARS' STOLEN BIKE

MIKE: "Sharon left the door open and she knows it."

SHARON: "That's such crap and Mike knows it. I wasn't even in the house. I can't believe Mike. You be Judge Judy on this one. Was it the English girl? Or the half-naked racing guy? Or maybe it was Kat with the rope in the dungeon. You know what, it was probably Legend. Legend did everything naughty in that house. I mean, can we talk about the copious amounts of turds that dog produced. And that dog is so tiny. It's scary!"

LARS: "I know it was one of the girls, probably Sharon or Jacinda. They kept leaving the door open. My bike and Neil's bag got stolen, on account. But we didn't really have a choice. We didn't have windows to open and we had to get fresh air into the house. We had about a hundred spotlights inside for filming and it got unbearably hot inside.

"That bike cost, like, $2,000. It was one of only twenty made worldwide. I used to run a mountain bike store in Germany and it was made for the store. When the bike got stolen, it was gone. I got nothing back. I spoke to MTV and asked if they'd reimburse me for it. They said, 'It got stolen out of *your* house.' They said, 'The door was left open. There wasn't a robbery!' And the insurance company said, 'Uh, no. Sorry.' So no one reimbursed me.

"At this point, I don't really care what happened to the bike. Had I taken it with me to New York, I'm sure it would've been stolen by now."

"Are you the guy? Are you *that* guy? That guy from that show?' That's what most people ask. I get recognized all the time. At airports. Even driving on the street. It's fun. It's weird. It's tough. It's uncomfortable. It's all sorts of things. How do I deal? I don't go out [laughing].

"But most people are real friendly. They want to know, 'Was it fun? What was it like? What are you doing now?' They're curious and they wonder if they could do it. A lot of people think it's staged. I tell them, 'What we say and what we do is real. But how they edit the show is up to them.'

"As for my so-called 'Big Ben' comment, they cut me off. What I said was, 'I know it's a clock. I was just kidding.' But they cut that out. That's what they do. **Watch. I might start a sentence in one room and finish it in another. Once, I started a sentence in a confessional and ended it on the racetrack in different clothes.**

"But I have few regrets. I wish I'd spoken my mind more, especially about certain incidents. Like the Ranch dressing incident. I mean, come on, that was stupid. But the reality is that everyone is bound to reveal a flaw over five months. 'Oh, my God. He's drunk!' or 'What a dork! How could he do that?'

**"Thankfully, we all got along. We were following San Francisco. The producers must have said, 'Let's put together seven people who can truly get along. We were just nice, friendly people. We fought about stupid stuff—about the dishes, or this or that—but any night of the week we could get together for dinner and have a good time.**

"I didn't want to leave in the end. I loved being in London, and not having much to do. I miss the friends I had, both in and out of the house. I'm still in touch with Jacinda, Kat and Lars. **The house was so cozy. I could've walked around naked, no problem. In fact, we all saw each other naked two or three times. No big deal.**

"I don't really know how the experience changed me. Well, I now know where Big Ben is [laughing]. **I do think *Real World* takes a part of your life away. You can't be the same Mike or Jacinda as before the show. In a sense, *Real World* takes your first twenty years from you.**

"As for the real, real world, I recently graduated with a bachelor of arts in business administration from Westminster College. I'm now running a race team in Orlando, where we compete in the Formula 4200 pro series. I used all my money from the show to buy half a race car. My entire *Real World* salary was gone in 24 hours. Of course, I'm still driving. How fast? Well, the fastest I've gone, so far, is 187 miles per hour.

"But my love life wasn't so speedy for a while there. All these girls would come up to me, but they just wanted to know about the show. When it was time to get dirty, they'd say, 'Oh, I have to go home now.' They wanted to know me, but not too close. I met my girlfriend, Cheryl, in a bar in Chicago. She's great! She had no idea I'd ever been on the show. Of course, she knows now."

?

**WOULD YOU DO IT AGAIN?**
**"I think all of us would do it again with a new contract for more money."**

**SHARON: "Mike was the shorts king. He never walked around naked. What's he talking about? Maybe he's thinking of his bath towel. That *was* pretty skimpy."**

**"We all saw each other naked two or three times. No big deal."**

# Mike

.IF *REAL WORLD* WAS MADE INTO A MOVIE, WHO WOULD YOU WANT TO PLAY YOU?
**"How about Dan from Miami?"**

**SHARON: "Mike is still Mike. Still doing his racing thing."**

**JAY: "Mike was my best friend in the house, probably 'cause we were the two good ol' American boys in a foreign land."**

**LARS: "I'm really close to Mike, so close we spent last Christmas together. He was my favorite roommate in London and we've just kept it going ever since. Mike is a really good guy—honest and a lot of fun. We're very different—he's a rich Midwesterner and I'm a whatever—but I totally respect him for what he is and what he's trying to do."**

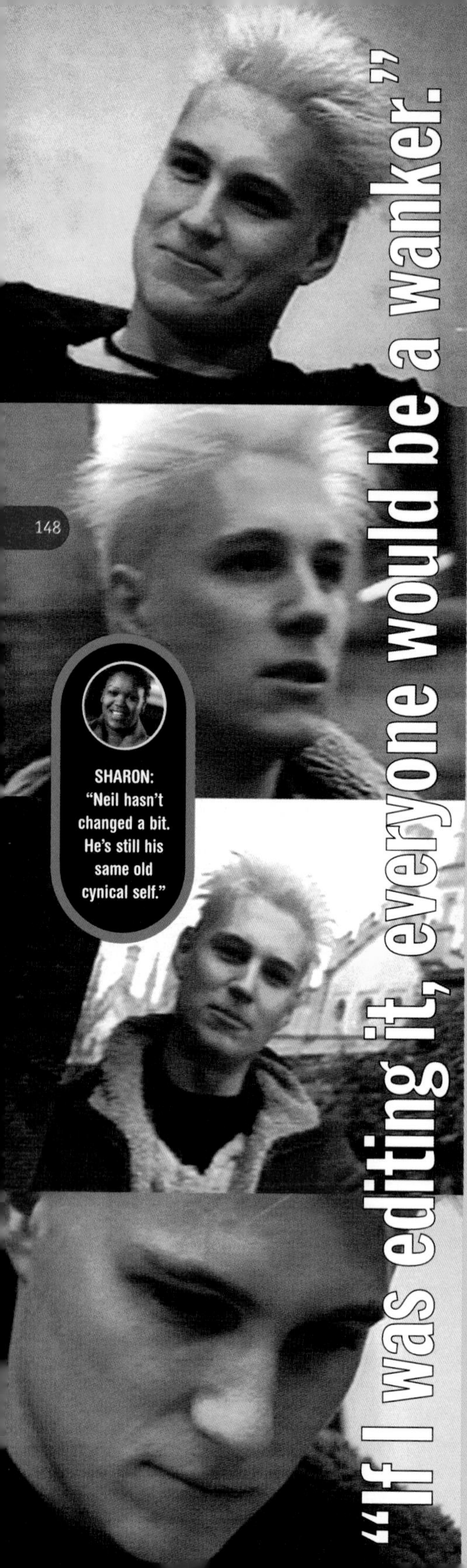

**"If I was editing it, everyone would be a wanker."**

**What surprised you the most about doing *The Real World*?** "First, the realization that being observed 24/7 is not the breeze I first imagined it would be. Witness the psychotic gleam in my eye the first couple of episodes. After reaching the breaking point, I realized there was no way to second-guess the behind-the-scenes process. So, I just got on with it. How that experience feels can only be understood by those who've been through it. Some appear to get along obliviously; some play up to the camera. For me, it was complete hell, at first."

**JAY: "Neil and I gave each other plenty of space, especially after things went down between him and Kat. I don't think that whole episode was such a good thing for Kat, and my allegiances were to her."**

**SHARON: "Neil hasn't changed a bit. He's still his same old cynical self."**

**Do the cameras lie?** "Cameras don't, but story editors are a little 'creative' with the truth, shall we say. Then again, with 99 percent of the footage ending up on the cutting-room floor, **I'm surprised they chose to show people in such a good light. If I was editing it, everyone would be a wanker."**

**Do you think you were accurately portrayed?** "Well, the show does tend to have an agenda when it comes to portraying characters. Me, I was supposed to be the cynical Yank-hating punk rocker. Having a sense of humor as well would be *far* too much to cram into those lovely little ten-second sound-bites that they base their narrative on."

**How would the experience have been different if no cameras had been around?** "Difficult to say. I probably would've done a number of things differently had I known I could've 'gotten away with it'..."

**Is *Real World* just a TV show or something more?** "As far as capturing the Gen-X zeitgeist, I never really believed that at all. I honestly didn't believe the show could educate young people in a meaningful way. However, if one kid in Hicksville feels more confident to tell the jocks to f**k off as a result of watching the show, then it's served that purpose."

**How did the experience change you?** "For the better, it let me experience fame with the minimum effort. Tried it. Don't like it much. For the worse, it made me a bit more prone to paranoia than I was beforehand."

# Neil

**Did *Real World* help or hinder your career?** "I spent over a year trying to use the show to get preferential treatment from record companies in the States and found it made little difference. Speaking of which, you folks can now buy the new Unilever CD—*Smorgasbord*—from Malkin Records via the Internet! The address is: http://www.escape.com/~toneman/malkin.htm."

**DID NEIL AND RACHEL HOOK UP AT THE REUNION?**

RACHEL: "Oh, my God. Where did you hear that? How do you know? I don't know if Neil would get pissed, but if he admits to it…well…sure.

"It was kinda weird. He had a girlfriend at the time and I was seeing someone too. Neil and I relate on this really bizarre level. NEIL IS AN INTELLECTUAL VERSION OF PUCK. He is very rebellious and I've always liked the bad boys. I'm toning that down a bit; after all, I *am* 25. But don't get me wrong, I don't want a boring accountant or anything."

NEIL: "Well, actually Rachel made it onto our new Unilever album—*Smorgasbord*—in a song I wrote called 'Delirium.' Two of the verses go like this:

*i'm dancing with the devil in the*
*land of the free*
*you're so stupid, you straight up*
*ask me,*
*'what is this?'*
*i'm looking listless?*
*nah, just minding my own from*
*an ironic distance*

*king size bed with a girl*
*that's pint sized*
*never thought I'd fall for that*
*beach chic style*
*she's standing in the corner*
*different from the rest*
*a prophetic message scrawled*
*on her chest.*

So, now you have your answer."

i was standing proud
til you kicked the sticks
bounded and in control
no wall between me and
the world
except my own
under glass i threw my stone,
petulant, dogged survivor.
nothing shattered.
bulletproof.
just a gentle tap tap tap from
here to there, reduced
to flaying electrons against a
cathode tube.

i pulled out my feathers
I picked at the locks
idly plotting futures
that never fruit
gone to seed
watching others choose
coke and a smile.

—NEIL (1997)

"I stole a whole bunch of books, but no big souvenirs."

**What else are you up to now?** "I'm working on a number of other musical projects, including a 'Trauma House' band called, 'thetinyorganismsthatliveinside-virgiliulamsbody,' which *Real World* viewers saw on the 'Tongue' episode; an experimental hip-hop project called, 'Scurvy'; an 'un-easy-listening' project called 'Return to Netley, Things Have Changed'; and, of course, 'Fish*Pie*Chicken,' the 'acoustic cabaret' band that performed the 'egg and cheese' song on the 'Confessional' episode. I've also formed my own Internet systems design company with a friend just over a year ago, which keeps me in beer money. My tongue is fine, my hair is blonde (after being black, then blue) and my fingernails are silver."

**IF *REAL WORLD* WAS MADE INTO A MOVIE, WHO WOULD YOU WANT TO PLAY YOU?**
**"Dennis Hopper."**

**Any roommates?** "I'm living in the East End of London with an old school friend. I've known him since I was about 12. Just a couple of mates who like to booze it up."

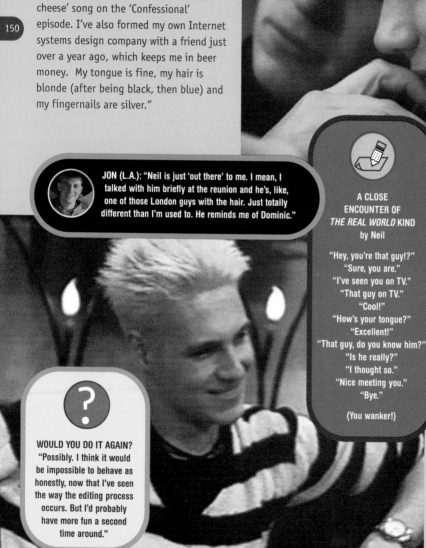

**JON (L.A.): "Neil is just 'out there' to me. I mean, I talked with him briefly at the reunion and he's, like, one of those London guys with the hair. Just totally different than I'm used to. He reminds me of Dominic."**

**A CLOSE ENCOUNTER OF *THE REAL WORLD* KIND**
**by Neil**

"Hey, you're that guy!?"
"Sure, you are."
"I've seen you on TV."
"That guy on TV."
"Cool!"
"How's your tongue?"
"Excellent!"
"That guy, do you know him?"
"Is he really?"
"I thought so."
"Nice meeting you."
"Bye."

(You wanker!)

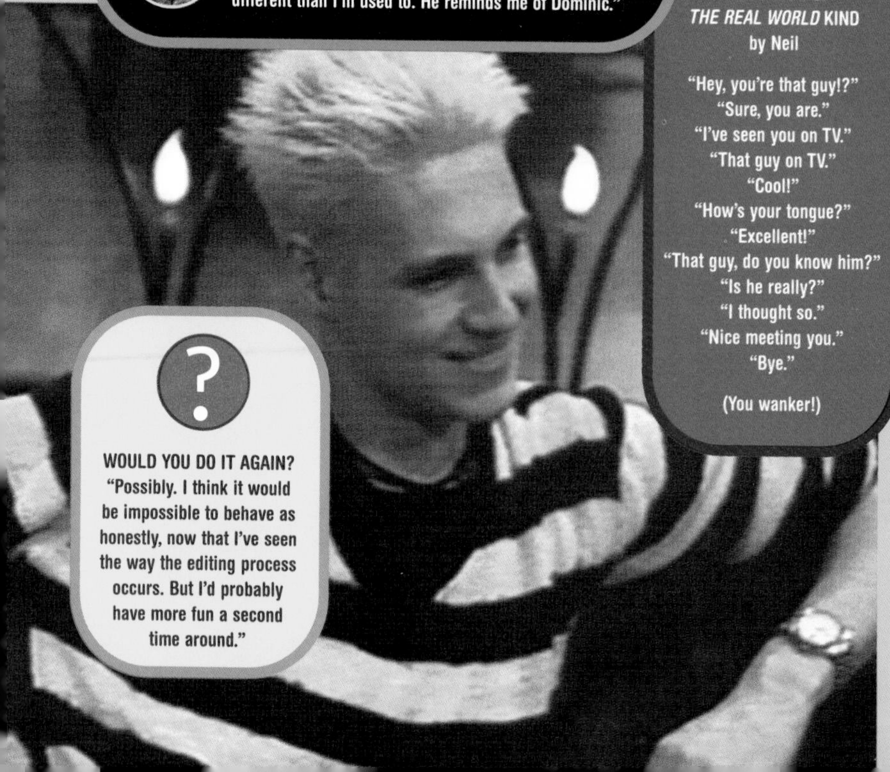

**WOULD YOU DO IT AGAIN?**
**"Possibly. I think it would be impossible to behave as honestly, now that I've seen the way the editing process occurs. But I'd probably have more fun a second time around."**

# Sharon

"At the time, I was living in England and on holiday in New York. I went to meet a friend to go shopping. She was auditioning for *Real World,* so I waited outside the casting office for her to finish.

"I think I'd seen three episodes from the first season. All I remember was how nice the apartment was. Eric arrived with Becky and exclaimed, 'Oh, my God. I'm a king and you're a queen.' Well, the casting receptionist suggested I audition, too. I figured, 'What the heck. I wouldn't mind living in a place like that, especially for free!'

"Living with so many people was a first for me. I'm an only child. I wasn't used to opening my fridge

**"Jacinda and I used to flash the monitors when we came out of the shower."**

and finding my food consumed [laughing]. Not to mention, the gangrenous bread in the bread bin.

"Sometimes, you felt invaded by all the cameras. I felt like shouting, 'Get out of my home!' Jacinda and I used to flash the monitors when we came out of the shower. Just to be funny. We didn't know who was watching, but the gag reel has to be hilarious.

**"You know I was extremely aware that I'd be immortalized a certain way forever. That's why I made a deliberate decision not to have a boyfriend in front of the camera. I had two boyfriends off-camera. Not at the same time, of course. I don't operate like that. Fidelity all the way. I have a conscience [laughing].**

**"One guy was a real suit. He'd have none of the filming. The other one might**

IF *REAL WORLD* WAS MADE INTO A MOVIE, WHO WOULD YOU WANT TO PLAY YOU? **"I'm Edina and Patsy combined from the show *Absolutely Fabulous,* not including the narcotic tendencies, of course."**

"I took loads of books. Oh, boy! I raided the library. I think half of it's in my house now. There were two things I would've loved to get—the gorgeous sun mirror above our fireplace and the computer. I don't think anyone took anything of real value. Our cast was far too ethical for its own good."

**have gone for it, but I wasn't sure if he was an a**hole. I didn't want to look back four years from now and think, 'Why did I go out with him?' [laughing].**

"I'd say ***Real World* is not the whole truth and nothing but the truth. It's a partial truth. When people come up and say, 'I know you,' I say, 'Well, you don't *know* me, know me!'** No one wants to look less than perfect, especially at this stage of one's life. The show holds up such a huge mirror. Not only do you see yourself, you see how others perceive you.

LARS: "I talk to Sharon at least once a week and see her every other week. I consider her a very good friend. But I would never want to live with her again. She spends three hours in the bathroom every day, which drives me nuts. I wouldn't want to live with her, but I definitely wouldn't want to lose touch with her."

"I knew, to a certain degree, I was representing black people. But I've always been reared as an individual first, and a black person second. That means I have to be a decent person. Period! I hope I gave another perspective on black people that doesn't always come across through the media—bright, articulate. **I hope I came across as a woman, who is not afraid to voice ideas, who doesn't have problems with people of all colors...and who happens to be black.**

"In America, the race thing is so much more of an issue than it is in Europe. I wonder why that is. You've had longer to deal with a mixed bag of races. Yeah, I can understand why there's some anger. But eventually, you come to a point when you have to be responsible for yourself. Bottom line: If you apply yourself in school and make the effort, you have as much chance to excel as anyone else.

**"My mother always said to me, 'You do your duty. And the rest is up to the Lord.' Like in the episode about Outward Bound. My goal was to get to the top. Everyone was kidding me, although I know it was only in jest. Actually, some of the editing annoyed me. But the point is, I met my goal. I'm really satisfied when I meet my goals.**

"And let me say this about the editing. I didn't *quit* my waitressing job after one day. The waitress, who trained me, said, "Don't call us. We'll

SHARON'S ANSWERS TO YOUR TOP 10 MOST FREQUENTLY ASKED QUESTIONS

1. No, I didn't go to high school with you.
2. Yes, I was.
3. My throat's fine, thank you.
4. Yes, his tongue has healed.
5. No, the two of them did *not* do it.
6. No, we don't know who stole it.
7. It wasn't my fault, it was Jacinda's pet.
8. Yes, we keep in touch.
9. New York.
10. THANK YOU.

**DAVID (L.A.): "I think Sharon is cool, man. I love her accent. And she has charisma."**

**NEIL: "Sharon is Sharon is Sharon. I saw her recently in the States. She's still Sharon, only now she's living in New York. Seems like I'm the only one left in my home country."**

call you.' When I got home, it was Lars who said, 'You quit?' But my response was chopped off mid-sentence. I was so pissed. So pissed! And another thing. In twenty-two episodes, they couldn't once show Kat, Jacinda and me going out for coffee or shopping for clothes. We did that regularly.

**"In general, I think *I* was portrayed as the nice one—the grounded one, the Earth mother.** And that's real. I can't be mean. I don't believe in voicing negativity. I'll do anything to avoid conflict. I hate it. And yet, some people said I didn't stand up for myself, just because I didn't have a screaming fit or wasn't verbally abusive.

**"Most people, who know me, say I'm just like I was on TV. 'Real. Very real.' Some people come up to me and tell me I'm much slimmer, too (laughing.) I like that.**

"At the end of shooting, there were some people who said, 'Sharon, we feel like we don't know you.' I was surprised and hurt 'cause I thought I'd done my best to be open. But, the fact that I'm still extremely good friends with more than half the group suggests they got to know me well enough. I think we forged something very real in London. I lived with Jacinda in L.A. for six months *without* a camera crew. We got along great. We all did, more or less. To this day, I also have good, lasting friendships with Kat and Lars.

"Of course, I'm still singing and songwriting. I'm writing an album and I've started both a music publishing and production company. Someday, I'd like to get into music supervising and composing for movies.

"The notoriety from *Real World* has helped my career a bit. I get meetings I might not be able to get, or as quickly. But record companies aren't knocking down my door or clamoring to give me a deal. I've got to have the product, just like everyone else. It's talent they're looking for. It's going to be purely on the merits. Not 'cause I was on the show.

"From time to time, I randomly turn on MTV and there I am. Back in that house in London—talking back to myself. You know, it's sweet."

**JAY: "Sharon has such a motor running inside of her. She's *on* all the time. Sometimes, she's totally captivating and wonderful to be around. But other times, she's in a terrible state and a terror to be around. When the latter occurs, just give her space."**

# Quiz LONDON

## MULTIPLE CHOICE

1. **What prize did the roommates award each other on a weekly basis?**
   a. Slob of the Week
   b. Slut of the Week
   c. Slacker of the Week

2. **Where in London *didn't* the girls go on their day away from the boys?**
   a. The Tower of London
   b. Chippendale's of London
   c. The Thames River

3. **What was the name of Jay's play?**
   a. *Bedroom*
   b. *Bathroom*
   c. *Closet*

4. **What was Jay's play about?**
   a. A kid who can't fall asleep
   b. A kid who is stuck with six strangers in a house
   c. A kid who wants his MTV

5. **What did Neil's girlfriend, Chrys, send him for a Valentine's Day present?**
   a. A roasted pig
   b. A pig's heart
   c. A pig's knuckle

6. **What did Neil send to Chrys in return?**
   a. A dozen roses
   b. A box of chocolates
   c. A piece of barbed wire

7. **Why did a heckler try to bite off Neil's tongue?**
   a. 'Cause the heckler had promised it to *his* girlfriend for Valentine's
   b. 'Cause the heckler had seen the movie *Midnight Express*
   c. 'Cause Neil tried to kiss the heckler

8. **What secret, regarding the woman Mike met in a London nightclub, was he the last to learn about?**
   a. She's a kleptomaniac
   b. She's a drag racer
   c. She's a he

9. **What did Jacinda help Jay buy for his girlfriend back in Portland?**
   a. Liver
   b. Linguine
   c. Lingerie

10. **What did Jacinda buy for Kat to help cheer her up?**
    a. A Kat
    b. A Cat
    c. A Kitten

11. **What precious possession of Lars' was stolen from the house?**
    a. His cheekbones
    b. His bike
    c. His turntable

12. **What throat ailment did *not* force Sharon into a hospital?**
    a. Nodules
    b. Tonsillitis
    c. Screaming at her roommates

13. **What was Jacinda's dog, Legend, most infamous for dropping around the house?**
    a. His tail
    b. His tongue
    c. His turd

# DID THEY REALLY SAY THAT?

**Which lines were really said by cast members on *The Real World–London* and which lines are fake?**

14. KAT: "There are more pubs here than people."

15. NEIL: "I'm a sucker for people in distress."

16. MIKE: "No Ranch dressing. That's like a lifeblood, ya know?"

17. SHARON: "Everybody's got too much sexual energy."

18. JAY: "If I could have things my way, I'd just entertain."

19. LARS: "You know, you could get laid in a place like this."

20. JACINDA: "No, I don't know Crocodile Dundee!"

## MULTIPLE ENGLAND

**21. When Sharon uses the slang word "snog," what does she mean?**
a. Sneezing
b. Sniffling
c. Kissing

**22. When Neil says he's looking for a "rubber," what is it he's looking for?**
a. A pencil eraser
b. A condom
c. A pair of galoshes

**23. When Mike says he needs "some Ranch dressing," what does he really need?**
a. Some sexual deviancy
b. Some peace and quiet
c. Some Ranch dressing

**24. What is "Big Ben"?**
a. Legend's waste product
b. A famous bell
c. Lars' privates

**25. When the girls went to see the crown jewels, where did they find them?**
a. In the Tower of London
b. At Buckingham Palace
c. Down Neil's pants

## SCORING GUIDE

20-25: Wow! Hugs from everyone and a snog from Neil (just as long as you leave his tongue intact). Take a victory lap with Mike.

15-19: Pretty impressive. You've earned a magnum-sized bottle of Ranch dressing on the house.

10-14: Not bad. On account, Lars has left two tickets for you at the door under the name "Big Ben."

5-9: For your efforts, you've earned a ride on Lars' bike. Oh, that's right...

0-4: Did you forget to pay your cable bill? Or did you really intend to buy the Beavis & Butt-head book?

ANSWER KEY: 1.c 2.b 3.a 4.a 5.b 6.c 7.c 8.c 9.c 10.c 11.b 12.c 13.c 14.did 15.did 16.did 17.did 18.did 19.did not 20.did not 21.c 22.a 23.c 24.b 25.a

# San Francisco

## POP CULTURE LANDMARKS

TV shows set in S.F.:
Full House • Hotel • Ironside
My Sister Sam • Streets of San Francisco
Too Close for Comfort

Movies set in S.F.:
Basic Instinct • The Conversation
Dirty Harry • The Enforcer
Escape from Alcatraz • High Anxiety
Mrs. Doubtfire • Play It Again, Sam
The Rock • Shattered • Sister Act
So I Married An Axe Murderer
Star Trek IV • Sudden Impact
The Towering Inferno • View to a Kill
Vertigo • The Woman in Red

## MUSIC

Some famous S.F. bands:
Big Brother and the Holding Company
(with Janis Joplin) • Counting Crows
Creedence Clearwater Revival
The Dead Kennedys • The Doobie Brothers
Faith No More • Grateful Dead
Huey Lewis and the News • Chris Isaak
Jefferson Airplane/Jefferson Starship
Journey • Metallica • Santana
Steve Miller Band

## S.F. MUSICAL HIGHLIGHTS

- The Beatles played their final paid concert at Candlestick Park on August 29, 1966.
- The Sex Pistols played their last gig ever at the Winterland in S.F. (1978).
- Peter Frampton recorded *Frampton Comes Alive!* at the Winterland arena.

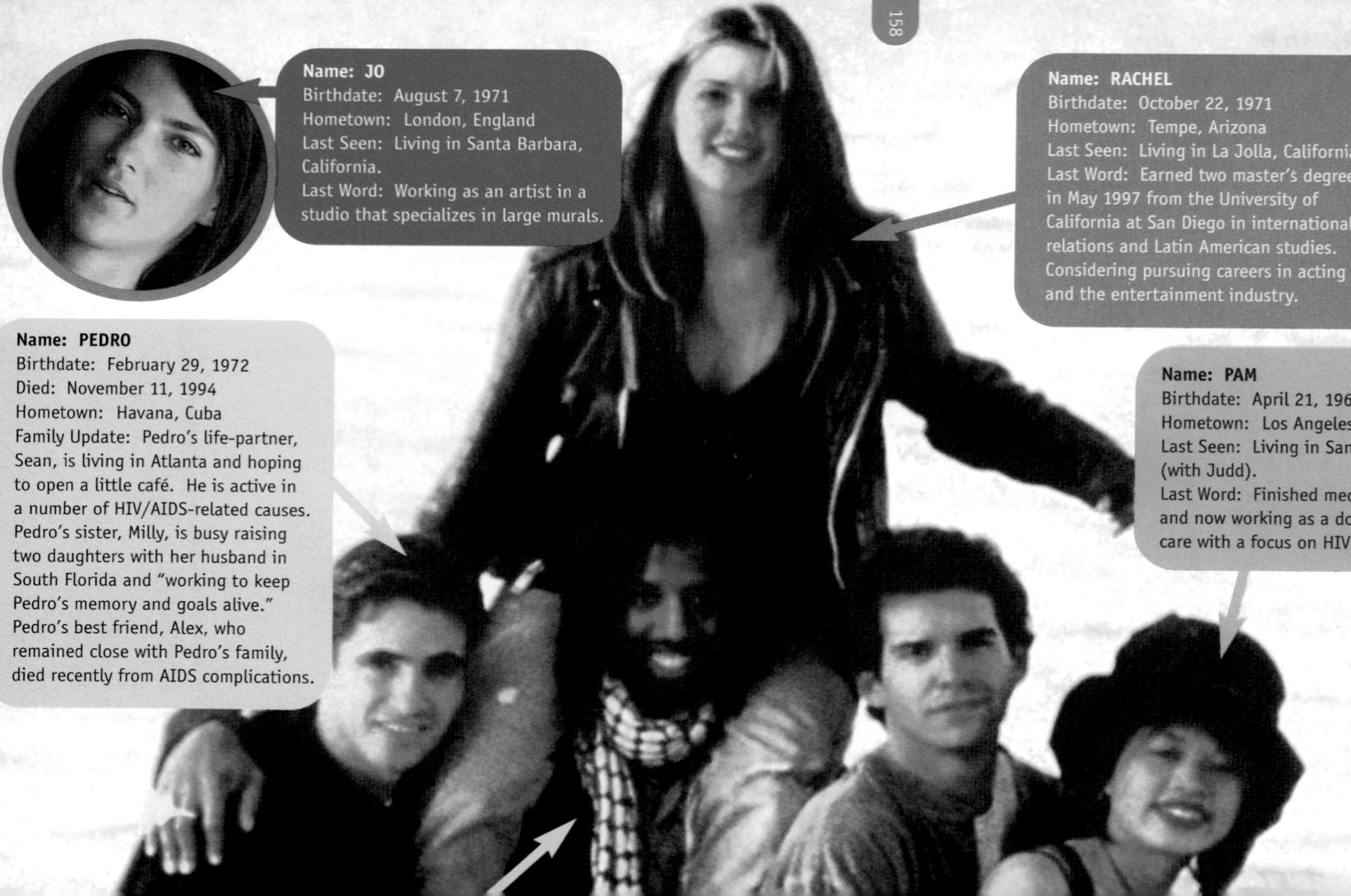

**Name: JO**
Birthdate: August 7, 1971
Hometown: London, England
Last Seen: Living in Santa Barbara, California.
Last Word: Working as an artist in a studio that specializes in large murals.

**Name: RACHEL**
Birthdate: October 22, 1971
Hometown: Tempe, Arizona
Last Seen: Living in La Jolla, California.
Last Word: Earned two master's degrees in May 1997 from the University of California at San Diego in international relations and Latin American studies. Considering pursuing careers in acting and the entertainment industry.

**Name: PEDRO**
Birthdate: February 29, 1972
Died: November 11, 1994
Hometown: Havana, Cuba
Family Update: Pedro's life-partner, Sean, is living in Atlanta and hoping to open a little café. He is active in a number of HIV/AIDS-related causes. Pedro's sister, Milly, is busy raising two daughters with her husband in South Florida and "working to keep Pedro's memory and goals alive." Pedro's best friend, Alex, who remained close with Pedro's family, died recently from AIDS complications.

**Name: PAM**
Birthdate: April 21, 1968
Hometown: Los Angeles, California
Last Seen: Living in San Francisco (with Judd).
Last Word: Finished medical school and now working as a doctor in primary care with a focus on HIV and AIDS.

# Class of '94

## The San Francisco Cast

**Name: MOHAMMED**
Birthdate: March 28, 1970
Hometown: Washington, D.C.
Last Seen: Living in San Francisco.
Last Word: Touring with his band, Midnight Voices. Writes a column for *The Bay Guardian*. Writing a book on cultural diversity. Speaking and performing his poetry at colleges around the country.

**Name: PUCK**
Birthdate: July 18, 1968
Hometown: San Francisco, California
Last Seen: Living in Los Angeles.
Last Word: Modeling and acting. His television appearances have included MTV's *Beachhouse*, *The John Larroquette Show* and *The Jon Stewart Show*. He was also featured in the movie *Jury Duty*.

**Name: JUDD**
Birthdate: February 12, 1970
Hometown: Long Island, New York
Last Seen: Living in San Francisco (with Pam).
Last Word: Created the comic strip *Frumpy the Clown,* now syndicated in thirty newspapers. Illustrates the *Idiot Guide* series of computer books. He and Pam hosted the MTV home video, *What Now? A Guide to Jobs, Money & the Real World.*

**Name: CORY**
Birthdate: August 28, 1973
Hometown: Fresno, California
Last Seen: Living in Los Angeles (and rooming with Norman).
Last Word: Working on television and commercial projects.

# the house

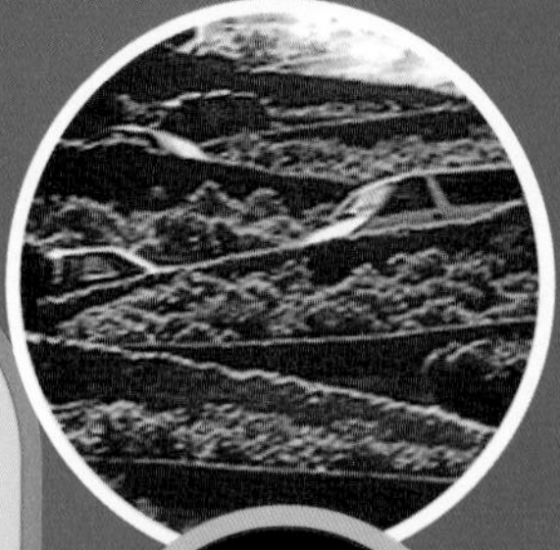

## SAN FRANCISCO TREAT!

Live on one of the most famous streets in America. 4-story, 4-bedroom house. 5,000 square feet. Outdoor balcony. Great views. Pool table room. Fireplace. Fish tank. Bike messenger on call. Dream house for cartoonists and characters.

History: The show's producers selected the house after the original location fell through at the last minute. Three families agreed to be relocated during the filming (in exchange for a "healthy sum") and extensive remodeling needed to be done beforehand. Several multi-generational families live there now, but none of the *Real World* furniture remains.

**PEDRO: "Lombard Street is the crookedest street in the United States, which I find kind of interesting, because I pretty much don't want anything straight in my life."**



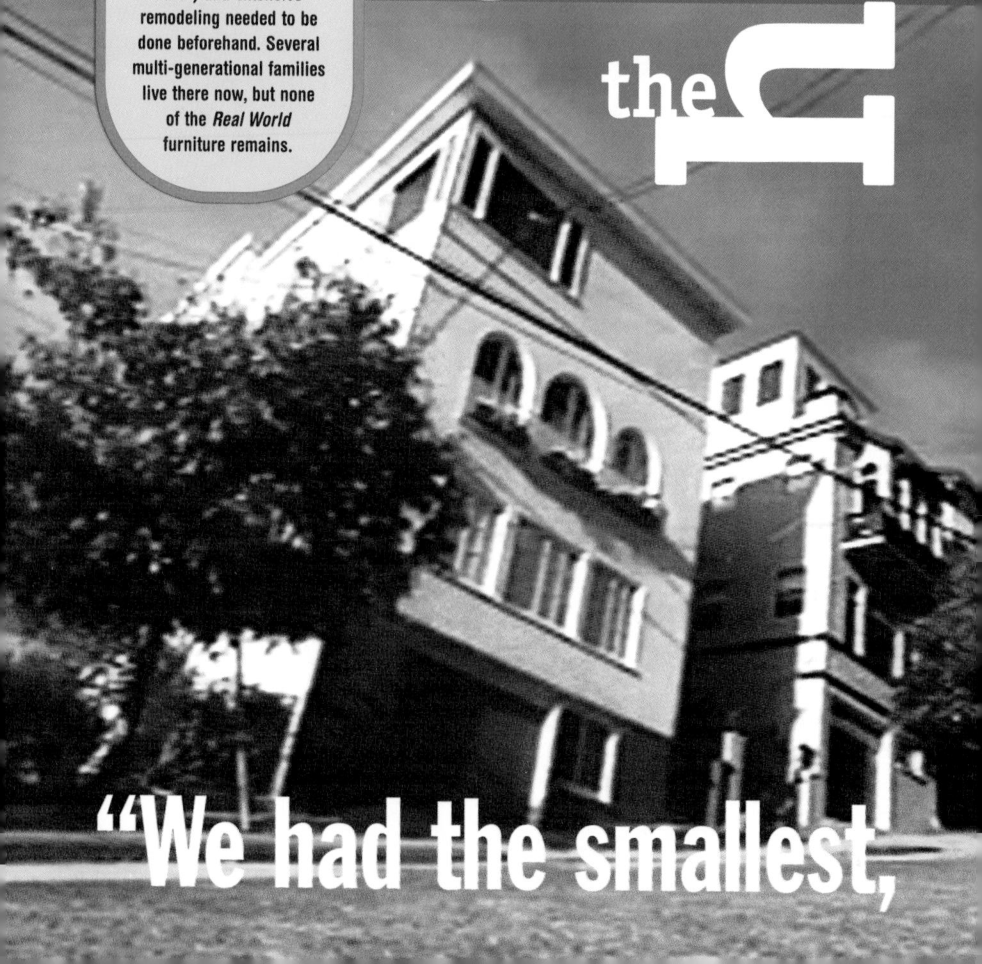

"We had the smallest,

## FOUL OR FINICKY

MOHAMMED: "I said to Puck, 'That's your side and this is my side. Now, keep your s**t over there.' After he left, I cleaned up his side and, man, there was some serious gook over there. He didn't just leave behind a dust bunny. He left behind a dust elephant."

PAM: "Our house was not clean. They used to stop filming in my room 'cause it was so messy. Pedro made a video of our house and showed it to his family in Miami. My room was so horrible I was horrified. You couldn't even see the floor. And, of course, Pedro's room was really neat."

RACHEL: "I wasn't as neat as I normally am. You just get tired of cleaning up after other people. And Pedro was neat enough for everybody."

PAM: "We had the smallest, wimpiest house of all, but I still miss it. I had my own room, which became my sanctuary. There were no doors anywhere in the house, so you would never feel too far from your housemates. And I loved the purple chaise near the video phone. I would have stolen it, if I'd had the chance."

JUDD: "For the record, we had the smallest place of all the shows, without question. At the time, we thought it was great. But they've gotten better and better each season. You see that Miami house? Good Lord, that place was ridiculous."

wimpiest house of all..."

RACHEL: "I miss the couch in the living room. That couch was soooo comfortable."

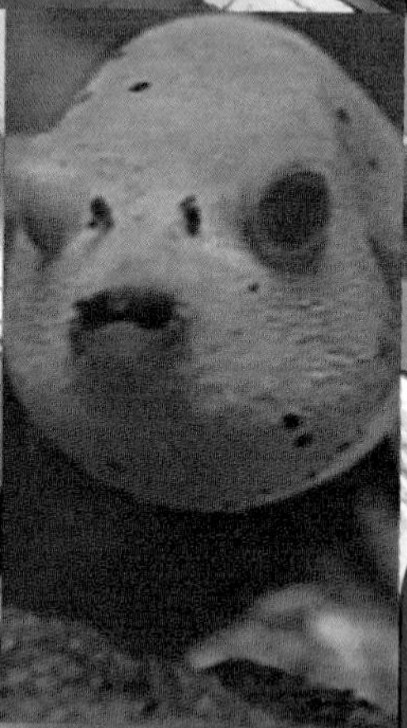

MOHAMMED: "I liked the couch in the main living room the best. That's the couch I was sitting on when we kicked out Puck. And I liked the little den. That's where I'd go to write."

## design tip

**from JOSH KORAL (Designer, *RW–S.F.*): "The key is to go to flea markets, buy things cheap. Then alter it, paint it, sand it. Be eclectic. Use vintage fabrics from discount stores. Make it yourself. You don't have to go to designer stores."**

**SEAN**
Pedro's shining knight.

## PEDRO

Arrived HIV+; Left legacy; Discussed AIDS; Disgusted by Puck; Pushed self; Struggled with health; Met Sean; Married Sean; Hid little; Changed many.

## CORY

Arrived on train; Complained she was "boring"; Bonded with Puck; Berated by Puck; Hiked with Rachel; Climbed with Jo; Departed with Pam, Judd and Pedro.



**TONI**
Puck's derby queen.

## PUCK

Arrived on bike; Rocketed snot; Refused to shower; Boxed soap; Biked messages; Scabbed; Peanut-buttered; Kissed Rachel; Kicked out by roommates.

## MOHAMMED

Arrived as writer/musician; Performed with Midnight Voices; Voiced anger at Puck; Made out with Sadie; Made up with Stephanie; Craved solitude; Rejected attitude.

**STEPHANIE**
Mohammed's midnight voice.

## JUDD

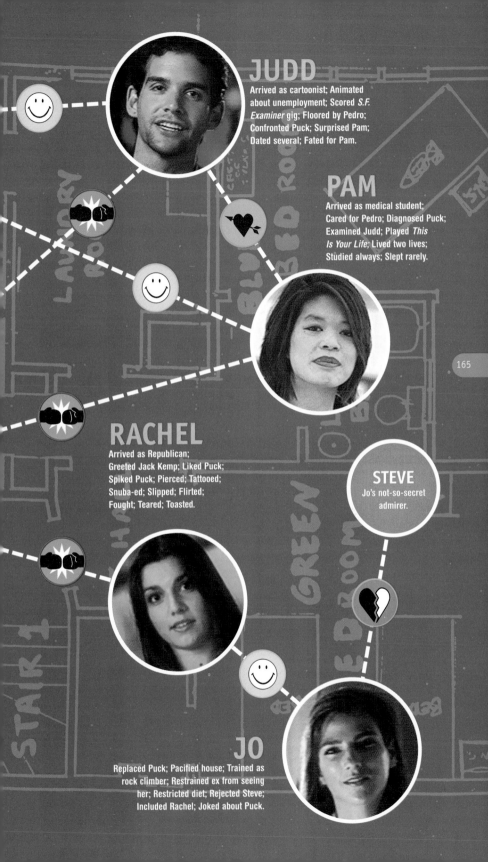

Arrived as cartoonist; Animated about unemployment; Scored *S.F. Examiner* gig; Floored by Pedro; Confronted Puck; Surprised Pam; Dated several; Fated for Pam.

## PAM

Arrived as medical student; Cared for Pedro; Diagnosed Puck; Examined Judd; Played *This Is Your Life;* Lived two lives; Studied always; Slept rarely.

## RACHEL

Arrived as Republican; Greeted Jack Kemp; Liked Puck; Spiked Puck; Pierced; Tattooed; Snuba-ed; Slipped; Flirted; Fought; Teared; Toasted.

### STEVE

Jo's not-so-secret admirer.

## JO

Replaced Puck; Pacified house; Trained as rock climber; Restrained ex from seeing her; Restricted diet; Rejected Steve; Included Rachel; Joked about Puck.

"Cory is this edition's designated Charming Wide-Eyed Innocent."
—*Entertainment Weekly* (July 15, 1994)

# Cory

**RACHEL: "I talk with Cory all the time. There's just a connection we have because of the show. A definite connection you just can't feel with anyone else who hasn't gone through it."**

"I felt like everybody on our show was so incredible and had so much to offer. But every time Puck appeared, he took away from that. He had to be the center of attention and everything had to be about him and no one else.

**"I think the last reunion gave people a sense of how Puck overpowered our entire experience. The audience was really excited about having Puck come out. But by the end, they just wanted him to leave. That just about summed up what happened in the house.**

"Just prior to the reunion, I spoke with Rachel and Judd and they were extremely nervous about seeing Puck again. We just knew he was going to make a scene. I even expected a confrontation between Mo and Puck, although it surprised me that it nearly got physical. But sometimes, you know, Puck just makes you want to hit something.

**"Yes, I understand Puck must be hurting. I do have compassion for him and I don't hate him. He's only doing it for the attention, so I know I can't totally hate him for it. But I don't know why he chooses to deal with his anger and hurt in that manner.**

"But I never let Puck spoil the *Real World* experience for me. I met too many wonderful people for that to happen, both inside and outside the show. And I've met some really, really great fans of the show, too. I get approached fairly often, usually by people who feel a connection to my character. And then, of course, there are some people who just feel like they know me from somewhere, but can't exactly place me, like, 'Did we party together?' [laughing].

"A lot of people ask me, 'Was it hard living with the cameras?' Yes, but just like anything else, you adjust. When people go to a foreign country, they adjust to the new environment. *Real World* was a new environment—a new world—that just

**"...there are some people who just feel like they know me from somewhere, but can't exactly place me, like, 'Did we party together?'"**

**KEVIN (N.Y.): "Cory is so nice. How could anyone ever say anything bad about Cory?"**

happened to include cameras. In fact, I forgot how stressful the cameras were until they were gone. **The first few times I watched our show I thought, 'That's not how it was. That's not what I'm like.' But eventually I had to admit, everything they showed, I actually did.**

"Perhaps, the hardest part of living with the cameras was not being able to interact with the crew. Your instinct is to cling to everyone, and I mean *everyone,* who is sharing this experience—so new, so unfamiliar, so unique. On top of that, the crew knew so much about us and we knew nothing about them. But even though they rarely spoke to us, we sensed the crew's support just by how energetic they all were.

"Without question, however, the hardest part of the entire *Real World* experience for me was the period just after filming ended. I had just shared this intense experience with six strangers and nobody else around me could understand what I'd been through. I returned a very different person to the world I left just six months before. I found it very hard fitting my new experiences back into my old, familiar places. So, I ended up moving around a lot, burying myself in my schoolbooks, and trying to figure out where I fit in again."

**"Without question, however, the hardest part of the entire *Real World* experience for me was the period just after filming ended."**

**PAM: "One thing I always hate hearing from people is that Cory is 'whiny and cries all the time.' That's totally untrue. There were four shows in a row in which she cried, so people say, 'Gosh, that blond girl cries all the time.' I always have to tell people that Cory isn't dumb and doesn't cry all the time. She was a straight-A student."**

# Jo

**On being cast:**
"Random chance. I was a student living in Tahoe and hostessing part-time in a restaurant. One night, this group came in and asked me if they could put some of their stuff down. I got to talking to them and it turned out they were a bunch of producers and directors, who were in town for a ski vacation.

"Well, I happened to be in a really good mood 'cause I'd been out climbing that day, so I was really chatty and bubbly. I started telling them about all the stuff that I do—the mountain biking, the climbing—and they kept asking me question after question. They said they were doing this show, *Real World,* which I'd never seen before. And they asked me if they could interview me the next day. I just went, 'Yeah, yeah, whatever,' and put their card in my pocket. You know, I thought they were trying to pick me up or something. So I just forgot about it.

"Well, the next morning I got a call and it was them. I decided to do the interview, then several more over the ensuing two weeks. Finally, they called me one weekend and said, 'Pack some stuff. We're gonna send three people into the house, and if you get picked you're moving in.' I said, 'Okay,' grabbed my things, and, well...you've seen the rest."

**On her favorite *RW* moment:**
"I'll never forget the day we all went diving in Hawaii. That was my first experience diving and it inspired me to get certified after the show."

**On her least favorite *RW* moment:**

"I was really upset when they showed me dropping my English class. I'm a good student, but that incident made it look like the exact opposite."

**On the crew:**

"Sometimes, all we did was sit on the couches in the living room and do nothing. You could tell the crew would get really bored. They were like, 'Come on, guys. Do something!' Well, one day, all the crew started laughing and laughing. They had to rush into the other room, just to pull themselves together. But even after they returned, they couldn't film us with a straight face. They were laughing so hard their cameras kept wobbling back and forth. This went on for hours, but nobody would tell us what was so funny. Eventually, we all became really self-conscious.

"Well, no one told us what had happened 'til months later. It turns out the crew had *Beavis & Butt-head* speaking dolls down in the control room. The directors had gotten so bored themselves, they'd begun playing the dolls into the crew's headsets, saying over and over again, 'This sucks. This sucks. This sucks....'"



## The Reunion

**On Puck:**

"Prior to the taping, I went to use the studio bathroom and Puck was inside.

"He screamed at me, 'F**king get out of here.'

"And I'm like, 'What are you talking about? Don't pull that s**t with me.'

"And he's like, 'F**king get out of here.'

"So I ignored him and walked toward the bathroom door. Well, he jumped in front of me and slammed the door shut.

"I yelled at him, 'Puck, don't pull that s**t with me.'

**PUCK: "I don't think Jo is that rad of a rock climber."**

"He screamed back, 'Use the other bathroom. This is *my* dressing room.' Well, I could see he had this little entourage back there, so I went somewhere else.

"Afterward, I told Puck that I thought his behavior was unacceptable. He apologized to me, which was cool. The whole San Francisco segment on the reunion show was a brawling, tiring mess. I was glad Puck came back after he stormed out of the studio. I guess he just needed to cool down."

**On Judd:**

"I thought Judd's confrontation with Puck was a little over the top. If it were me, I'd have spoken to Puck in private. Not in front of an international television audience. But I guess Judd had something he needed to say and his point was valid. Those two guys should get together and talk it out. But I don't think they ever will."

**On Mohammed:**

"I kind of expected a little confrontation between Mo and Puck because they'd had a tiff the last time they were together. When Mo got real heated during the taping, I just held his hand and tried to calm him down. I kept saying to him, 'It's not worth it...it's not worth it.' I think Puck did the smart thing moving to the other side of the room."

"I think Andre said, 'Being on *The Real World* is like going to the moon. You can describe it to people. You can show them the pictures. But until you've actually been on, you really don't know what it's like.'

***"The Real World* was easily the greatest and worst experience of my life. To do this show, you have to be something of a pig.** You have to have the confidence that you can survive being on television. And you have to have the attitude that you have something important to say. I think every one of us has had their own bill of goods to sell, whether personal or professional.

"In most respects, it's just a TV show. They shoot 70 to 90 hours during the week, which they edit down to 22-minutes-and-30-seconds without commercials. They mix it up with Smashing Pumpkins and Green Day.

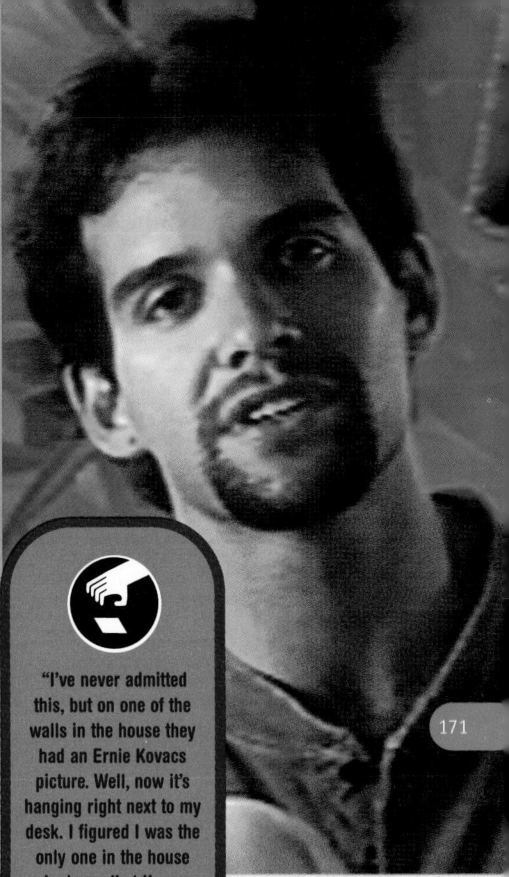

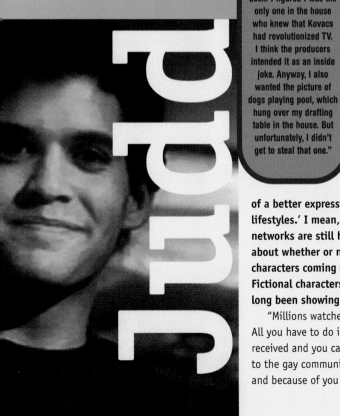

**"I've never admitted this, but on one of the walls in the house they had an Ernie Kovacs picture. Well, now it's hanging right next to my desk. I figured I was the only one in the house who knew that Kovacs had revolutionized TV. I think the producers intended it as an inside joke. Anyway, I also wanted the picture of dogs playing pool, which hung over my drafting table in the house. But unfortunately, I didn't get to steal that one."**

And then they present it as real life. That's not life. It's TV!

**"But I do think important subject matter has been aired on the show, including, for lack of a better expression, 'alternative lifestyles.' I mean, it's 1997 and the TV networks are still hemming and hawing about whether or not to show fictional characters coming out of the closet. Fictional characters! *Real World* has long been showing the *real* thing.**

"Millions watched Pedro's story. All you have to do is look at the mail he received and you can tell his importance to the gay community: 'I'm a 15-year-old and because of you I'm coming out for

**RACHEL: "I think Puck is a lot more fun to hang out with than Judd. I used to say I'd have traded Judd for someone in one of the other casts."**

**IF *REAL WORLD* WAS MADE INTO A MOVIE, WHO WOULD YOU WANT TO PLAY YOU?**
**"I've heard everything from Menudo to Paul Reiser, which is more about me being neurotic and Jewish than anything else. But I'd like to see Albert Brooks do it."**



the first time...' Or those married, heterosexual couples, who understood for the first time that the gay experience could be just like their *own* experience—two people, in love, just wanting to share their lives together.

**"Listen, I think everyone realizes they'll never get another season as good as ours. I mean, first we had Puck and then Pedro. On top of that, how can they find an honest cast at this point? Everyone is just too hip to the way the show works. Frankly, I thought they would've wrapped up *Real World* after four seasons. But I guess they're well beyond caring about nice press write-ups anymore.**

"Do I have any regrets? Not really. There's nothing I did that I'm ashamed of. Would I have shot my mouth off more? Probably. Would I have been more sarcastic? Probably. But sarcasm doesn't play very well on TV.

**"I sort of wish I'd kept my composure at the last reunion, though. That's the first time anyone, other than my family, has seen me lose my s**t like that. I guess a combination of things were responsible. Puck had said some really horrible stuff about Pedro after he died—insane stuff. And then, there was Puck on-stage playing this part and interrupting everybody. I'd planned to talk to him after the show, but he just got to me. And well, you all know what happened.**

"Anyway, enough about that. Of course, these days I'm still doing my

# "To do this show, you have

## "It's 1997 and the TV networks are still hemming and hawing about whether or not to show fictional characters coming out of the closet. Fictional characters! *Real World* has long been showing the real thing."

cartooning. *Frumpy the Clown* is syndicated in thirty papers and has a web page at www.frumpy.com, and I'm illustrating the *Idiot Guide* book series. I've often been asked if *Real World* has helped my career as a cartoonist. I'd have to say a little bit. But most newspaper editors are over 35, so they're generally not big MTV watchers. Thankfully, they don't hold *The Real World* against me, either.

**"I know many find it tough adjusting to life after the show. If you don't have something going on right away, you can feel like you're washed up at 23. One cast member even told me how unbearable it was being recognized at the unemployment office. I guess I'm real lucky that I have something to do that I love.**

"Do I miss *The Real World?* Well, I still live with a former cast member. I do have my privacy back. But, Pam and I do miss the view [laughing]. And, of course, we miss Pedro very, very much. Pam and I are lucky we can comfort each other and get to honor his memory. But we miss him terribly. **We were all going to live together in San Francisco—Sean and Pedro on the upper floor, Pam and me below. How cute would that have been?"**

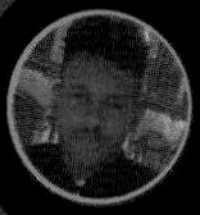

**KEVIN (N.Y.):** "I like Judd a lot. I think of all the people outside of my *Real World,* he's probably the one I'm the most into. I met him in New York, when the show was inducted into the Museum of Television and Radio. I just think he's really intelligent. And I respect everything he's done in Pedro's memory."

# to be something of a pig."

**PUCK:** "I harbor the most animosity toward Judd. He's just a puss. It's not my fault. I didn't make him live with his mom. He wears suspenders and he has no butt."

**DAVID (L.A.):** "If you put Judd and Puck at a table and just let them talk it out, I think those guys would come to an understanding. Or it could be that they don't even give a s**t. Maybe, they don't even want to understand each other. It could be that too, you never know."

# Mohammed



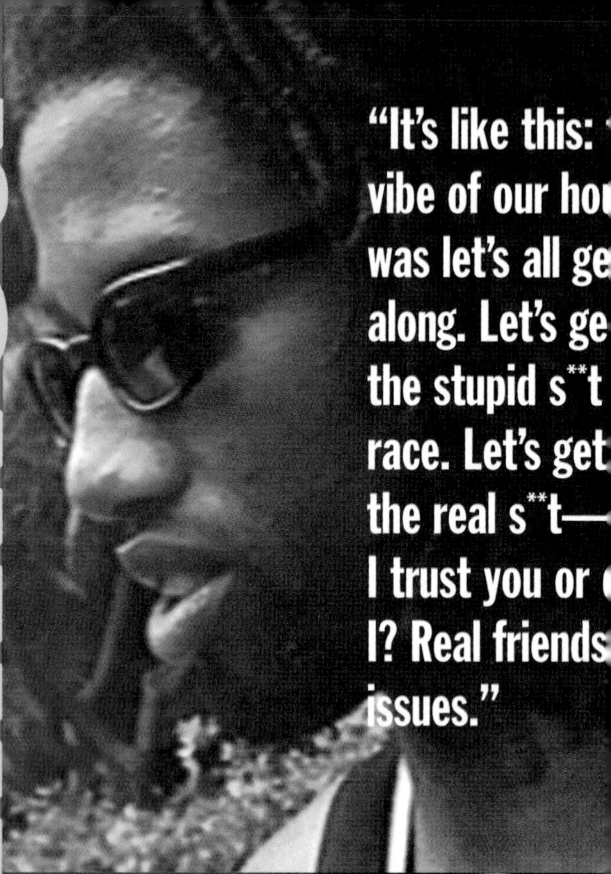

"It's like this:
vibe of our ho
was let's all ge
along. Let's ge
the stupid s**t
race. Let's get
the real s**t—
I trust you or
I? Real friends
issues."

JUDD: "Mo is the most patient, spiritual, level-headed guy you can meet in your whole life. But if you start with him and get him going, you'd better hope God gets you first. I think that's the way Puck felt at the reunion after he pissed off Mo. Because suddenly Puck was ripping off his microphone…and went to sit on the other side of the room."

"I have few complaints with *The Real World*. I think I came across as a pretty decent and intelligent guy. No one hates me or loves me to death. I wasn't extreme. Listen, I coulda kicked Puck's ass or hung on a ledge to get more airtime. But that's not me. I'm that peace-loving, dreadlocked poet-musician you saw [laughing].

"What bothered me more than anything was the way they edited Pedro to look like this whiny homosexual, which he wasn't. And they made Puck into this rebellious, misunderstood guy, which is a stretch, to say the least. They never showed Puck walking around the house saying, 'Faggot,' ten million times. I think audiences saw our whole issue with Puck in a twisted way. **It wasn't Pedro vs. Puck. It was the whole house against Puck.**

"No matter what else happens on *The Real World,* it's all about making money. And the producers expected to cash in on Puck. He was *The Man.* That's why they got so tripped out when we kicked him out. The producers flew immediately to San Francisco: 'Oh, my God, our star is gone. What do we do?'

"But if you ask any of us, none of us *wanted* to kick Puck out. We gave him so many chances. All we wanted to hear from him was, 'I'll *try* to be more civil.' But he couldn't or wouldn't do that. It bothers me that people think we decided, 'Oh well, L.A. kicked out Dave, so let's kick out Puck.' Puck needed to get kicked out. Puck knew full well what he was doing.

**"Puck also knew not to f**k with me. You could see that at the last reunion. They cut our microphones when I was like, 'Puck, I will f**k you**

**RACHEL: "Mohammed is so restrained and when he tipped Puck's hat at the reunion...If anybody else had tipped Puck's hat like that, Puck would've clocked him. But you could just see the fear in Puck's eyes. He was very afraid of Mohammed. And deep down, I kind of wanted Mohammed to hit him. But it didn't happen, unfortunately."**

**CORY: "I don't stay in touch with Mo very often, but I think about him a lot. He had an incredible impact on my life. Just going to the Upper Room with him was an experience. I mean, he just gave me so much and taught me so much."**

**PUCK: "Mohammed is a poet, but in my eyes he has no business being a front man in a band. I call his band 'The Mediocre Choices' because they're weak. I lied on TV. I said they 'rocked.' But I was just doing them a favor, a press boost."**

**up.' That's why he raised his hand and asked to move. He was afraid I'd hit him. But I wouldn't have lost it. Why fight him? I know I can beat him, so violence isn't necessary.**

"It's like this: the vibe of our house was let's all get along. Let's get over the stupid s**t about race. Let's get to the real s**t—do I trust you or don't I? Real friendship issues. That's what it boiled down to with Puck. We just didn't trust him, period!

"And I know I'm still representing *The*

**IF *REAL WORLD* WAS MADE INTO A MOVIE, WHO WOULD YOU WANT TO PLAY YOU?**
**"I like Denzel [Washington], but I'm not so sure we're the same type."**

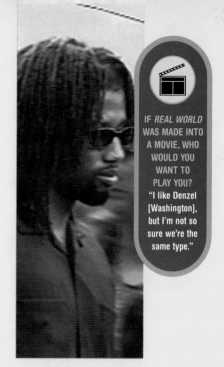

## "If I felt any pressure at all, it was the self-imposed pressure of being the sole African-American in my cast. Anytime you do a show like this, I believe you're representing the entire African-American diaspora. But then again, I feel like I'm representing, even when I'm walking down the street."

*Real World.* A day doesn't go by without someone recognizing me from the show. It still takes a little getting used to. I get asked all sorts of questions from 'How's Stephanie?' to 'What's up with Midnight Voices?' Well, I'll tell you:

"Stephanie is dancing for the Dance Theatre of Harlem. We're still great friends, although not boyfriend and girlfriend at the moment.

"And I'm still touring with Midnight Voices. We got lots of terrific exposure out of being on *The Real World,* which has created the 'Purple Panty' phenomenon. They used to go see Prince 'cause he wore purple panties. But once they realized what kind of a musician he was, they came back to hear his music. That's the way it's been with us. The promoters love us for the *Real World* gimmick, but our audiences love us for the way we play."

**WOULD YOU DO IT AGAIN?**
**"I won't live with six people again. I only want to live alone or with a significant other."**

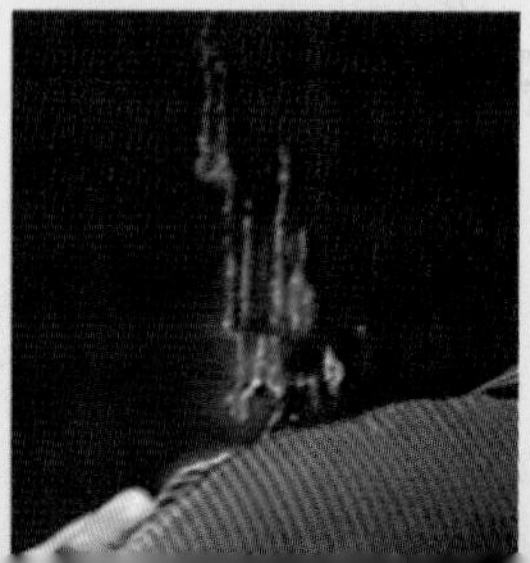

# Pam



**"A lot of things have changed in my life since the show. I have a new boyfriend, a new place and a renewed commitment to medicine.**

"I guess I'd say I went through a tumultuous period around the time our show aired. Much of it had to do with Pedro dying. On top of that, I broke up with my boyfriend of eight years and later moved in with Judd. It seemed like almost every relationship and element in my life was changing.

**"It's impossible to say what would've happened without *Real World.* But I know, I wouldn't have met Pedro. I wouldn't have met Judd. I wouldn't have taken a year off from school. And I probably wouldn't be focusing as much of my work on HIV and AIDS patients as I am now."**

"Yes, I think our season was the best. I'm proud of some of the things we portrayed. I think people found moving things and role models, especially because of Pedro. People say they appreciated how Judd and I treated Pedro. And some even tell us they thought it was great we didn't freak out when he and Sean were kissing. God, that's just common decency.

"I still get recognized plenty at the hospital, usually by the younger patients or the older ones with kids. It's kind of funny—that instant flash of recognition. I'll be doing my rounds and suddenly some new patient will yell, 'You're that TV woman!' Everyone is real nice about it. Many want to talk about Pedro.

# "Much of my work involves providing primary care for HIV and AIDS patients. My own experiences with Pedro taught me so much about what patients and their families go through. I've been the close friend to the family before, so I think it may give me a unique perspective."



**JUDD: "Walking around with Pam makes it difficult to blend in. I sort of look like a typical white guy. But Pam is an Asian woman with colored hair, so they pick us out of a crowd immediately. And then they come over in droves."**

"That may explain why my work is so overwhelming at times. I have a lot of trouble leaving it all behind at the hospital, especially when a patient of mine is dying. When I'm not *working on* that patient, I'm *thinking about* him and his mom...a lot.

"One of the most positive things I've noticed recently has been the increased level of tolerance for people living with HIV, especially within families. I think Pedro was very influential in bringing about that change through greater sensitivity and awareness.

"I've seen most of our shows only once. Unlike Judd, I don't like watching them too many times and analyzing what went on. I'd rather safeguard my memories."

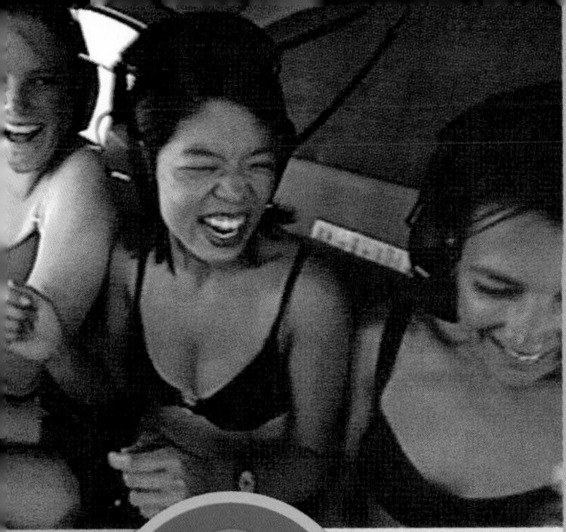

“Despite the violent streaks in her hair, [Pam is] the most mature of this bunch, and frighteningly self-assured.”
—*Entertainment Weekly* (July 15, 1994)

**WOULD YOU DO IT AGAIN?**
“Knowing what I know now, I think I’d do it again. It was a very interesting and unique experience for me. I think it really enriched and changed my life in ways I had not expected, especially because of Pedro and Judd. But I probably wouldn’t recommend it for other struggling medical students, because it’s crazy trying to do it along with med school.”

**MOHAMMED:**
“I don’t think we got to see enough of Pam on the show. They spent so much time focusing on Puck, there wasn’t enough time to develop any of the other characters. I, myself, was interested in Pam’s character. I never got to see why she wanted to be a doctor.”

# Pedro

*Pedro's Story*

Teen With AIDS Virus Tries to Teach Youths Some Lessons for Life

At Miami Schools, He Talks About Sex, Pain, Death

**Pedro's sister, Milly:** "When my brother told me he wanted to do *The Real World,* he said, 'I think it's a great opportunity for me to reach everybody I can. Milly, please support me.' Of course, I told him I would. But, of course, I wanted him to stay.

"Ever since Pedro was infected with HIV as a high school senior, we knew each moment with him was precious and few. Six months does not seem like a long time to be away, but when you're terminally ill, it is really a lifetime. I was also very worried about who would take care of Pedro when he was in San Francisco. Who would make sure he took his medication and got plenty of sleep? But no matter what I said to Pedro, I just knew he was going to go to San Francisco anyway.

"When Pedro came to visit midway through the show, I could already see his health had changed a lot. He was very thin and he was forgetting things that he'd never have forgotten normally, like how to get to certain places in the neighborhood. I could tell that everyone involved with the show loved Pedro very much. But I could also see how much pressure he was under. I talked to him about staying behind in Miami, but he insisted on returning to San Francisco to finish the show.

"I'm glad, for his sake, that he did finish and that he was on *The Real World.* I think he accomplished exactly what he hoped it would. He reached more people with his message and touched more people with his life than anyone, including him, could have imagined. Of course, I wish I had those six months back with him. But, I'm also glad our family got to share Pedro with rest of the world, too.

"When Pedro was very sick, he said, 'I'm not afraid to die. I'm afraid of

what's going to happen to my family. And who's going to continue my work?' I told Pedro, 'Don't worry, little brother. We'll take care of each other. And I'll do whatever I can do to continue your work. You know, I won't be able to do it as well as you—my English isn't very good and I have to take care of my two children—but I'll do the very best I can for you.'

"Well, I try to do my best. Every Wednesday I volunteer at Mercy Hospital in Miami, bringing food to people with AIDS. I also help out at two support groups at my local church—one for people with HIV/AIDS and another for mothers with children suffering from the

**"He reached more people with his message and touched more people with his life than anyone, including him, could have imagined."**

disease. Our mother died in 1985 and, in many ways, I felt like a second mother to Pedro. So, when I talk to these mothers who are suffering, I feel like I know firsthand what they're going through.

"I have no words to describe how hard it's been without Pedro. But I could cry and cry in my home and say, 'Oh, my little brother is gone.' Or I could remember him by working with people, just like Pedro, who also have HIV and AIDS. You know, every time I look in those people's eyes, I see my brother's face.



"I think Pedro's death has been hardest on my father. He always says, 'Why not me? I'm the older one. Why take the little one?' He had eight children—two girls and six boys—and Pedro was the baby. Pedro always needed to be involved in everything. Everything! He was always doing something that brought the entire family together. For that reason, I think it's especially hard for my father to be at large family gatherings. He always leaves early 'cause it makes him too sad that Pedro isn't there.

"I've told my two daughters all about their Uncle Pedro. That he worked hard in school. That he embraced the whole family. That he was very open with everybody. I hope my daughters are as open with me as Pedro was. Pedro was the most open person I ever met.

"It's not easy to admit you're gay, especially in the Spanish community. One day when Pedro was 13 years old, he came to me and said, 'Milly, I'm gay.' Just like that. Well, I was just 20 at the time, so my reaction was, 'Pedro, are you crazy? What's wrong with you? Did something happen to you when you were a child? Go see a psychologist.' In fact, I took Pedro to see a psychologist and the doctor said, 'There's nothing wrong with Pedro. Maybe *you* need to see a psychologist yourself' [laughing].

"Gradually, I learned to accept my brother's lifestyle because that was who he was. And I'm very careful to tell my young daughters the truth about Pedro. I explain that he got AIDS through sexual transmission. I think it's very important that they understand the truth and the risks out there.

"It's important everybody understands the truth about this disease. I just don't want my brother's life to be in vain. Please, take care of yourselves. If you want to have sex, please use a condom. Too many lives have already been lost because people didn't take care of themselves. Think of Pedro. Think of your mother. Your father. Yourselves!

"I'm so grateful to Pedro's *Real World* friends for their love and support. Cory is such a sweetheart and Judd, well, I just love that person. He has taken care of everything having to do with Pedro—the press, the tributes, the speeches....He's incredible. You just have no idea what

**"It's not easy to admit you're gay, especially in the Spanish community. One day when Pedro was 13 years old, he came to me and said, 'Milly, I'm gay.' Just like that. Well,... my reaction was, 'Pedro, are you crazy? What's wrong with you? Did something happen to you when you were a child? Go see a psychologist.' In fact, I took Pedro to see a psychologist and the doctor said, 'There's nothing wrong with Pedro. Maybe *you* need to see a psychologist yourself' [laughing]."**

kind of friend he's been to our family. And Pam, too. She's been so wonderful about continuing the work of Pedro. Pam and Judd are a very nice couple. I hope they get married [laughing].

"Everybody knows Pedro because of *The Real World*. Whenever I go to the hospital, the AIDS patients say, 'Oh, my God. Look, it's Pedro's sister.' They say so many beautiful things about my brother. So many people have said so many beautiful things about dear Pedro.

"And so, I continue to do Pedro's work. I do it for Pedro and for my two daughters."

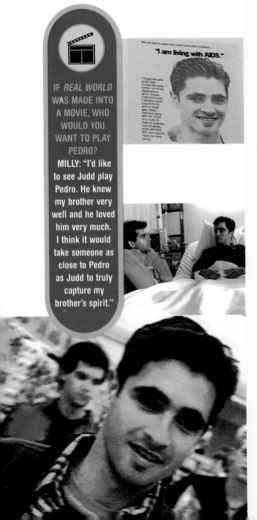

IF *REAL WORLD* WAS MADE INTO A MOVIE, WHO WOULD YOU WANT TO PLAY PEDRO?

**MILLY: "I'd like to see Judd play Pedro. He knew my brother very well and he loved him very much. I think it would take someone as close to Pedro as Judd to truly capture my brother's spirit."**

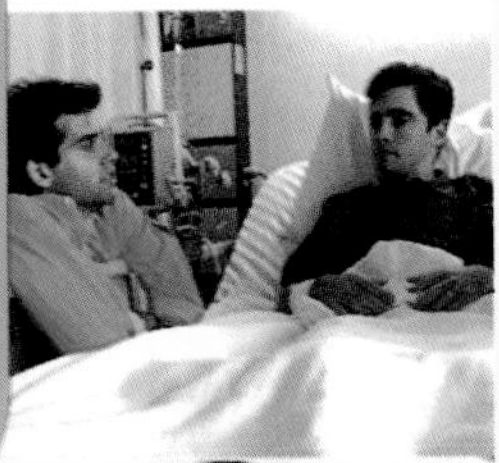

# About Pedro

JUDD: "After his son died, Paul Newman said, 'It doesn't become better. It becomes different.' Pedro's death is still very, very sad for me, but I've tried to stop being so angry at the senseless loss of life. You know, Pedro had so much more he wanted to accomplish. He was going to walk the halls of Congress and pass a bill. He was going to hang out with Elton John. That was his due. Stuff that would have been plain old fun.

"People say Pedro accomplished a lot, and he definitely did. But he wanted to do so much more. I guess that's why it makes us crazy sometimes to think that he could've been around six more months to a year, if he'd only been better about taking his medications. But we realize, we'll just make ourselves crazy thinking about that.

"After Pedro's death, it was well over a year before I could even look at the show again. Pam and I went on the road for most of that year speaking about HIV/AIDS education and prevention, carrying on Pedro's message. We just wanted to do something in his honor. Prior to that, Pam was undecided about what type of medicine to pursue. Pedro solidified it for her. Now, she's in primary care with a focus on HIV/AIDS care. That's what Pedro did for her, and so much more.

**"Pam and I joke about what a drama queen Pedro was [laughing]. I mean, he died hours after the last episode aired. It was astounding! He could have died two days later or two days earlier. Instead, he picked *the* moment when all the obits around the country would say, 'Pedro Zamora died hours after the last episode aired...' That was just *soooo* Pedro."**

# About Pedro

PAM: "Knowing Pedro changed my life in so many ways, including my relationship to medicine. Before Pedro, I'd had an academic interest in HIV/AIDS. My first patient in medical school died of AIDS. So, I'd seen the face of the disease. But I'd never known it in such a personal way. I felt like Pedro was walking me through the disease and through death, the way a close friend might take your hand for a stroll. It gave me a totally different level of awareness than anything I might've ever experienced as a medical student, or even as a doctor."

CORY: "As an AIDS educator, Pedro taught me so much about what it's like to live with the disease. He dispelled so many stereotypes and questions I once had like, 'Is it safe to get close?' But more importantly, Pedro taught me how to stand up for what I believe. To not be afraid of what others might think. 'People love you the most,' he would tell me, 'when you're honest and passionate about life. Don't hold back because you're afraid of offending people. Stick to your guns.' That's what Pedro's legacy meant to my life."

MOHAMMED: "I don't think anyone could have lived with Pedro and not gotten a lasting effect from the experience. The stuff that tripped me out about him were the smaller things. Like, he would receive more than ten letters a day from people all over the world. And he'd sit down, respond to every one of them that day and send them back out. There was this drive in him to connect with every person. That was one of the most amazing things about him."

PUCK: "Pedro accomplished with his life exactly what he set out to accomplish. He informed the public about his disease. He had something to say and he said it. That's why I was so offended when they kicked me out of the house because I had something to say, too."

**"...he would receive more than ten letters a day from people all over the world. And he'd sit down, respond to every one of them that day and send them back out. There was this drive in him to connect with every person."**

"...You have to love a kid in this day and age who says right out, 'I give thanks every day that I live in America,' perhaps especially when he is saying it on MTV."
—*The Washington Post* (June 23, 1994)

**JIM KEY (L.A. Gay & Lesbian Center):** "On July 20, 1995, we opened the nation's first HIV/AIDS clinic specifically for gay youth, **The Pedro Zamora Youth HIV Clinic,** to care for a segment of the population where the infection rate is increasing at an alarming rate—gay men under the age of 25.

"Pedro really symbolized the face of HIV/AIDS today—young gay men 'of color.' According to a recent medical study, gay men under the age of 25, most of them minorities, account for half of all new HIV cases nationwide.

"The goals of **The Pedro Zamora Youth HIV Clinic** were best stated by Pedro himself during testimony he gave before Congress: 'If you want to reach me as a young, gay man, especially as a young, gay man of color, then you need to give me information in a language and vocabulary I can understand and relate to. I'll be much more likely to hear the message if it comes from someone to whom I can relate.'

"To accomplish Pedro's objective, the L.A. Gay & Lesbian Center established an HIV/AIDS clinic staffed by specially trained peer counselors and medical personnel sensitive to young people's needs.

"For many young people, HIV/AIDS is their first time ever dealing with a health-related concern, not to mention their own immortality. **The Pedro Zamora Youth HIV Clinic** was designed specifically to help young people navigate through the challenging emotional, physical and medical hurdles associated with this disease.

"We're open six days a week and our staff provides health services ranging from HIV/AIDS education and prevention to anonymous testing and comprehensive treatment. All services are provided free of charge to those people who can't afford to pay.

**"I'm often asked, 'What was the impact of Pedro Zamora on the HIV/AIDS communities?' I can simply say that Pedro did more to sensitize people around the world to the realities of being a young, gay man with AIDS than anyone ever has. And that's why it's perfect that the first clinic in the nation for gay youth bears Pedro Zamora's name."**

**JOSÉ ZUNIGA (AIDS Action Foundation):** "Pedro injected humanity into our fight against HIV/AIDS. He was a voice for so many young people—gay and straight—who don't have a voice in places like Capitol Hill. He sensitized our lawmakers to issues of vital concern to young people concerning the disease. In terms of HIV/AIDS education and prevention, Pedro did as much as anyone ever has to ensure that there will come a day when no other person, especially young person, is infected with the disease.

"Unfortunately, two young people are now infected every hour in this country. So following Pedro's death in November 1994, the Zamora family established **The Pedro Zamora Memorial Fund** at our nonprofit AIDS Action Foundation, where Pedro had been a board member. The fund's principal aim has been to continue the work that Pedro did when he was alive, ensuring that young people, people of color, women and the poor receive the HIV/AIDS education they need.

"As an act of remembrance on the first anniversary of Pedro's death, we established **The Pedro Zamora AIDS Public Policy Fellowship Program.** The program provides young adults, ages 18 to 25, the opportunity to participate in the development of federal HIV/AIDS policy. Six Zamora fellows are selected each semester from around the country to work at AIDS Action in Washington, D.C., where they develop skills so they can become AIDS advocates in their own local communities. Fellowships are available three times a year and anyone wishing to apply should contact us at AIDS Action in Washington, D.C., or through our e-mail: **HN3384@handsnet.org.**

"Most recently, we established **The Pedro Zamora Memorial Award for Youth Advocacy** honoring a young person living with AIDS who has demonstrated Pedro's leadership qualities. This year's recipient was Hydeia L. Broadbent, a 12-year-old who has lived with AIDS since birth and who addressed the Republican National Convention in 1996.

"Her citation read, in part: 'Hydeia has shown America and the world another face of the epidemic...she has forged a unique leadership position—in the tradition of Pedro Zamora—as the clear, strong voice of youth...sharing her experiences and educating others about AIDS.' We know Pedro would've been proud!"

WOULD YOU DO IT AGAIN?
"I'd definitely do this again. I got my dream. I'm accessible now. That was great for me."

**KEVIN (N.Y.):** "I think Puck is a victim of self-hatred, like so many young people in this country. He doesn't really care about himself, so why would he care about anybody else....Puck has nine lives, that's all I can say, man. But, you know, what do you do after the ninth life is over, Puck?"

# Puck

**JUDD:** "It took a full week, no lie, for Mohammed to get the stink of Puck out of his room."

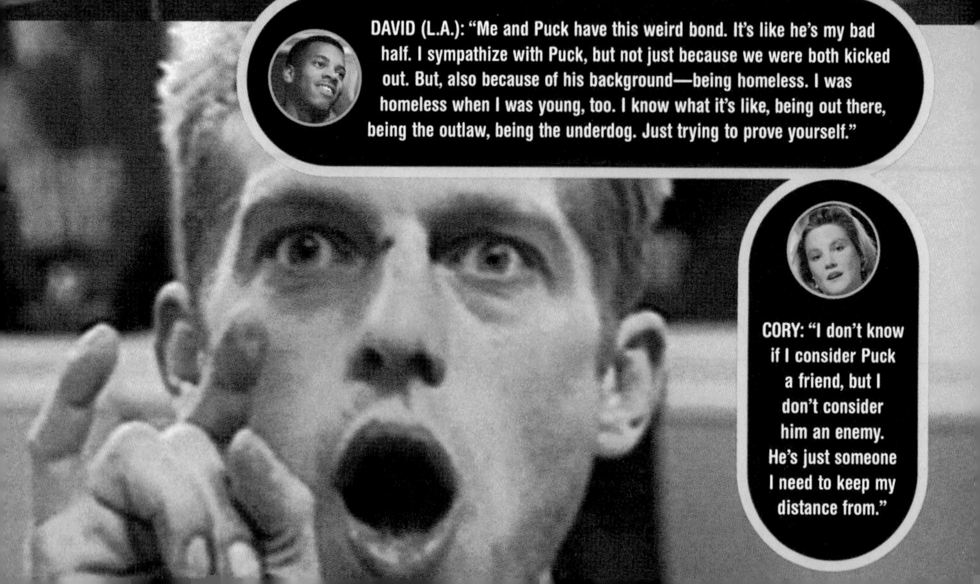

**DAVID (L.A.):** "Me and Puck have this weird bond. It's like he's my bad half. I sympathize with Puck, but not just because we were both kicked out. But, also because of his background—being homeless. I was homeless when I was young, too. I know what it's like, being out there, being the outlaw, being the underdog. Just trying to prove yourself."

**CORY:** "I don't know if I consider Puck a friend, but I don't consider him an enemy. He's just someone I need to keep my distance from."

**On the reunion:**
"I wasn't looking forward to seeing anybody at the reunion. Quite honestly, I did it for the money. That's the bottom line. I don't give a crap about all those kids, man. They're fly-liners.

"I already knew I was going to hear Mohammed call me a racist; Judd call me a homophobe, and Rachel call me an a**hole. I mean, so what.

"Okay, so I showed up at Universal Studios with a plan. I was going to be really gnarly backstage and freak everybody out. I wanted to get people running back and forth shouting, 'Puck is here and he's acting really gnarly.' Then, I was going to walk out on-stage and be real nice and calm. I was going to be the good Puck. I even had cheat cards in my pocket with little constructive things to say.

"But the moment I walked out there, everybody was ready to get me. That constructive guy got lost in the gunfight. Listen, man, I'm John Wayne. If you draw your gun, I'm going to draw my gun, too. I can't help it. It's in my gene pool. My grandpa is straight-up John Wayne.

"Anyway, that's exactly what happened. We all drew our guns and bullets went flying. Except, everybody had a peashooter and they were trying to shoot this elephant. It just wasn't going to work, man. Everybody was jumping in there, throwing in their two cents. It wasn't fair, you know. They might see it as, 'I'm only throwing in my two cents.' But eventually it adds up to be like...forty-two cents.

"Man, I was ready to punch someone out. So, I left for a few minutes. I went out the back, slammed the door, cried, left in the car, smoked a cig, came on back, no shirt, tattoos blazing....I'll tell you what, those guys were fools for letting me leave and come back like that. I could've returned with a gun and killed everybody like Woody Harrelson. I could've gone postal. I definitely had Allison Stewart going. She was reeling against the ropes. But instead, I just laid down and was real mellow.

"I thought what Judd did was really untactful, losing his temper like that. He accused me of saying something about Pedro, but he was too busy grandstanding to let me clarify what I'd actually said. For the record, what I said was 'I'm happy for Pedro that he's dead.' But not in the ha-ha funny sense. I meant that his struggle through life was over. He didn't have to worry about bills or cost of living anymore. He was free.

"Listen, I admit I was a complete butt-head out there. I know it. I just let myself go fourth grade. That's me, that's my defense mechanism. I don't know where everybody lives, but my defense mechanism is to recede to fourth grade and bust out mom caps on people. That's not really me. That's my outer extremity.

"Inside me lives this other guy, who's a little more tactful about what he says and does. His name is Dave. But you've got to prove to me you're worthy of meeting Dave. He's a hard man to get out of his shell. My man, Dave, lives in the woods."

**On his interview for *Real World*:**
"Mary-Ellis Bunim, the producer, told me not to eat during my interview. But I was like, 'Hey man, I don't care how much money you've got, I'm eating food right now. That's it.' Plus, I know it's the rudest thing you can possibly do during an interview, just a big-old-mouth-full-of-food."

> "Puck [is] a free-spirited Lord of the Flies who can also be an obnoxious pest."
> —*The Washington Post* (June 23, 1994)

**On being cast:**
"I was so stressed out when I heard. I went over to my friend's house to mellow out and I got hit by a car. I mean, if that's not God striking me in the head with a lightning bolt for doing TV, then I don't know what is. He's like, 'You're such a jerk, man, take a shot in the head.'"

**On watching the show:**
"The hardest moment for me to watch is my grandfather at the soap box derby 'cause he died, you know, and it's really a bummer."



**On being kicked out:**
"It wasn't like they were just kicking me out of the house. It was like they were stealing away a camera from me. They were taking away a story I had to tell."

**On role models:**
"I like being a role model. I think it's cool."

**On political correctness:**
"I don't have to be P.C. for anybody, man. I make all my own choices. I think that's pretty well documented."

**On *Real World*-ers:**
"Most of the people who've been on *Real World* are knuckleheads. They just think they're cool 'cause they're cool. What they don't realize is it takes work to be cool."

**On Hollywood:**
"I am Hollywood. I'm glam rock to the bone. I think The Puck has found his little nook for at least a couple of years. I'm just going to hang out and do this little Hollywood thing. Do movies and stuff. I just like to stay busy."

**On San Francisco:**
"I can barely go back to San Francisco. I'm just too hot for that town."

**On what question are you most frequently asked by fans:**
"Did I poke Rachel?"

**On what question are you second most frequently asked:**
"Did I deserve to be thrown out of the house?"

**On your answer to the second most frequently asked question:**
"I think they kicked me out of the house because they were intimidated by me, not because of my actions."

**On the comment you hear most often from fans:**
"'Yo, man, you got robbed.'"

**RACHEL: "Puck makes you laugh. He's a lot of fun. Okay, sometimes he reeked. But he liked to exaggerate that. He just wanted that image—hardcore and all."**

**JO: "I've hung out with Puck several times and he's never, ever been 'The Puck' with me. I like Puck. I can't say I don't, 'cuz I do. He's just this really insecure person, who feels like everyone is picking on him."**

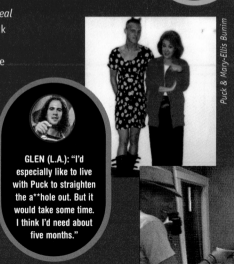

*Puck & Mary-Ellis Bunim*

**GLEN (L.A.): "I'd especially like to live with Puck to straighten the a**hole out. But it would take some time. I think I'd need about five months."**

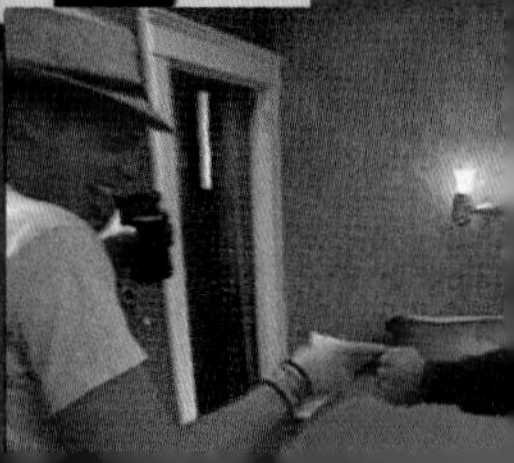

# Rachel

"Rachel [is] a female Dan Quayle."
—*The New Yorker* (July 25, 1994)

"You know what I find lame? Guys who tell you they're too cool to watch *Real World* and then tell you everything that ever happened on it. Some people even remember what I did in, say, episode three. Stuff I can barely remember myself.

"I recently met this person from a foreign country, who quite honestly never heard of the show. Well, when he mentioned my name to his friends, they all asked him, 'How can you hang out with her? She's such a bitch.' Obviously, *they'd* seen the show [laughing]. Well, I'll tell you I'm not that same person anymore. I've changed a lot.

"Not only am I no longer a bitch [laughing], but I've changed a lot physically, too. God, I looked really ugly on those shows. In a few episodes, I looked downright scary. I went to this drag show in L.A. and these drag queens were complimenting me, but they were saying all this other noncomplimentary stuff, like, 'Glad you lost the weight.' Or, 'You look fabulous. What happened?' Thanks... I guess.

**"I think we had the coolest cast, by far. But there's no question, we all came in with our own agendas. First and fore-**

**IF *REAL WORLD* WAS MADE INTO A MOVIE, WHO WOULD YOU WANT TO PLAY YOU?**
**"Selma Hayek. Yeah, I wish [laughing]."**

"Rachel is so physically attractive that her views generally are mitigated in the minds of her male roommates."
—*L.A. Daily News* (June 23, 1994)

# "I think we had the

**most was Pedro, then Mohammed, Judd, me...everyone with the exception of Cory. We all arrived thinking, 'I'm going to use this experience. I'm not going to let them twist my views.' And in Pedro's case, 'I'm going to show my views.'**

"I developed some amazing relationships through the show, especially with the crew. I was always talking and flirting with them, even though they weren't allowed to talk back. I was so flattered when they actually wanted to hang with me after the show. I mean, they'd seen just about all my bad sides.

"I'm still amazed at how many people have watched our shows. I'm famous and it feels like for no apparent reason [laughing]. One moment, I was just a teacher's assistant and then suddenly my first-year students were freaking out over me.

"A lot of my students asked why we kicked out Puck. After the reunion show, I think people understood why we did what we did. **Puck is a lot of fun, if you don't have to share a house with him.**

"Most fans are very respectful and friendly. I rarely hear annoying comments. I did get a few letters from viewers advising me on how to deal with my mother. I was like, 'Huh! You don't know me.' I don't have to sit and explain to every fan that my relationship with my mother is a cultural thing. Only white mothers say, 'Dear, that's a bad idea. Time out.' My mother chooses to speak to me and my siblings in her own way. It's not 'cause she doesn't love me. No one loves her children more than my mom does.

"I'm at a bit of a crossroads now, as to what to do. I recently earned two master's degrees—one in Latin American studies and the other in international relations. The next step would be for me to get a doctorate, but I don't know about that. It's been a long haul just getting to this point.

"Most importantly, I've been through some pretty traumatic s**t the past couple of years and I'm slowly beginning to find happiness again."

**BECKY (N.Y.): "I roomed with Rachel at the reunion and I thought she was great. She's like completely the opposite of me in a lot of ways. Well, I guess, I used to be a bit of a party girl myself, if you want to call it that. And she's very smart, too."**

**PUCK: "Rachel is going to college and she's groveling. That's what I see. I don't have nothing to say to Rachel."**

# coolest cast, by far."

**CORY: "My friendship with Rachel has gotten stronger since *Real World.* Sometimes it's easier to just be friends, instead of roommates."**

"We had this library of books in the house, which the producers had put together based on what they thought we'd like to read. There were all these Catholic books, political books and gay books. So during the season, every time a friend of mine had a birthday, he or she got a book from the house."

**WOULD YOU DO IT AGAIN?**
**"There's no way I could ever live again with six people. I live alone now and frankly, I don't know if I'll ever get married 'cause I love living alone so much. I'm so neat and tidy, and I don't want anyone putting their yucky furniture all over my house."**

# RACHEL'S ACCIDENT

"My boyfriend, a friend of his and I were driving back from Yellowstone Park, when all of a sudden we looked up and saw headlights bearing down on us. A gentleman had fallen asleep at the wheel and merged into our lane.

"I was in the emergency room, when the coroner came up to me and said, 'Is this your purse?' I said, 'Yeah, that's my purse. Where's my boyfriend?' And he said, 'Everybody died except for you.'

"My boyfriend and I had been talking about marriage on that trip. I was all for it. I thought I'd found the perfect guy. And I did. I really did.

"I have a relative, whose spouse died in a car accident, and she just said, 'It hurts and it hurts and it hurts...and then one day, you just wake up and it doesn't hurt the same way.' I'm just waiting for that day to happen.



"I never knew how important flowers were until I was hospitalized in both Wyoming and Phoenix. The flowers I received from fans and friends were overwhelming. The nurses said they'd never seen such a quantity of flowers in all their years. My boyfriend died, my leg was in really bad shape and they didn't know if I would ever walk again, so how could flowers help in that situation? Well, they did...a lot. And I can't thank you all enough for sending them to me. It meant a great deal.

**"I...received some very powerful letters from fans, who have lived through similar experiences. You can imagine how easy it is to feel sorry for yourself. But the letters helped me understand that I wasn't alone..."**

"I also received some very powerful letters from fans, who have lived through similar experiences. You can imagine how easy it is to feel sorry for yourself. But the letters helped me understand that I wasn't alone and I wasn't being punished for something I did. Just hearing about other people's experiences, even the ones of complete strangers, was extremely comforting.

"Going back to school definitely helped me cope. It gave me something to do. I try and stay focused now. I'm doing a lot better. I'm not disabled. I'm walking. And I'm generally just taking it one step at a time."

# Happily Ever After

## (Pam and Judd)

**Opening statement:**

**JUDD:** "For those of you who haven't heard already, Pam and I are dating, we're in love, we're a couple, we're an item, we're significant others, we're partners of the opposite sex sharing the same living space—is that what they say now? And all I can say is, 'Thank God!'"

**PAM:** "We're in love. We're actually very much in love."

**Unrequited love:**

**JUDD:** "By the time I left the house, I was fall-ass backward, head-over-heels in love with Pam. But unfortunately, she was dating Christopher at the time."

**CORY:** "Judd confided in me how much he really liked Pam. We were sitting over coffee and he told me he just couldn't do anything about it 'cause Pam had a serious boyfriend."

**PAM:** "I guess I didn't see it coming."

**First signs of love:**

**JUDD:** "The first time we saw 'it' together was in the lounge at St. Vincent's Hospital in New York. Pedro, Sean, Pam and I were watching tapes of the show on a VCR. We were watching the episode where Pam goes off with Christopher. I noticed I had this little look on my face. And I remember thinking, 'Good thing no one else caught it.' Well, duh! Like a million people did."

**PAM:** "People come up to me all the time and say, 'I knew you guys would get together 'cause in episode 12 there's this *look* on Judd's face...' Oh, my God. People really *do* watch this show. They notice stuff I didn't see."

**The letter:**

**PAM:** "Even when Judd and I were staying in Miami to see Pedro, I didn't think Judd's interest in me was anything more than as a friend. I was kind of wondering, 'What's his deal?' So, I decided to snoop through his stuff and I found a snooper's dream—a letter addressed to me."

**JUDD:** "I didn't think she'd go digging

like that. It was deep inside my notebook. She just happened to be lucky enough to open it up to 'Dear Pam.'"

**PAM:** "Of course, I *had* to read a letter if it says, 'Dear Pam...' Who's not going to read something like that? The letter said he 'loved me' and that if he never told me directly how he felt, he'd still walk around with these feelings for me forever. The hardest thing was pretending like I'd never seen the letter."

**JUDD:** "Three weeks later, I actually gave it to her."

**PAM:** "Right, and then I..."

**JUDD:** "...Feigned surprise. It was a full month 'til she admitted she'd already 'found' it in Miami."

**PAM:** "Well, I had to work my way up to it."



**Living together:**

**PAM:** "We don't clean the house. Neither of us do, until his parents come to visit [laughing]. Other than that, we share chores and things. Judd is based in the house and I'm in the hospital. It's great that I can come home and talk about *Frumpy the Clown,* when I need to get away from it all."

**JUDD:** "Having done those six months in the house together, which was stress like nobody's business, and after taking care of Pedro in Miami, we feel like any problems we might encounter are cake compared to what we've been through."

**Being recognized:**

**JUDD:** "It's much easier for people to recognize us, now that we're together. I'm sure people walk by us all the time and say, 'Hey, is that the guy from *Real World?*...Oh, wait a second...That looks like the girl, too. Man, that's got to be them.'"

**JO: "We all knew it was coming. We all knew they were going to get together."**

**PAM:** "It's the worst when you're in a hurry. You rush out to buy a magazine and some person is like, 'Oh, my God! Blah, blah, blah, blah....[laughing].' It's much nicer that we both have to deal with it. I think it would drive me crazy, if I had to stand and wait for someone who was constantly being stopped."

**Stupid questions:**

**PAM:** "A lot of people ask us, 'Are you still living in the house?' I feel like telling them, 'Yeah, and they left the cameras running. But they've decided not to show the footage [laughing].'"

**Marriage?**

**PAM:** "We hear that question all the time."

**Well, what's the answer?**

**PAM:** "We're not in a hurry. Oh, my God, a wedding has to be one of the most stressful things you can do. But eloping isn't a bad idea. If we elope, we'll call you. But I have a feeling it won't be for some time."

**JUDD:** "We want to get married. We want to be together. We are head-over-heels in love."

**So, what about children?**

**PAM:** "Pedro's roommate, Alex, started speculating, 'Well, if Pam and Judd get married and have a kid, they can name

him after Pedro.' Well, then we'd have a son named Pedro with a Chinese middle name and a Jewish last name. He'd be like, 'No, man, my mom's Chinese and my dad's Jewish...I don't know why they named me Pedro.'"

**JUDD:** "Black bean, won-ton, matzo ball soup is now being served in the house."

**CORY: "Pam and Judd seem like such an odd couple. But as soon as you're with them, you realize just how perfect they are for each other. They click in a weird way. And they just adore each other. It's soooo cute!"**

On Sunday, August 10th, 1997 Alex Escarano died of AIDS complications.

Alex was 40.

The viewers of *The Real World* knew Alex best as Pedro's best friend and roommate from Miami. Alex was actually the one who was responsible for Pedro's involvement on *The Real World.* It was at his insistance that Pedro audition. So, at the very least, the world owes him a great debt because of that.

Alex was a true Renaissance man. A graduate of Duke University, an accomplished painter, actor, producer of television, and comedy writer.

But most importantly, Alex was an AIDS activist who fought tirelessly for the rights of PWAs (people with AIDS) and for the education of young people.

Alex was one of the greatest people we knew. He always gave so much more than he got, and our lives are diminished in his absence. We loved him dearly, and not a day will go by that we won't think about him.

—Pam Ling and Judd Winick

**MOHAMMED: "Judd and Pam are together once again. I say, 'Again,' because we all observed a lot of kinetic energy flowing in the house between them. I don't know what transpired in the house, outside of a really intimate, nonsexual relationship, but it's no shock to any of us that they're now together."**

# SAN FRANCISCO Quiz



## MULTIPLE CHOICE

**1. What name did the roommates give their special club on Valentine's Day?**

a. The Stinking Rose Club
b. The Lonely Hearts Club
c. The Get the Puck Out Club

**2. At what event did Pedro and Sean meet?**

a. At a "Get Out the Vote" march
b. At a "Get Out Puck" march
c. At a "Gay and Lesbian" march

**3. How did Judd surprise Pam at her birthday party?**

a. Playing *This Is Your Life*
b. Playing doctor
c. Playing with himself

**4. What did Rachel get for a tattoo?**

a. A picture of a rose
b. A picture of a heart
c. A picture of Puck

**5. For what public offense did Pam and Rachel receive a police citation?**

a. Displaying too much affection in Golden Gate Park
b. Climbing the Golden Gate Bridge
c. Breaking out of Alcatraz

**6. What did the roommates accuse Rachel and Jo of doing?**

a. Sharing a shower with Melody the Waitress
b. Stealing Lars' bike
c. Excluding them from their friendship

**7. Mohammed's band, Midnight Voices, was the opening act for what performer?**

a. Michelle Shocked
b. Jerry Garcia
c. Huey Lewis

**8. What is the name of Judd's comic strip?**

a. *Nuts & Bolts*
b. *Puck S**ks*
c. *Pam's My Ma'am*

**9. What underwater activity did the cast learn to do on their vacation in Hawaii?**

a. Snuba
b. Snicker
c. Snuggle

**10. What was the nickname of the guide who led the grueling bike tour?**

a. Kamikaze Ken
b. Cruiser Bob
c. Pam's Pain

## DID THEY REALLY SAY THAT?

**Which lines were really said by cast members on *The Real World–San Francisco* and which lines are fake?**

11. CORY: "I never felt so white."

12. JO: "What's the difference between Puck and a pool table? The pool table's still in the house."

13. JUDD: "We're all pigs. We all did this for attention—except Cory."

14. MOHAMMED: "If I were any more laid back, I'd be sleeping."

15. PAM: "I have no trouble just being friends with a guy I'm attracted to."

16. PEDRO: "I don't like my peanut butter with scabs."

17. PUCK: "I'm humming—can you see the stink coming off me?"

18. RACHEL: "He's got a lot of nerve. I am not interested in dating Puck."

## MULTIPLE PUCK

**19. Who did Puck claim to be?**
a. The Mario Andretti of Soap Box Derbies
b. The Shaquille O'Neal of TV
c. The Oscar Madison of Roommates

**20. What infamous actress does Puck claim to have dated?**
a. Traci Lords
b. Madonna
c. Jenny McCarthy

**21. What did Rachel give to Puck?**
a. Her undying love
b. Her virginity
c. Her finest manicure

**22. Why did Puck like sodas that were blue?**
a. They reminded him of the ocean
b. They reminded him of sunny skies
c. They reminded him of glass cleaner

**23. What was Puck's favorite thing to blow?**
a. Snot rockets
b. Bubbles
c. A rent-free apartment

**24. How did the roommates kick Puck out of the house?**
a. By bike messenger
b. By smoke signals
c. By phone

**25. On what sitcom did Puck guest star?**
a. *Men Behaving Badly*
b. *Beavis & Butt-head*
c. *The John Larroquette Show*

### SCORING GUIDE

20–25: Great! So great, in fact, that Puck might even take a shower in your honor.

15–19: Good! So good, in fact, that Puck might even take you for a spin in his soapbox.

10–14: Okay! So okay, in fact, that Puck might even share his blue soda with you.

5–9: Poor! So poor, in fact, that Puck might even shoot a snot rocket at you.

0–4: Bad! So bad, in fact, that Puck must now share a room with YOU!

ANSWER KEY: 1.b 2.c 3.a 4.a 5.b 6.c 7.a 8.a 9.a 10.b 11.did 12.did 13.did 14.did not 15.did not 16.did 17.did 18.did 19.b 20.a 21.c 22.c 23.a 24.c 25.c

# Los

## POP CULTURE LANDMARKS

TV shows set in L.A.:
The Adventures of Ozzie & Harriet
The Adventures of Superman
The Brady Bunch • Charlie's Angels • CHiPs
Dragnet • It's a Living • L.A. Law • Lou Grant
Melrose Place • Remington Steele
Set in Beverly Hills: Beverly Hills 90210
I Love Lucy • The Beverly Hillbillies
Set in Malibu: The Rockford Files
Set in Santa Monica: Baywatch
Set in Venice: Three's Company

Some famous movies set in L.A.:
Beverly Hills Cop • Blade Runner
Body Double • Car Wash • Chinatown • Colors
The Crow: City of Angels • Devil in a Blue Dress
Die Hard • Dragnet • Earthquake • Falling Down
Fletch • 48 Hours • Heat • L.A. Story
Lethal Weapon (I, II, III) • Men in Black
Menace II Society • Pretty Woman • Pulp Fiction
Rebel Without a Cause • Rising Sun • Shortcuts
Speed • Stand and Deliver • Swingers • Terminator
To Live and Die in L.A. • The Usual Suspects
Volcano • White Men Can't Jump

## MUSIC

Some famous L.A. musicians' deaths:
Janis Joplin overdosed on heroin in a Hollywood motel on October 2, 1970. Blues Brother John Belushi overdosed at Hollywood's Chateau Marmont hotel on March 5, 1982.

Some famous L.A. music acts:
The Bangles • The Beach Boys • The Byrds
Concrete Blonde • The Doors • Go-Go's
Guns N' Roses • Poison • Red Hot Chili Peppers
Van Halen • Frank Zappa and Captain Beefheart

# Angeles

City of
Los Angeles
VENICE
Bel Air
U.C.L.A.
Brentwood
Heights
Century City
20th Century Fox Studios
West L.A.
Santa Monica
Santa Monica Mun. Arpt.
Santa Monica State Beach
Venice
Marina Del Rey
USTOR

# Class of '93

## The Los Angeles Cast

**Name: KITTY**

**Name: BETH S.**
Birthdate: February 14, 1969
Hometown: Garfield Heights, Ohio
Last Seen: Living in Santa Monica, California.
Last Word: Starting a film production company to produce independent films. Has appeared as an actor in several low-budget movies.

**Name: JON**
Birthdate: July 30, 1974
Hometown: Owensboro, Kentucky
Last Seen: Living in Kentucky.
Last Word: Performing country music and looking for a record deal.

**Name: IRENE**
Birthdate: August 14, 1967
Hometown: Covina, California Last Seen: Living in Covina.
Last Word: Working as a bailiff with the Los Angeles County Sheriff's Department. She and her husband, Tim, have a 3-year-old son.

**Name: GEORGE**

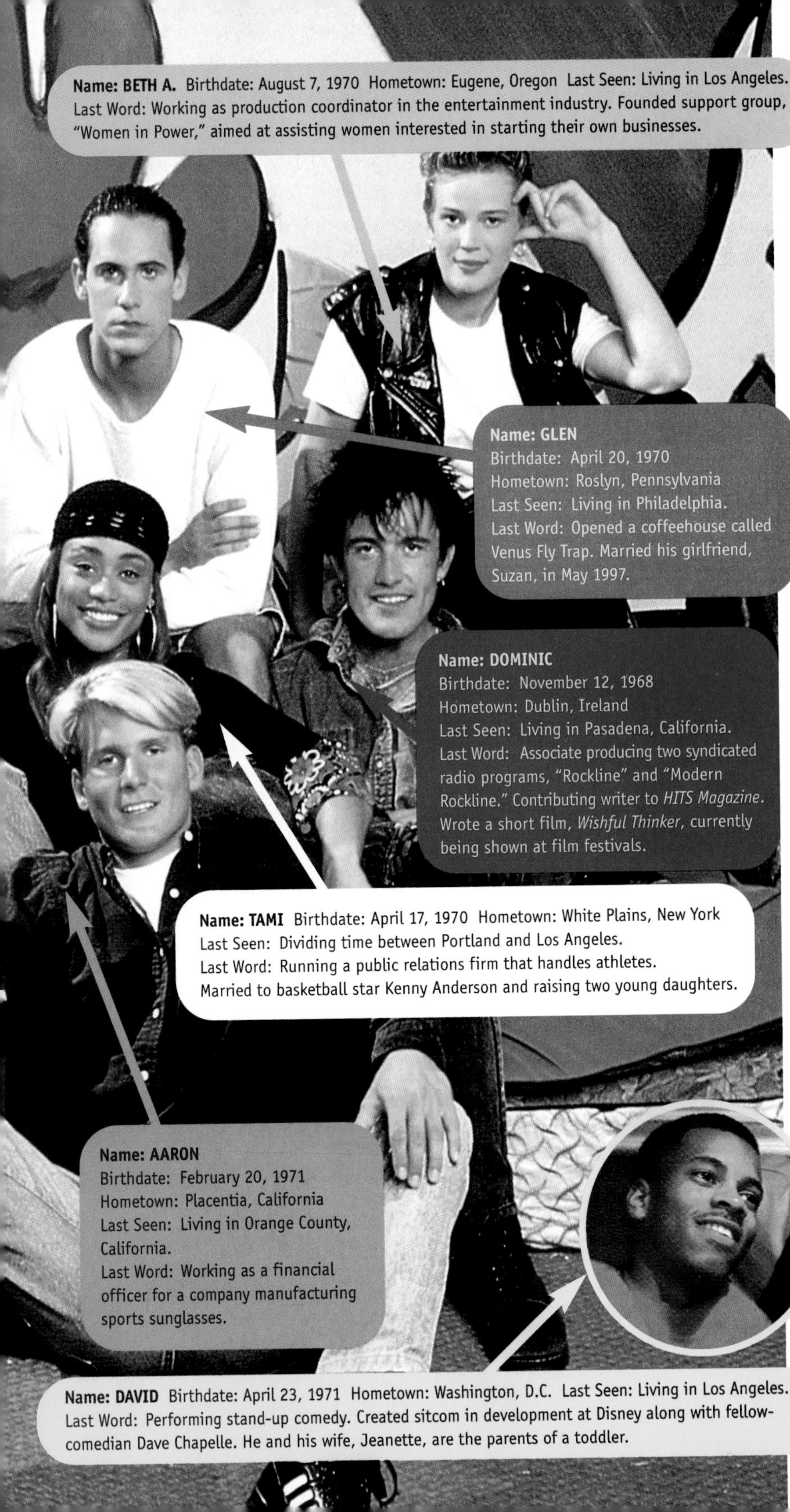

**Name: BETH A.** Birthdate: August 7, 1970 Hometown: Eugene, Oregon Last Seen: Living in Los Angeles. Last Word: Working as production coordinator in the entertainment industry. Founded support group, "Women in Power," aimed at assisting women interested in starting their own businesses.

**Name: GLEN**
Birthdate: April 20, 1970
Hometown: Roslyn, Pennsylvania
Last Seen: Living in Philadelphia.
Last Word: Opened a coffeehouse called Venus Fly Trap. Married his girlfriend, Suzan, in May 1997.

**Name: DOMINIC**
Birthdate: November 12, 1968
Hometown: Dublin, Ireland
Last Seen: Living in Pasadena, California.
Last Word: Associate producing two syndicated radio programs, "Rockline" and "Modern Rockline." Contributing writer to *HITS Magazine*. Wrote a short film, *Wishful Thinker*, currently being shown at film festivals.

**Name: TAMI** Birthdate: April 17, 1970 Hometown: White Plains, New York
Last Seen: Dividing time between Portland and Los Angeles.
Last Word: Running a public relations firm that handles athletes.
Married to basketball star Kenny Anderson and raising two young daughters.

**Name: AARON**
Birthdate: February 20, 1971
Hometown: Placentia, California
Last Seen: Living in Orange County, California.
Last Word: Working as a financial officer for a company manufacturing sports sunglasses.

**Name: DAVID** Birthdate: April 23, 1971 Hometown: Washington, D.C. Last Seen: Living in Los Angeles. Last Word: Performing stand-up comedy. Created sitcom in development at Disney along with fellow-comedian Dave Chapelle. He and his wife, Jeanette, are the parents of a toddler.

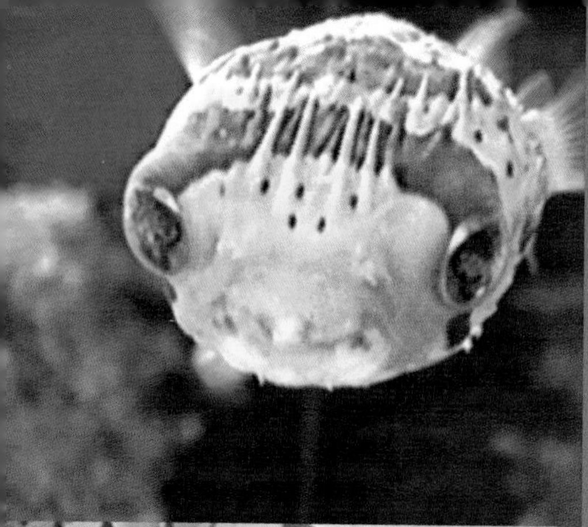

### VENICE VISION!

Surfer's paradise. 3-story, 3-bedroom dream house located one block from Venice Beach. 6000 square feet. Ocean view. Roof deck. Spa deck. Billiard room. Painted murals. Great place to kick back or kick out.

HISTORY: The rumor mill is most active on *The Real World–Los Angeles* house. One source said a member of Madonna's entourage bought this place, so she could preserve its *Real World* state. Another one claimed a not-so-enthusiastic neighbor purchased and gutted it, so there'd be no reminder of the previous tenants. Either way, there's no truth to the rumor that David bought it, so he could move back in.

BETH S.: "The closet was my favorite spot, as if you needed to ask."



# the house

BETH A.: "I loved the slipcovers on all the furniture. I wanted to steal them."

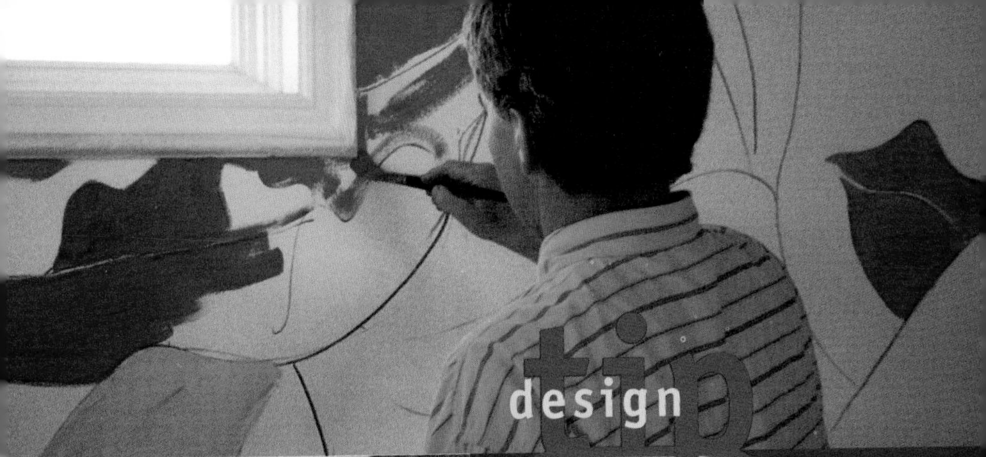

## design tip

from NAOMI SLODKI (Designer, *RW–Los Angeles):* "The biggest bang for your buck is paint! Strong colors show up a room. We did a lot of murals."

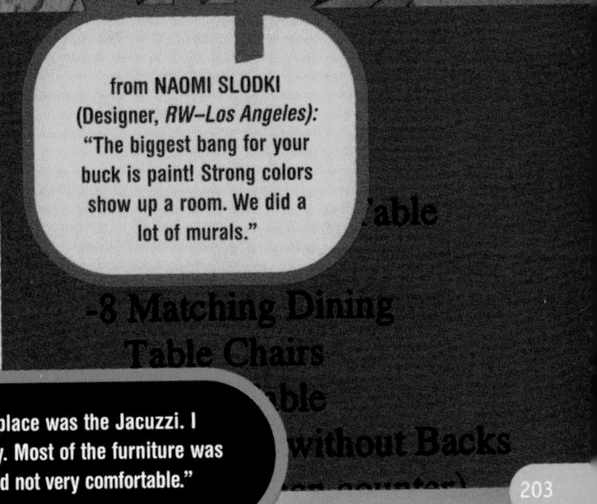


JON: "My favorite place was the Jacuzzi. I was in it every day. Most of the furniture was real artsy-fartsy and not very comfortable."

IRENE: "The closet was my favorite place. We told all our secrets in there 'cause there were no microphones inside."

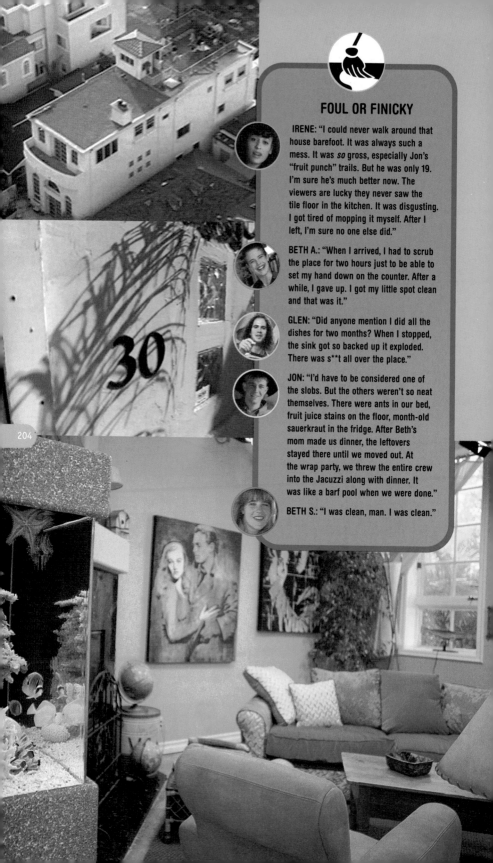

## FOUL OR FINICKY

IRENE: "I could never walk around that house barefoot. It was always such a mess. It was *so* gross, especially Jon's "fruit punch" trails. But he was only 19. I'm sure he's much better now. The viewers are lucky they never saw the tile floor in the kitchen. It was disgusting. I got tired of mopping it myself. After I left, I'm sure no one else did."

BETH A.: "When I arrived, I had to scrub the place for two hours just to be able to set my hand down on the counter. After a while, I gave up. I got my little spot clean and that was it."

GLEN: "Did anyone mention I did all the dishes for two months? When I stopped, the sink got so backed up it exploded. There was s**t all over the place."

JON: "I'd have to be considered one of the slobs. But the others weren't so neat themselves. There were ants in our bed, fruit juice stains on the floor, month-old sauerkraut in the fridge. After Beth's mom made us dinner, the leftovers stayed there until we moved out. At the wrap party, we threw the entire crew into the Jacuzzi along with dinner. It was like a barf pool when we were done."

BETH S.: "I was clean, man. I was clean."

DAVID: "I liked the wall, especially when the camera-man crashed into it. That was hilarious."

GLEN: "The long sofa was my favorite hangout. I slept on it a lot. And the fish tank, of course. But Jon didn't know how to feed them and killed them all."

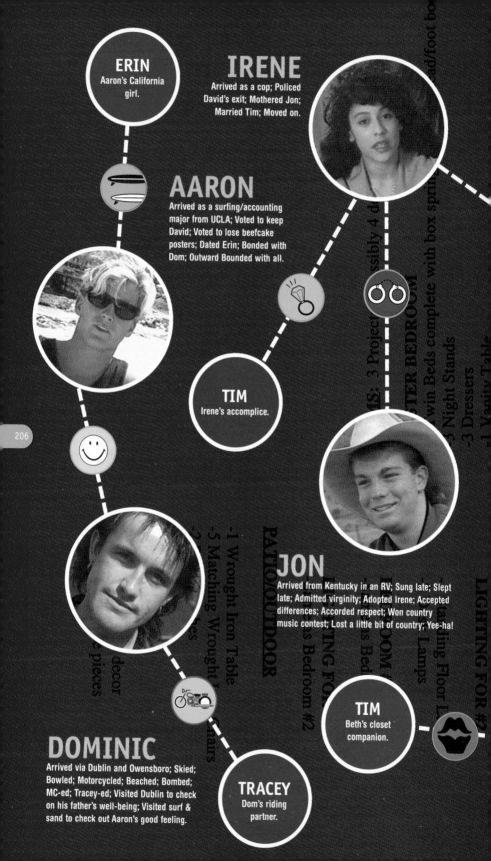

**ERIN**
Aaron's California girl.

## IRENE

Arrived as a cop; Policed David's exit; Mothered Jon; Married Tim; Moved on.

## AARON

Arrived as a surfing/accounting major from UCLA; Voted to keep David; Voted to lose beefcake posters; Dated Erin; Bonded with Dom; Outward Bounded with all.

**TIM**
Irene's accomplice.

## JON

Arrived from Kentucky in an RV; Sung late; Slept late; Admitted virginity; Adopted Irene; Accepted differences; Accorded respect; Won country music contest; Lost a little bit of country; Yee-ha!

**TIM**
Beth's closet companion.

## DOMINIC

Arrived via Dublin and Owensboro; Skied; Bowled; Motorcycled; Beached; Bombed; MC-ed; Tracey-ed; Visited Dublin to check on his father's well-being; Visited surf & sand to check out Aaron's good feeling.

**TRACEY**
Dom's riding partner.

# DAVID

Arrived as the comic; Joked on Jon; Tattooed with Tami; Pulled covers off Tami; Apologized to Tami; Booted out by Tami (et al.).

**TOOTIE**
Tami's Mr. T.

# BETH A.

Replaced Irene; Catered for movies; Served the homeless; Wore on Tami's nerves; Kickboxed with Beth S.; Kicked back with Glen; Shared her past; Prepared for future.

# TAMI

Arrived with Dom and Jon; Wired mouth; Rigged *Studs;* Irritated by Perch; Dated; Dumped; Tooti-ed; Tami-ed; Volunteered; Persevered; Listened; "Lip-synched"; Introduced Mom; Delayed motherhood.

# BETH S.

Arrived as aspiring actress; Inspired David's premature departure; Denied masturbating; Cried "Rape"; Auditioned for movies; Costarred with Tim in the closet; Crashed her moped; Paintballed her roommates.

**PERCH**
Arrived with Glen.

# GLEN

Replaced David; Perched with bandmates; Annoyed some roommates; Clicked with Beth A.; Clanked with Beth S.; Dressed in drag; Raged on stage.

# Aaron's California Dream

**BETH A.:** "I think if I could've chosen seven people from all the *Real Worlds* to live with, I'd have loved for Aaron to be one of them."

**JON:** "Aaron wanted to come across as the stud."

GLEN: "Aaron is a funny guy, even though that didn't come across on TV. We'd go for our beer runs and had so much fun. I only had a problem with him the first week 'cause he was wary of me. That's just the way he is."

# Aaron

"For people who haven't seen the show, I tell them it's about seven people living in hell."



# Beth A.

"*The Real World* wasn't pressure. It was a pleasure.

**"For people who haven't seen the show, I tell them it's about seven people living in hell [laughing].** I'd never seen it before, so I wasn't certain of what to expect. All I knew for sure was that my grandparents were going to watch. I just saw it as a great way to educate young people that it's possible to get past differences. I figured I'd be a young, gay female role model. That I'd help break the boundaries of ignorance.

**"Having Tami there helped. She was so ignorant and asked such dumb questions, which was great. The line that most people remember was: 'Well, should I tag my friends at the door and let you know who is gay and who is not?'**

"It was an interesting experience. But by the end, I couldn't take it anymore. It's an interesting phenomenon. Here, you have this great chance to show what society could be. Unfortunately, no one really takes advantage of that opportunity, or responsibility for that matter. Except Jon. He stuck to his guns and made his positions clear.

"I held back a lot. I didn't want to deal with the very immature level of confrontation going on. Now, I wish I'd expressed more of an opinion. All I did was hold back my own

opportunity to educate people. Still, I was quite happy with the way I was portrayed. I had dignity and poise and integrity. I think I also showed that lesbians transcend shape, size and color.

"It wasn't the show, itself, that changed me the most. Dealing with all those personalities just felt like high school. No, it was my own self-esteem. Until *Real World*, I'd been trying to finish projects and accomplish things. I'd had a lot of opportunities, but taken advantage of few of them. Perhaps I was too scared of my own power. As a result of my experiences on the show, I felt I could do anything.

"I still do craft services, preparing holistic food for production companies. But I'm also doing a project now called Women In Progress (W.I.P.) and it's pretty exciting. I'm working on a line of merchandise—T-shirts and postcards—based on feminist symbols from the women's movement. I'm donating 10 percent to nonprofit organizations fighting against AIDS. I've already done some garage sales. And I plan to provide grants for women who are opening their own businesses. I'm 26. It's now time to do something important!

"As for my love life, Becky and I have decided to be apart for awhile. We're still totally together, but we're taking one year apart. It's hard to live with someone. It's hard, but I want to work on it 'cause we love each other.

"As for *Real World*, I got to do a lot of wonderful things because of it. I met incredible women writers and young people. Even now, people still come up to me to talk about the show. And it's still a pleasure."

**GLEN: "Beth A. loves me. She loves me. Doesn't matter that she's a lesbian. She sees beyond the sex."**

**WOULD YOU DO IT AGAIN?**
**"I wished I had utilized the experience more. I was intimidated by the energy of the other people. The next time I'd throw my hair back and not care as much about the others' energy. At the end of *Schindler's List*, Schindler says, 'God, this ring could've been one more...I could've done more.' I wish I'd done more with the opportunity, like showing recycling. We can make this a better world."**

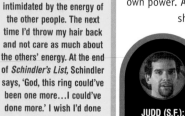

**JUDD (S.F.): "I met Beth A. for the first time at a benefit for Pedro in Los Angeles. She is incredibly sweet. She can come up to the Bay Area and crash with me and Pam anytime."**

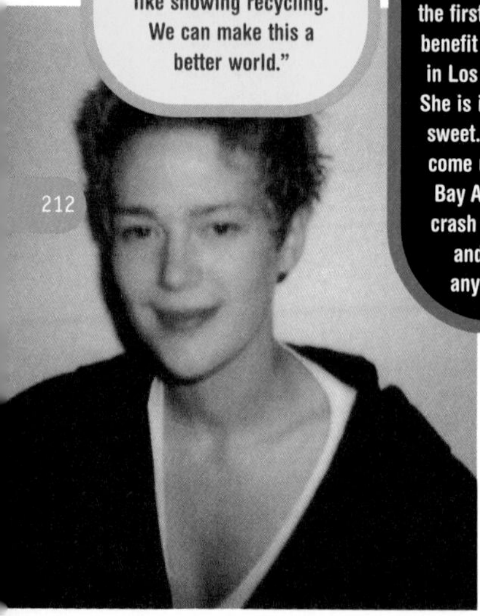

**"I took everything. I took a year's supply of cotton swabs and shampoo. No one else wanted it. Actually, I had cotton swabs for years [laughing]. I took my bedding as well. But I'm so honest, I told MTV I was taking it. They made me pay $20. Dead serious! They made me pay for my blanket. I should've stolen it, but it's against my nature."**

**IF *REAL WORLD* WAS MADE INTO A MOVIE, WHO WOULD YOU WANT TO PLAY YOU?**
**"Glen in drag!"**

"So, did you ever do it with the cowboy?' I get asked that question the most.

**"My answer—'No. Not yet'... just kidding.**

"Listen, Jon's my little brother. Yes, I think he's cute. Would I like to date him? No, I don't think so. He's still going through growing pains right now. Let's see where Jon is five years from now. Let's wait 'til he gets through puberty and we'll see [laughing]. But I told Jon if I'm not married by the time I'm 32, I'm coming after him. And seeing as I'm 28 and single, it looks like I might be coming after all [laughing].

"Speaking of love life, that's one thing of mine that's really gotten screwed up by *Real World*. It's gotten to the point where I refuse to date anyone who recognizes me from the show. That's turnoff number one. If they recognize me, I figure they're only interested in me because of *Real World*. On top of that, it's just too weird knowing the guy's got all this information on me, when I know nothing about him.

"Of course, my rule on dating limits the talent pool, since it seems like everybody still recognizes me from the show. Just the other day, a carload of guys pulled up alongside me, screaming 'Hey, it's Beth from *The Real World*. Pull over.' Yeah, right. They even started following me. Thankfully, they drove away.

"On the plus side, *Real World* has given me a nice little taste of celebrity-hood. It's like going to 'Celebrity Training School.' I get into clubs for free, good tables at trendy restaurants and drinks on the house. If I

**"I got stuck in the wrong house."**



# Beth S.

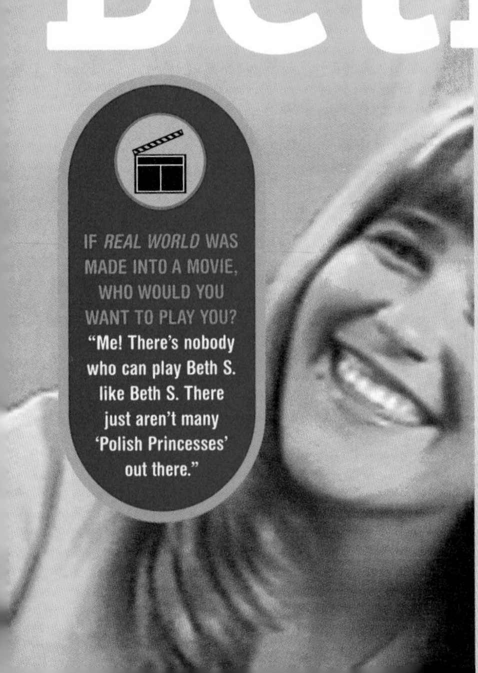

IF *REAL WORLD* WAS MADE INTO A MOVIE, WHO WOULD YOU WANT TO PLAY YOU?

**"Me! There's nobody who can play Beth S. like Beth S. There just aren't many 'Polish Princesses' out there."**

**DAVID: "When I look at Beth S., I can tell she knows it was f**ked up what she did. You know, it's weird that you can look at somebody's face and you don't even have to hear the answer. You can just tell. At least, Tami was decent enough to say, 'Yeah, I was wrong. I'm sorry.' Beth just tried to shut it off. She was just, 'Heh, heh!' Playing it off. But I'm not going to strap her down and make her say it."**

really wanted, I could party every night for almost nothing. And I've gotten to meet some pretty cool people, too, including Ben Stiller. Oh, my God—Ben Stiller. Now, he's the 'King of Sex Men.' I mean, that guy can make me cry.

"Of course, *The Real World* hasn't transformed me from a struggling actor into a major movie star. A lot of casting agents know who I am because of it. Some of them tell me they thought I was a major, major bitch on the show. Unfortunately, they haven't cast me to play any major, major bitches in the movies, just yet. I'd love to do that. Hey, anyone can play nice [laughing].

**"'Do you keep in touch with your housemates?'** I get that one, too.

**"My answer—'I got stuck in the wrong house.'**

"I get along better with people from the other casts than the people from my own. I talk to Cory and Norman just about every day. And I see Rachel, Jacinda and Neil whenever they're in L.A. When fans see us all together, they assume we're taping another *Real World* reunion. In fact, we all met at the last reunion and had a great time. It's like we've formed some kind of support group—'*Real World*'s Not-So Anonymous.'

"As for my cast, I speak with Jon nearly every week. I talk to Irene from time to time; and I see Beth A., whenever she comes to town. But that's it! **Quite frankly, if I don't talk to Glen, Aaron or Dominic again for the rest of my life, I wouldn't miss it at all.**

"I never really got to know any of them. I just didn't feel like sharing myself with people who weren't willing to make an effort to share themselves. I felt like, 'These people don't deserve to know me.' Too bad for them and too bad for me.

**"'Why did you throw David out of the house?'** That's a fan favorite.

**"My answer—'David deserved to be thrown out.'**

"First of all, I never called David 'a rapist.' You can look it up on the videotape. And I wasn't the only person in the house who wanted David thrown out. We all wanted him out. For David to rant and rave that I was responsible for influencing

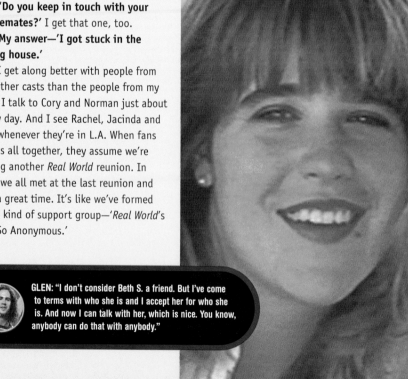

**GLEN: "I don't consider Beth S. a friend. But I've come to terms with who she is and I accept her for who she is. And now I can talk with her, which is nice. You know, anybody can do that with anybody."**

"I don't know what I was thinking, but I didn't steal anything good. And I'm good at that sort of thing. I'm the 'Queen of Scams.'"

Angie Everhart. I'm also starting a production company with a friend to produce independent, festival-type films. And lastly, I'm the vice president of an Internet company that caters to actors and writers in the entertainment industry.

"As for my love life, I'm still looking for my 'Prince Charming.' My dream is to find a male virgin, but I don't think that's likely to happen. Well, come to think of it...Jon's still a virgin."

**DID SHE OR DIDN'T SHE...IN THE CLOSET ON HER EX?**
**BETH S.: "Ah, man...I will never live that down. Okay, the answer is...yes. Now leave me alone. Because of that incident, my friends now call me the 'Queen of Oral Sex' [laughing]."**



Tami is absurd. Excuse me, but nobody could talk Tami into doing anything.

"Some people say we had no right kicking David out 'cause it's just a TV show. Well, hello! It wasn't just a TV show for us—we were living it. If I'd had my way, I would've kicked David out two days after we moved in—right after he choked Jon. Or the fourth day, when he pulled his pants down in front of me. David had no respect for anyone.

"**'So Beth, what are you doing now?'** Of course, everyone asks me that one.

"**Answer—'Keeping busy.'**

"My acting career is coming along fairly well. I've been cast in several low-budget movies, most recently as a snooty TV reporter in *Dillinger in Paradise*, starring Maria Conchita Alonso and

**WOULD YOU DO IT AGAIN?**
**"If you throw me in a house with some hot guys, I'd do it again in a heartbeat. How 'bout Eric, Lars, Jon, a heterosexual Dan, and throw in Beth A., too, because I know she wouldn't be stealing any of the guys."**

# David

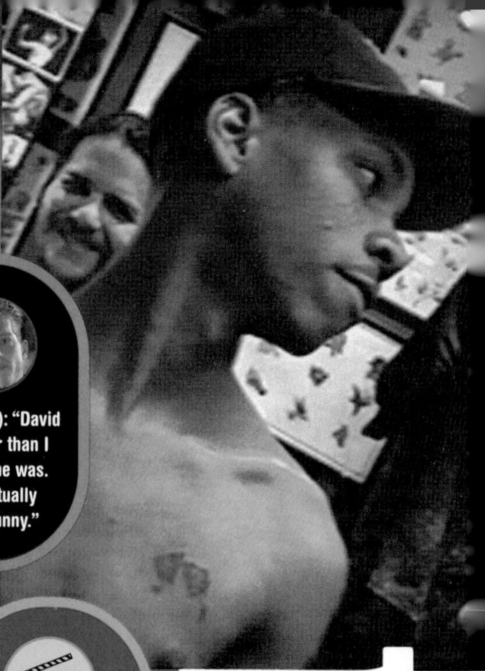

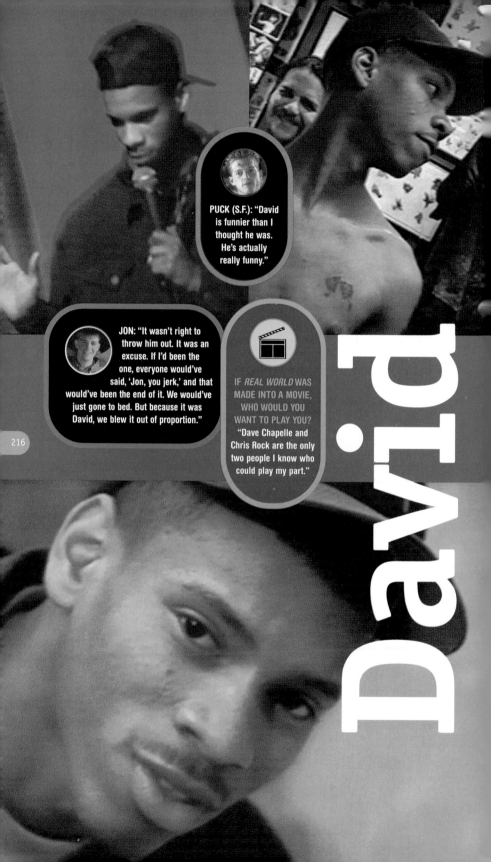

**PUCK (S.F.):** "David is funnier than I thought he was. He's actually really funny."

**JON:** "It wasn't right to throw him out. It was an excuse. If I'd been the one, everyone would've said, 'Jon, you jerk,' and that would've been the end of it. We would've just gone to bed. But because it was David, we blew it out of proportion."

IF *REAL WORLD* WAS MADE INTO A MOVIE, WHO WOULD YOU WANT TO PLAY YOU?

**"Dave Chapelle and Chris Rock are the only two people I know who could play my part."**

"**Getting kicked out was one of the best things that could have happened to me.**

"Look. I got on their nerves. I don't blame them. When I think about it, I think, 'Hey, I would've kicked me out, too [laughing]!' I was pushing buttons. But what else was I supposed to do? I'm a comedian!

"But listen, if they'd played that tape of the Tami incident for the others, I never would've been asked to leave. I never understood why they didn't just play it for us. Put on the VCR and let us see that segment. You can hear Beth egging Tami, and so was Irene. Irene said 'rape,' too. And she's a police officer. That's outrageous! I think Beth was just getting back at me for a fight we had a bit earlier. Jon, Aaron and I had teased her about some date, who was on his way over. I teased the s**t out of her. I kept ringing the doorbell and making her run down the stairs to answer it for no reason. She was furious.

"Fact is, I don't think it would've worked anyway. Look at the personalities they chose. There was going to be plenty of pressure in that house, even before they added the cameras.

"I don't think the others knew where I was coming from. None of us spent enough time getting to know each other. We could've asked each other more questions. Maybe it would've lessened the conflict. But if we'd done that, it would've been a show about hippies and not about Gen-X kids.

**"Getting kicked out was a big deal for me. Real big. I can still hear my keys hitting the table. That was one of the most dramatic and emotional experiences of my life.**

"It reminded me of when my mother put me out when I was 14. Mom and I are the best of friends now, but I was a little pigheaded when I was younger. I wasn't a bad kid, just had a mouth on me. One snowy night, she said to me, 'You're just like your father. Get out.' That hurt! It hurt a lot. I bounced around for a while. The police came looking for me. They put me in a receiver home, but I escaped. Eventually, my mother's best friend adopted me for a couple of years. Then, I found comedy.

"So when my roommates kicked me out, I was scared. Real scared. I was crying in Jon and Mary-Ellis' office. I had no place to go; no place to live. I had this little check from *Real World* and I had to get an apartment. I found this little, sh**ty place with holes in the wall. It was in a bad neighborhood. Motherf**kers kept fighting over dominoes. There were f**king orgies and s**t. And no cable, either [laughing]. I'm thinking, 'What am I going to do?'

"And then it hit me like a vision. I better get working before this s**t hits the air. I have three months before it goes on. I have to get an agent and some scripts right away. I started crashing auditions, literally picking s**t off the floor. I got *House Party 3* from off the floor. I went in for an audition and boom! Then I got *In Living Color* during their last season.

"I got so busy I forgot about *The Real World* s**t myself. That was until Jamie Foxx and Tommy Davidson came up to me and said, 'Man, are you living with seven people?' I thought, 'Uh-oh!'

"Soon as they aired the incident, the industry froze on me. I had management leave. Agents rearranged. Motherf**kers



**"Getting kicked out was one of the best things that could have happened to me."**

**IRENE: "Dave and I talked at the reunion. Everything was cool. We put it in the past, so it's in the past. I think he's grown a lot from it, too."**

got scared. **They thought I was on *Court TV*. They didn't know what the f**k I was on [laughing].** It took about six months for people to get the hang of it. It was weird. Thank goodness they did a good job editing it. I have no complaints there.

"People still stop me just to talk about the *incident*. They can't wait to tell me how much they want to kick Tami and Beth's asses. I have to tell them, 'They're not so bad. I'm over it.' It's, like, 'Yo. I'm okay. It's just a show.' I don't know if things were patched up at the reunion. It was more like closure. It's like we put a Band-Aid and a little ointment on the wound.

**"I'm not bitter, nor do I regret anything I did. Some people hold me in this category, like O.J. or Woody Allen. Yeah, I got accused. But falsely. There was no trial. No police. My life wasn't ruined, but it definitely changed.**

"Now, I'm a happy man. **A HAPPY MAN**. I have a beautiful one-year-old baby girl and a beautiful wife. My wife has a great sense of humor. When I get on her nerves, she brings up the show. 'That's why they threw your ass out, and I can throw your ass out, too' [laughing]

"As for my career, I recently wrapped up a college tour and am appearing in a documentary, *King of the Park*. Dave Chapelle and I have a sitcom in development at Disney, where we play two jazz musicians and best friends. Our characters live together...and I don't get kicked out!"

**TAMI: "I think David has matured so much. I guess it's like that old saying about getting a chance to step outside yourself and look in. You get to see how other people see you. He's realized he may have been a little jerky at times and he's made a change for the better. I'm real proud of him for that."**

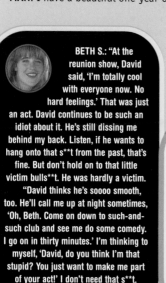

**BETH S.: "At the reunion show, David said, 'I'm totally cool with everyone now. No hard feelings.' That was just an act. David continues to be such an idiot about it. He's still dissing me behind my back. Listen, if he wants to hang onto that s**t from the past, that's fine. But don't hold on to that little victim bulls**t. He was hardly a victim.**

**"David thinks he's soooo smooth, too. He'll call me up at night sometimes, 'Oh, Beth. Come on down to such-and-such club and see me do some comedy. I go on in thirty minutes.' I'm thinking to myself, 'David, do you think I'm that stupid? You just want to make me part of your act!' I don't need that s**t. Of course, I never go."**

**WOULD YOU DO IT AGAIN?**

**"If history were to repeat itself, I wouldn't change one single thing. I did some stuff I'm not proud of, but it doesn't outweigh being there. I only have good memories, so I don't regret any of it."**

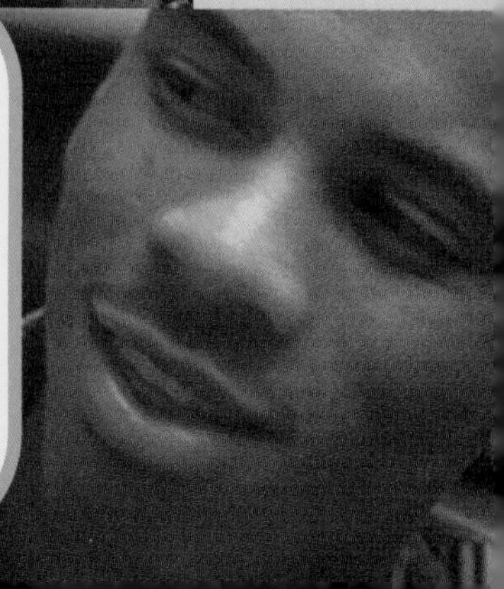

# Dominic

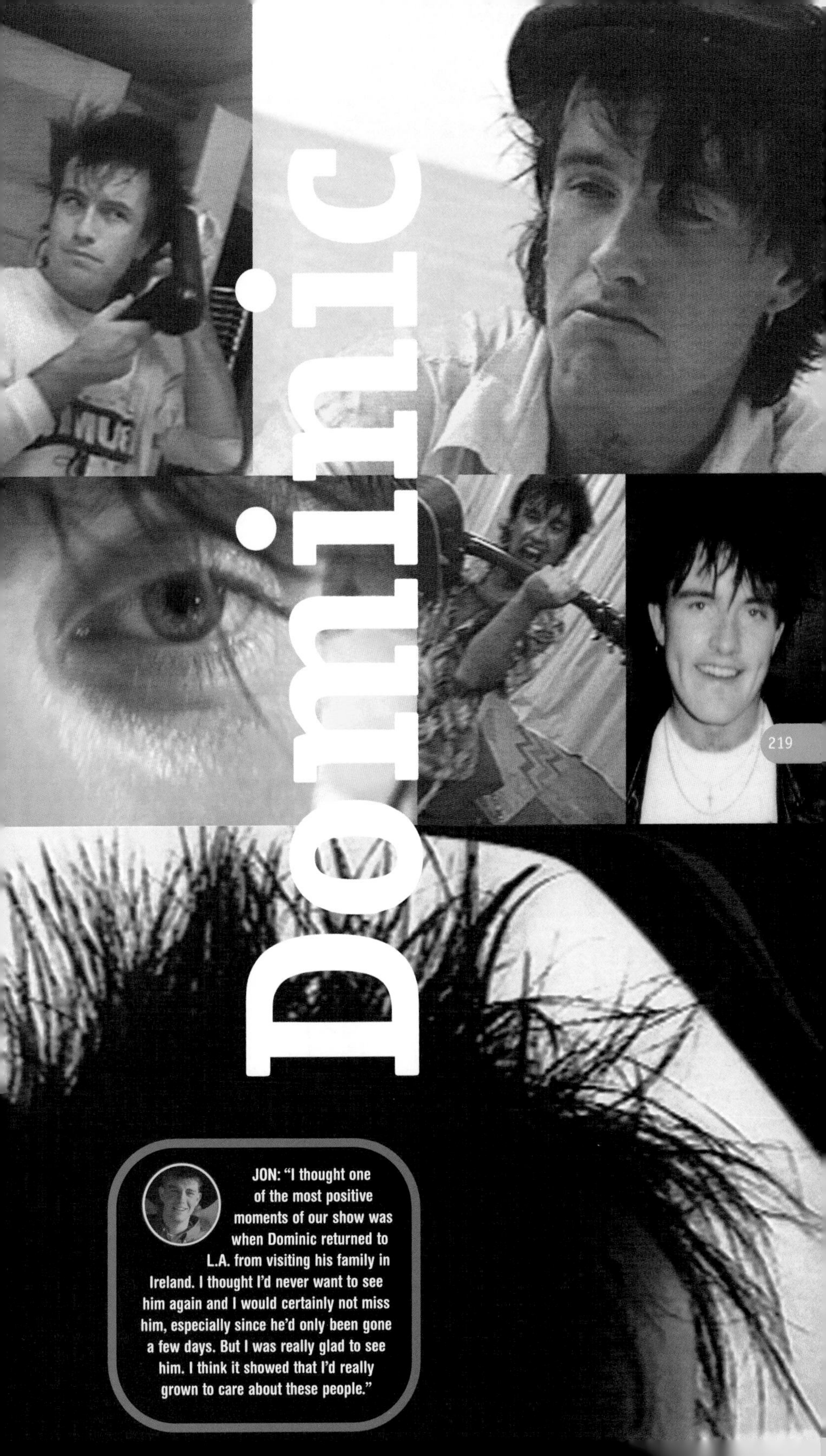

**JON:** "I thought one of the most positive moments of our show was when Dominic returned to L.A. from visiting his family in Ireland. I thought I'd never want to see him again and I would certainly not miss him, especially since he'd only been gone a few days. But I was really glad to see him. I think it showed that I'd really grown to care about these people."

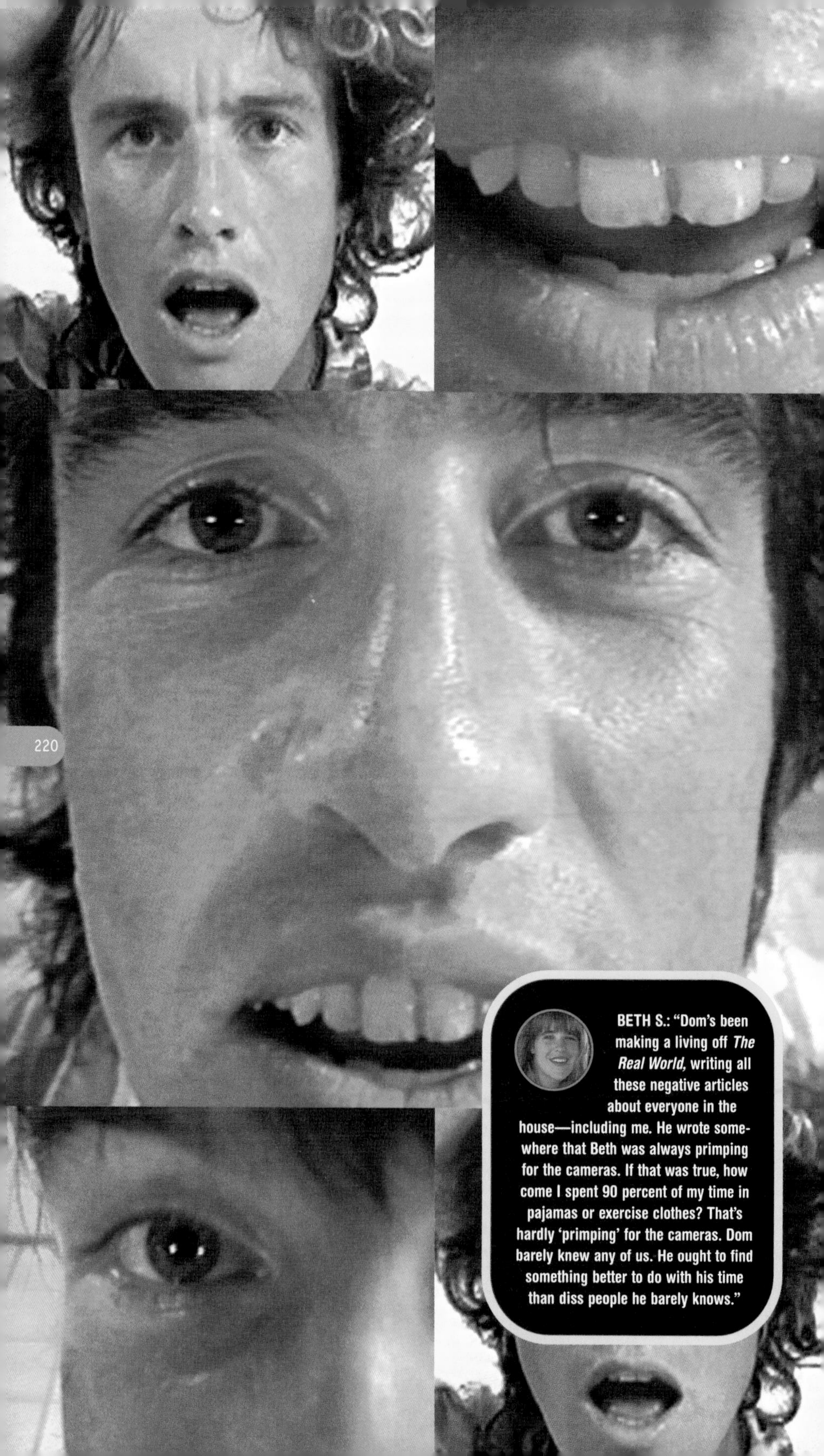

**BETH S.: "Dom's been making a living off *The Real World,* writing all these negative articles about everyone in the house—including me. He wrote somewhere that Beth was always primping for the cameras. If that was true, how come I spent 90 percent of my time in pajamas or exercise clothes? That's hardly 'primping' for the cameras. Dom barely knew any of us. He ought to find something better to do with his time than diss people he barely knows."**

# "If they weren't going to be open, why should I be?"

"At first, I hated the whole experience. I think everyone thinks that if they're on the show, they'll manage fine. But everyone finds out it's not what you think it's going to be.

"I guess I touched a lot of nerves when I moved in. My closest friends have always been people I *didn't* get along with at first. So I figured I'd work things out. But I think they thought I was an a**hole. **And I just got mad at them. If they weren't going to be open, why should I be? I always thought, being from the East Coast, that people on the West Coast were so cool. I should've known better.**

"Strange thing is, I now miss 'em all. Honestly, I do, especially hanging out with Dom. I went to the *Real World* reunion, but I didn't know how to talk to everyone all at once. I just can't do that. I have to meet people gradually.

"I was a mess after the show ended. I stayed in L.A. and lived in a house a few doors down from *The Real World* house. It was incredibly depressing watching the owners gut the interior. It felt like they were taking something away from me.

"I pursued music off and on with Perch and movie production on my own. I was an extra in several flicks, mostly low-budget ones, including *Reality Bites.* You can see me in the bar when Ethan Hawke punches the wall fighting with Winona Ryder. I'm only on-screen for a second, but a lot of people have come up to me and said, 'Hey, man, I saw you in *Reality Bites.*'



# Glen

"The more I lived in L.A., the more I thought I was going to end up like the homeless people living in my neighborhood. I was unemployed a lot, and I began to think I might end up on the

Glen and Suzan on their honeymoon

Venus Fly Trap >

street, too. So after two years, I left L.A., moved to San Francisco and, ultimately, back to Philadelphia.

"I'm still playing with Perch, although the band is now made up of people from both Perch and Magnetic Jesus, the other band I performed with.

"I've also started a nonprofit organization called Junto, which is aimed at reminding people that at any age you can remain youthful. Junto was the name of a social club founded by Benjamin Franklin in the 1700s to foster the exchange of ideas among people of all ages.

"Toward that end, a friend and I opened a two-story coffee dive in South Philly called Venus Fly Trap. It's as wacky as Perch—both have just a little bit of everything. We've got food, we've got music, we've got poetry.... Hopefully, Venus Fly Trap will serve as a prototype for what I want Junto to be—a place where the young and the old can respect and learn from each other. Someday, I hope to create youth centers all across the country for children of all ages—from 7 to 70. **I know it's going to be a lot of hard work, but nothing comes easy. You just gotta make choices in life.**

"The best choice I've made so far was getting married this past May to Suzan, whom I'd been going out with for over a year. We didn't have a wedding—we eloped...with our parents. Yes, that's right, with our parents. We told our parents we wanted them to go on a short trip with us. We picked them up, drove to a church, where we had a minister standing by, and got married. And it was the first time our parents had ever met."

**BETH S.: "I don't talk to Glen. I really don't have any desire to."**

**WOULD YOU DO IT AGAIN?**
**"I'd like to sit with all those people again and say, 'We're in this million-dollar house. Let's enjoy it. They should send us all to some island for two weeks and let us film it."**

**BETH A.: "Glen was very young and immature at the time of the show. He was in a radical phase, always attacking people. He holds true to what he believes. And now he's doing incredible things with his life. He has that strength. If I was straight, I'd probably marry him. But that's not going to happen [laughing]."**

**"I took my comforter and I got in trouble for taking it. They told me to bring it back. They let us take some towels—the ones with stains all over them."**

**IF *REAL WORLD* WAS MADE INTO A MOVIE, WHO WOULD YOU WANT TO PLAY YOU?**
**"I'd want to play myself. But Rob Lowe would be good. He's played a lot of creeps lately."**

JON: "Irene is very caring. She is classy and has morals. I respect that."

"I had my eye on the pay phone, but I didn't get it. I took the towels instead. I really did. As a matter of fact, I use one in my police locker as a rug. It's bright blue [laughing]. How's that for grand larceny?"

# Irene



"The majority of people who recognize me now are custodies. They do get cable in jail, you know [laughing]. That's scary when the criminals know who you are. And I do get a lot of jurors here that recognize me. I'm always flattered if someone recognizes me. It makes me feel good inside. It means they liked me on some level.

"Being on TV was weird. It was a time for me to play. I got some fan mail. I got to encourage some females to join law enforcement and the military. But now, I'm back to being a wife and mom and all that other good stuff.

"I didn't want to stay in show business. I got a few inquiries about modeling, but I had a job and wasn't interested. To me, my police work and family are *my* real world. My job is the most secure thing around. I didn't want to trade that in for insecurity. I still come to the same job every single day. *The Real World* gave me a lot of confidence. I'm not afraid now to talk to anyone. And I'm not afraid to give an order...and mean it. With confidence!

**"But by the end of my stint, I needed to get out of there. Honestly. When they showed me crying, it was tears of joy [laughing]."**

## "When they showed me crying, it was tears of joy."

When I told David to leave, that was Irene, the cop. But the mom side of me was also concerned for David's future well-being. I talked with David at the reunion. Everything's cool.

"I still keep in touch with some of the group. Jon and I talk just about every week. He's a friend for life. And I recently visited with Beth S. We've gotten together for barbecues and stuff. That's the beauty of the show. They put seven people together from different cultures and backgrounds to see what would happen. We either liked each other or didn't."

**IF *REAL WORLD* WAS MADE INTO A MOVIE, WHO WOULD YOU WANT TO PLAY YOU?**
**"The girl that played Selena, Jennifer Lopez. Definitely her!"**

"I wouldn't have done anything differently. Well, I guess I'd have loved to change the others, but that wouldn't have been possible.

"Everyone changed in front of the camera. I think David did the most. I was careful not to reveal everything. No way. I was told by the police department before I went on, 'Don't embarrass us.' So, I couldn't talk so openly or candidly. Truth is, you never, ever forget the cameras are there. I don't care what people say. You may forget it's a camera, but you know it's there. I never forgot.

"What folks saw was two different Irenes—Irene, the cop, and Irene, at home. During the David-Tami incident, both sides came out.

**TAMI: "I saw Irene at *The Real World* reunion. I wanted to let her know I was very upset she hadn't come to my wedding because I'd forgotten to put Tim's name on the invitation. I was very upset about that. So, I talked to her about it. She apologized for not coming and I apologized for not putting Tim's name on the invitation."**

**WOULD YOU DO IT AGAIN?**
**"It was hard, but I'd do it again. The friendships I made were so special. And it was an interesting world to play in for a little while. But I was mighty glad once I got out [laughing]."**

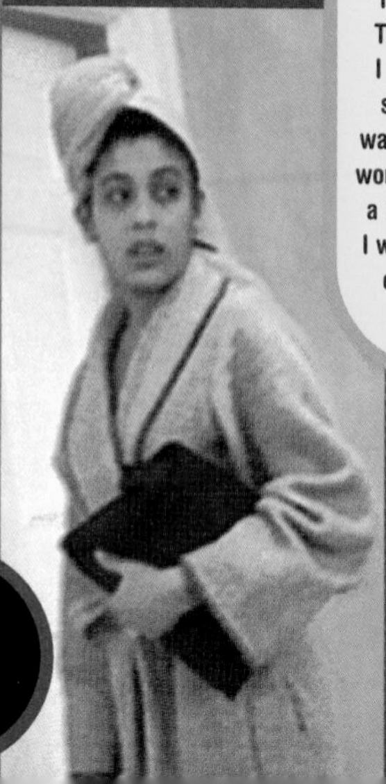

**GLEN: "Irene is great. I love her. But poor Irene gets caught between me and Jon. He just doesn't like me for some reason."**

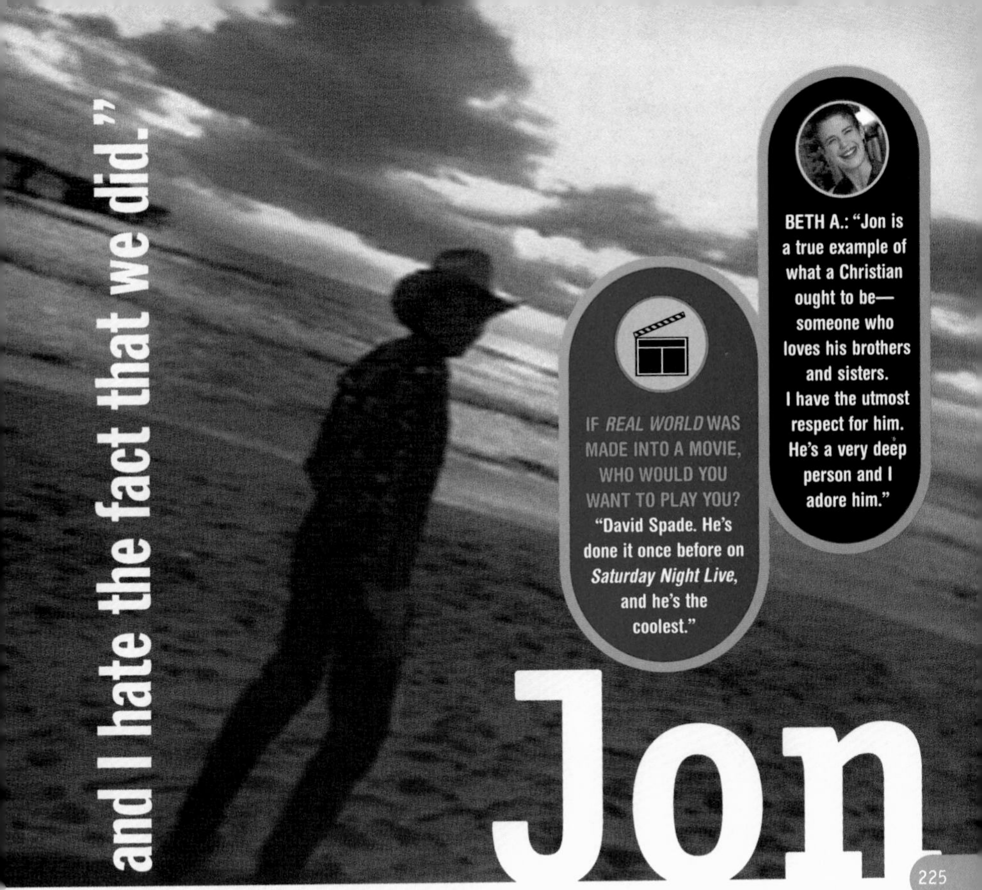

# Jon

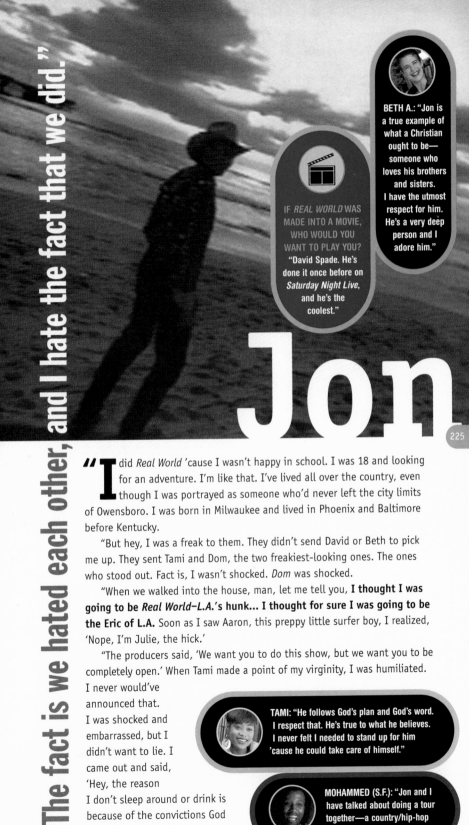

"The fact is we hated each other, and I hate the fact that we did."

**BETH A.: "Jon is a true example of what a Christian ought to be—someone who loves his brothers and sisters. I have the utmost respect for him. He's a very deep person and I adore him."**

IF *REAL WORLD* WAS MADE INTO A MOVIE, WHO WOULD YOU WANT TO PLAY YOU?
**"David Spade. He's done it once before on *Saturday Night Live*, and he's the coolest."**



"I did *Real World* 'cause I wasn't happy in school. I was 18 and looking for an adventure. I'm like that. I've lived all over the country, even though I was portrayed as someone who'd never left the city limits of Owensboro. I was born in Milwaukee and lived in Phoenix and Baltimore before Kentucky.

"But hey, I was a freak to them. They didn't send David or Beth to pick me up. They sent Tami and Dom, the two freakiest-looking ones. The ones who stood out. Fact is, I wasn't shocked. *Dom* was shocked.

"When we walked into the house, man, let me tell you, **I thought I was going to be *Real World–L.A.*'s hunk... I thought for sure I was going to be the Eric of L.A.** Soon as I saw Aaron, this preppy little surfer boy, I realized, 'Nope, I'm Julie, the hick.'

"The producers said, 'We want you to do this show, but we want you to be completely open.' When Tami made a point of my virginity, I was humiliated. I never would've announced that. I was shocked and embarrassed, but I didn't want to lie. I came out and said, 'Hey, the reason I don't sleep around or drink is because of the convictions God

**TAMI: "He follows God's plan and God's word. I respect that. He's true to what he believes. I never felt I needed to stand up for him 'cause he could take care of himself."**

**MOHAMMED (S.F.): "Jon and I have talked about doing a tour together—a country/hip-hop thing. That would be *phat!*"**

**JUDD (S.F.): "I consider Jon a friend. In a lot of ways, we were in the same boat, but working different sides of the fence. We were both the nice white guys in the house—that was our role."**

**ELTON JOHN: "God, how many times have I fallen in love with somebody on *The Real World?* The country-western singer with the big hat?...Whew! How typical, you always go for the ones you can't get, right?"**—*speaking at the Gay and Lesbian Center's 25th Anniversary ball*

**JON'S RESPONSE: "I don't agree with homosexuality. It's just wrong. However, I've been an Elton John fan for a long time. I'm flattered he knows I exist. That's cool. But he's old enough to be my grandfather."**

**PUCK (S.F.): "Jon, I love you. I dig you, man. I wear cowboy boots just for you. There's a lot of country in this kid, too."**



has placed in my heart.' I still feel that way. **My morals are the same. If I haven't sacrificed them on *The Real World*, why now? I'm still a virgin 'cause I'm still following God.**

"But I don't want to sound like I haven't changed at all. Aaron said that I came on the show to prove I wouldn't change and I didn't. I think I did! Before *Real World*, I would never have lived in a house with someone having an abortion...or with a homosexual. In fact, I think I came across as the most compassionate.

**"The fact is we hated each other, and I hate the fact that we did.**

"It's like this. I tried to have a relationship with everyone in the house. I hung with Dominic. I hung with Tami and with Aaron a couple of times, too. I hung with both Beths, David and Irene. But Dom and Beth dodged each other. Aaron would have nothing to do with Beth A. Beth S. hated Glen, and vice versa. All the girls didn't like Tami. It was ridiculous. The goal of the show was to interact. Yet, everyone else was too busy dodging each other. I feel they missed out on the experience.

"The show is supposed to break down stereotypes, but I'm afraid it only reaffirmed them. It made blacks into stereotypes and me into the country hick. Tami came off as promiscuous, which is the way she was. And money-hungry, which is the way she is. I could tell you things that would shock you. And David was loud and obnoxious, nothing like Mohammed, who made black people look good.

**"As for me, I was treated like a hick, even though I was born in Wisconsin and I've never lived on a farm in my life. I'm from a city—small compared to New York—but 85,000 people isn't so tiny. I said 'Yee-haw!' just to be obnoxious.**

"Recently I coached a high school basketball team and they were real curious about *Real World*. Particularly, about the gay people. I told them the ones I met through the show—Norman and Beth—were the nicest people on *The Real World*. They're the most loving, most compassionate, not to mention most fun, people I've ever been around.

**"When the show ended, the producers hired a psychologist for us. He told us we'd miss the attention. That we'd miss feeling important enough to be filmed tying our shoes. Sometimes, I do. I can't lie. It's like Eric once said: 'We've been given a platform, whether you want it or not.' People look up to you. The show goes across the world. I'm not some character on a sitcom. I'm Jon from *The Real World*. People know me! That's cool.**

**"On the other hand, I don't want to be that guy from *The Real World* the rest of my life. That's like being asked about your high school days in every conversation. *Real World* is over! It's four years ago! It's past! It's reruns!**

"Now, I want to be Jon, the singer. Slowly, that's beginning to happen. I'm not taken real seriously in Nashville, yet. I'm still known as the kid from MTV. But I'm only 22. I have to do something bigger than *The Real World*, something of substance, to move on. I need to have a hit song.

"I'm out touring with my band these days, opening for country acts. I don't have a CD yet. I had a deal with a major label, but it fell through. Hopefully, another will come along soon. Until then, my dream was to be a country singer and I'm living it."

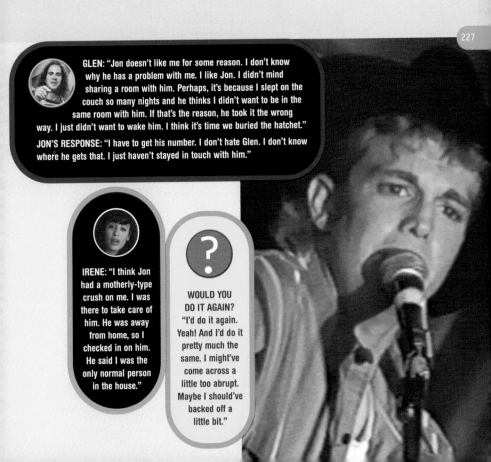

**GLEN:** "Jon doesn't like me for some reason. I don't know why he has a problem with me. I like Jon. I didn't mind sharing a room with him. Perhaps, it's because I slept on the couch so many nights and he thinks I didn't want to be in the same room with him. If that's the reason, he took it the wrong way. I just didn't want to wake him. I think it's time we buried the hatchet."

**JON'S RESPONSE:** "I have to get his number. I don't hate Glen. I don't know where he gets that. I just haven't stayed in touch with him."

**IRENE:** "I think Jon had a motherly-type crush on me. I was there to take care of him. He was away from home, so I checked in on him. He said I was the only normal person in the house."

**WOULD YOU DO IT AGAIN?**

"I'd do it again. Yeah! And I'd do it pretty much the same. I might've come across a little too abrupt. Maybe I should've backed off a little bit."

# Tami

## "I was very, very bitchy."

**JON: "I'd love to talk to her now. She could be the world's biggest you-know-what, but she could also be the sweetest person. When she was nice, nothing happened. But when she was the *b-word*, things just happened. And they showed most of the latter."**

**So, what was it like being filmed every waking moment?**

"Coming into it, I was a little nervous having the camera follow me around 24 hours a day. When the crew wasn't there, the stationary cameras were. So, it was a little hard getting used to. But by the second or third week, they all became commonplace. Like the couch or the TV. You know they're there, but you don't mind. It's unbelievable that happens, but it does."

**Were you pleased with what they showed?**

"I wish they'd shown more interaction between me and my mom, because she was around a lot. I wished they'd shown more of my job, instead of just showing the day Erin came to help me and I quit. And I wish they hadn't shown my relationship with Tootie. So many people come up and say, 'What the hell were you doing with that guy?' I get so much flak for that. But the truth is, everything they showed was real. They used what they wanted and got rid of what they didn't."

**How did you feel about the entire experience after it was over?**

"I felt like I'd learned so much about myself. I was very, very bitchy. That's all I ever showed. I think that's why there was so much anger toward me. I've learned how to talk to people now. To start thinking before I speak and not to offend others. I'm just so much more relaxed and at peace with myself. I try to portray that side of me now, instead of being so uptight all the time. I've tried to mellow out and take things day by day. I'm also not as rude as I used to be. People like me a lot better now."

**All that change because of *The Real World*?**

"I've also matured being a wife and mother. Having children really mellowed me out. I have a lot more patience. I'm trying to do more positive things and surround myself with positive people. Keep that positive energy flowing."

**BETH A.: "Here's this incredibly beautiful young black woman, who didn't take any responsibility for the image she was creating. To have her jaws wired shut like that was horrifying. I grew up on the streets. I'm used to knocking people out. And let me tell you, time after time it took all my strength not to hit her. I tried to maintain a calm mental attitude. I don't drink a lot of caffeine. Good thing! I'm sure I would've lost it, if I had."**

**Any advice for future *Real World*-ers?**

"Just be yourself. Be honest with yourself and don't try to let anyone change you. And stand behind whatever decisions you make on the show."

**How was it seeing David at the *Real World* reunion show?**

"When David hugged me, it felt like the natural thing to do. We don't hate each other. In fact, we didn't dislike each other from the beginning of the show. It was just an incident that happened and we all took the easy way out. We should've sat down, talked about it and really tried to work it out."

**Do you think he was kicked out unfairly?**

"Seeing the tapes, I can honestly see David's view of the incident. He felt it started as a joke and just continued as a joke. From my point of view, the David incident is resolved. It's over with! So please stop writing letters. Please stop coming up to me on the street saying, 'Why did you kick David out of the house?' It's over with. Move on!"

**GLEN: "One day, I was making chocolate-chip pancakes and Tami asked me to make her some. After that, I made them many times for her. I was trying to get in good with her. I mean, come on. I was attracted to her [laughing]. I would've kept hitting on her, if she had shown any interest in the white guy. Or maybe it was 'cause I had no money."**

**What about Beth S.?**

"I read that she said I 'probably got married for the money' and that 'I'm the biggest bitch she's ever known.' I wished she said those things when we were living together. I would've stayed away from her. I wasn't a fan of hers, either. Of course, being Tami, I had to confront her the moment I saw her at the reunion. She told me, 'You can't believe everything you read in the media.' She said she didn't say those things, so I left it at that."

**Do you believe her?**

"Personally, I think she said it and doesn't want to own up to it. That's fine with me. I'm moving on. If she says she didn't say it, that's where it lies."

**Did you speak with the other Beth?**

"I apologized to her for not having been comfortable living with a lesbian. I should've gotten to know her better and not been so defensive. I'm not apple pie all the time. I'm not sunshine all the time. I have my own problems, my own hang-ups, my own issues. I spoke with her, but she wasn't very positive with me. That's cool. I did what I had to do and I'm moving on."

**PUCK (S.F.): "Tami was the person I wanted to meet the least at the reunion. She's a sellout. I think her husband sucks, too. He's a horrible player."**

**Did you enjoy meeting the other casts?**

"People have a tendency to run all the seasons together. They think I lived with Eric, or I lived with Puck. I get questions about Lars, like, 'Is he really cute?' I don't know, I'd never met him. So the reunion was a great opportunity to finally meet 'em all."

**Looked like you and Heather sparred a bit.**

"I'd always wanted to meet her. I thought she'd seemed so one-dimensional during her episodes. I always thought if I met her, I'd discover another side to this girl. But when I finally did, she said she's just exactly like the girl on the show. What you see is what you get. She didn't want to get to know me at all. So, I didn't get much from meeting her."

**What's it like having people come up to you on the street?**

"It's really, really weird. They don't really know you. So, it's like, 'Did we go to college? Were you at my brother's wedding?' Then all of a sudden, they go, 'Hey, you're that girl from *The Real World*.' Most people don't come up to me with a lot of negativity. They say, 'I think you were great' or 'I loved you on the show.' It's nice. Of course, there are some ridiculous questions, like, 'Is it hard learning all those scripts?'"

**Well, is it?**

"So hard [laughing]! I'm sitting there thinking, 'Let me go over these so I can be the bitch at absolutely the right moment.'"

**Is there a question you get really sick of answering?**

"'Is my daughter the same baby I had on the show? Everyone, please do not keep asking me that question. I terminated that pregnancy. My daughter was born *after* the show. What happened on the show was real. But so is what has happened to me since."

**DAVID: "Someday I'll win an Academy Award and, in the middle of my speech, someone will stand up and yell, 'What about that bitch, Tami?' The award will fall out of my hand and everyone will point at me."**

**WOULD YOU DO IT AGAIN?**
**"Probably yes, but with some serious counseling. I've done it, so I know the aftermath."**

**BETH S.: "I don't speak to Tami—she's just not my cup of tea. It's unfortunate she's the kind of person that needs to put other people down to make herself feel better."**

# QUIZ

## LOS ANGELES

## MULTIPLE CHOICE

**1. What popular TV show was inspired by the cross-country travels of Dom, Tami and Jon?**

a. *Three's Company*
b. *The Dukes of Hazzard*
c. *Road Rules*

**2. What local delicacy did the trio eat on their drive out to L.A.?**

a. Rattlesnake
b. Bull's testicles
c. Roadkill

**3. What did Jon bring to L.A. that infuriated David?**

a. His virginity
b. His Garth Brooks collection
c. His Confederate flag

**4. On what game show did Tami appear?**

a. *The Dating Game*
b. *Studs*
c. *Wheel of Fortune*

**5. At what comedy club did David perform his stand-up routine?**

a. Laugh!
b. Cry!
c. Out!



**6. What activity did David and Tami do together and forever?**

a. Got tattoos
b. Got wired
c. Got along

**7. In what beefcake calendar did Aaron appear?**

a. "Men of Westwood"
b. "Men at Work"
c. "Men o' Pause"

**8. What did Irene threaten to do if David did not agree to move out?**

a. Get married
b. Resign from the force
c. Move out herself

**9. What did Beth S. deny doing in the closet with her old boyfriend?**

a. Phone sex
b. Safe sex
c. Oral sex

**10. What lesbian joke was inscribed on the T-shirt worn by Beth A.?**

a. "I'm not gay, but my girlfriend is"
b. "I'm not gay, but I watch *Ellen*"
c. "I'm not gay, but I voted for Candace Gingrich"

## DID THEY REALLY SAY THAT?

**Which lines were really said by cast members on *The Real World-Los Angeles* and which lines are fake?**

11. AARON: "I'm George Bush trapped in Fabio's body."

12. BETH A.: "I'm not gay but my boyfriend is."

13. BETH S.: "Tami, were those boxers or briefs?"

14. DAVID: "You can't fire me, 'cause I quit."

15. DOM: "Cats remind me of women and women have been pissing me off."

16. GLEN: "I liked the crew better than I liked my roommates."

17. IRENE: "I am the law twenty-four hours a day."

18. JON: "Don't argue with me because I'll win every time."

19. TAMI: "David, I have one word for you: So long!"

## MULTIPLE TRIPS

**20. Where did the L.A. cast do their Outward Bound adventure?**
a. At the Beverly Hills Hotel
b. Under the Hollywood sign
c. In Joshua Tree National Park

**21. What did Tami announce to her roommates near the end of that trip?**
a. She was missing David
b. She was afraid of heights
c. She was pregnant

**22. Where did the L.A. cast go on vacation?**
a. Kenya
b. Hawaii
c. Cozumel

**23. What did Beth A. crash while on vacation?**
a. A car
b. A moped
c. A party

**24. What did Beth S. and Tami confront Dom about during their vacation?**
a. Drinking too much alcohol
b. Inhaling too much sand
c. Growing too much hair

**25. How were the men dressed at the vacation pool party?**
a. As mariachis
b. As matadors
c. As señoritas

## SCORING GUIDE

20–25: Yee-haw! You deserve a fabulous night on the town, courtesy of Jon. All the bull's testicles you can eat for dinner. A little bronco bull riding and two-stepping afterward. And maybe, he'll even let you wear his hat.

15–19: Congratulations. You deserve a romantic night on the town with Tami, courtesy of Studs. Of course, that's only if she can rig the outcome.

10–14: Cool, dude. You deserve a day of surf and sand with Aaron. Perhaps, he'll even autograph a calendar for you.

5–9: Ouch! You deserve a long night handcuffed inside one of Irene's jail cells.

0–4: Out! You deserve the same fate as David.

ANSWER KEY: 1.c 2.b 3.c 4.b 5.a 6.a 7.a 8.c
9.c 10.a 11.did not 12.did not 13.did not
14.did not 15.did not 16.did 17.did 18.did
19.did not 20.c 21.c 22.c 23.b 24.a 25.c

## POP CULTURE LANDMARKS

TV shows set in Manhattan:
Amos 'n' Andy • Cagney & Lacey
The Days and Nights of Molly Dodd
Dream On • Fame • I Love Lucy
The Jeffersons • Kojak
Law and Order • Mad About You
The Man from U.N.C.L.E.
NYPD Blue • The Odd Couple
Saturday Night Live • Seinfeld
Spin City • Taxi • That Girl

Set in Queens:
All in the Family • Archie's Place

Set in Brooklyn:
Brooklyn Bridge • The Cosby Show
The Honeymooners • The Patty Duke Show • Welcome Back, Kotter

Set in the Bronx:
Car 54, Where Are You?
The Goldbergs • Rhoda

Some movies set in New York:
After Hours • An Affair to Remember
The Age of Innocence • Annie Hall (and nearly every other Woody Allen movie)
Arthur • Big • Bonfire of the Vanities
Breakfast at Tiffany's • A Bronx Tale
The Cotton Club • Crossing Delancey
Desperately Seeking Susan
Die Hard With a Vengeance
Donnie Brasco • Escape from New York
Fame • The French Connection
Ghostbusters • The Godfather
Goodfellas • Hair • King Kong
Last Exit to Brooklyn • The Mambo Kings
Midnight Cowboy • Miracle on 34th Street
New York Stories • The Pope of Greenwich Village • Ransom • Scent of a Woman
Sea of Love • She's Gotta Have It (and nearly every other Spike Lee movie)
Single White Female • Splash
Superman • Taxi Driver • Tootsie
Trading Places • Wall Street
The Warriors • West Side Story
When Harry Met Sally • Working Girl



## MUSIC

Some famous bands from NYC:
Beastie Boys • Blondie
Grandmaster Flash and the Furious Five
Public Enemy • The Ramones • Run-D.M.C.
Simon & Garfunkel • Patti Smith
Sonic Youth • Television • 3rd Bass
Velvet Underground

Some famous (or infamous) dates in NYC musical history:

- Bob Dylan's first paying gig was at NYC's Gerde's Folk City on April 11, 1960.
- The Beatles appeared on *The Ed Sullivan Show* in NYC on February 9, 1964.
- John Lennon was murdered outside the Dakota in NYC on December 7, 1980.
- The Beastie Boys wrote "Fight for Your Right to Party" during a night of partying at NYC's Palladium in 1986.

New York
42
HOUSTON
BOWERY
CANAL

**Name: ERIC**
Birthdate: May 23, 1971
Hometown: Ocean Township, New Jersey
Last Seen: Living in New Jersey.
Last Word: Hosted MTV's *The Grind* and a series of best-selling *Grind* workout videos. Has appeared in several films, including *The Brady Bunch Movie* and *Above the Rim*.

**Name: BECKY**
Birthdate: July 8, 1967
Hometown: New Hope, Pennsylvania
Last Seen: Living in the New York City area.
Last Word: Released her first album on Mercury Records.

**Name: KEVIN**
Birthdate: April 24, 1966
Hometown: Jersey City, New Jersey
Last Seen: Living in New York City.
Last Word: Authored a recently published book of personal essays, *Keepin' It Real*. Sold a screenplay to HBO. Writing for various magazines, including *Vibe* and *Rolling Stone*.

**Name: NORMAN**
Birthdate: March 6, 1967
Hometown: Williamston, Michigan
Last Seen: Living in Los Angeles (and rooming with Cory *(RW-S.F.)*).
Last Word: Working as an artist and art-directing for film, television and live events.

**Name: ANDRE**
Birthdate: September 10, 1970
Hometown: New Brunswick, New Jersey
Last Seen: Living in Detroit.
Last Word: Recording and touring with a new band.

# Class of '92

## The New York Cast

**Name: JULIE**
Birthdate: January 23, 1973
Hometown: Birmingham, Alabama
Last Seen: Living in Alabama.
Last Word: Teaching dancing and pursuing acting.

**Name: HEATHER**
Birthdate: November 13, 1970
Hometown: Jersey City, New Jersey
Last Seen: Living in New Jersey.
Last Word: Scored a rap hit with "All Glocks Down" and appeared in the movie *Dead Presidents*.

**Name: SMOKEY**

**Name: GOUDA**

# the loft

## SOHO SENSATION!

2-story, 3-bedroom, 3-bathroom loft located in New York's trendiest neighborhood. 3200 square feet. 14-foot ceilings. Second floor looks out over downstairs living room. Perfect place for trying out new ideas on cohabitation.

History: Ever dream of living in a *Real World* house? Well, now you can. The same loft where the cast of *Real World–New York* lived is now available to rent (though none of the show's furnishings remain). The owner—a woman in her mid-30s—rents the loft out each year for several months. Her asking price: $8,000 per month. But she'd "prefer a family or a single occupant."

What was your favorite part of the loft?
KEVIN: "I loved the room I shared with Eric because it looked out over the floor below. But I must admit, I was the grouch of the house. All I wanted to do was write and sleep, but the others wanted to party."

## design tip

from BRIAN BIGALKE (Designer, *RW-New York*): "Look for trash! Keep your eyes open while walking down sidewalks. People throw away the best things at night! Just take the stuff home and clean it up."

## BILL

A director who knew the true meaning of the word "action."

## ANDRE

Arrived as rocker; Rocked for roommates; Retrieved stray dog; Returned it to owner; Recorded video; Reigndanced.

## CARON

Eric's favorite grind.

## MISSY

Eric's on-again, off-forever.

## ERIC

Arrived as model; Posed in bikini briefs; Flirted with Julie; Grinded with Caron; Fought with Kevin; Wrestled with Heather; Sparred with Missy; Stormed control room.



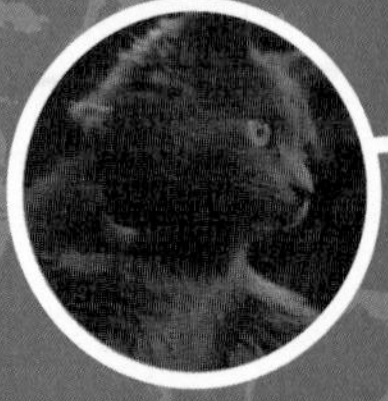

## SMOKEY

Heather's favorite feline.

## HEATHER

Arrived as rapper; Slanged a dictionary; Hung with Larry Johnson; Kicked back in Jamaica; Pushed back at party; Ushered out by police.

## GOUDA

Norman's best buddy.

## NORMAN

Arrived as artist; Painted loft for Jerry Brown; Walked Gouda; Rapped about sexuality; Revealed crush; Rallied for pro-choice; Amused; Admired.

## BECKY

Arrived as singer; Recorded *Mr. Sunshine;* Bra–ed in paper cups; Called "bitch" by Kevin; Hung out in Jamaica; Hooked up with director.

## KEVIN

Arrived as poet; Rhymed at café; Wrote to Eric; Complained about noise; Pained about racism; Insulted Becky; Argued with Julie; Taught many; Learned much.

## DARLENE

Julie's homeless friend.

## JULIE

Arrived from Alabama; Rode a Harley; Revealed her virginity; Flirted with Eric; Argued with Kevin; Daydreamed of dancing; Overnighted with Darlene.

# Andre

KEVIN: "I sort of wish for Andre's sake that he had come to the reunion. I think he could've gotten some closure to the whole *Real World* thing. He could've said in front of everyone, 'Reigndance, my band, is a real band. We didn't make it up for TV. We're not the Monkees. We have real songs, real instruments and we really sing.'

"But I think he took the same approach as he did on the show, which was to not participate when he felt misunderstood."

# Becky

"I ran into Peter Gabriel at Woodstock.

"He said, 'I know you.'

"I said, 'You do? I don't know you. I mean, I know who you are and I love your music, but I don't think we've ever met.'

"Well, he and I started comparing people we might know in common. And finally, he said, 'You're not from *The Real World,* are you?'

"So, wow! Even Peter Gabriel knows who I am. That's pretty wild.

"That was the incredible thing about the show. One day, I woke up and it seemed like everybody knew who I was. All of a sudden I belonged to the world. Everybody seemed to be calling out my name.

"At first, it was thrilling. But after a while, I felt like I was being spread thin. I had to create this chameleon-like vibe, where I could become unrecognizable. But most importantly, I needed to maintain a sense of humor about it all. Without a sense of humor, you'll go crazy the first moment *The Real World* airs. You can't take everybody's judgment seriously because everybody has a judgment.

?

**WOULD YOU DO IT AGAIN?**

**"I wouldn't do it again 'cause I've already done it. It would be too predictable for me. I think that's why being the first season was so great. None of us knew what to expect."**

"I needed to adjust to the show itself in the same way. The first few days in the house, everybody tried to be 'on.' But after a while, it was too exhausting to be 'on' anymore. All of us sort of broke down and just started to be ourselves. Julie was the only one who maintained an awareness of herself throughout the show. In a way, I sort of admire her stamina. **But I was like, 'Sooner or later they'll find out I'm just a big, old grump.'**

"Throughout filming, we all wondered what the crew thought of us. I figured they must've been making jokes about us and saying, 'I can't stand being with these people any longer!' But we didn't hear a peep from them 'til the end. They said nothing. Absolutely nothing. Totally poker-faced the entire time. It was a great relief when we learned they really kind of adored us. A real relief!

**"Nobody knows what that experience was really like, except us. I think that's why we feel real protective of each other now, and feel so much love as well. I love hearing what Heather and Julie are doing, and Norm too. I like reading something that Kevin has written or seeing Eric on TV. We have this bond that connects us, and always will.**

"My favorite part of our experience was going to Jamaica with Heather and Julie. It was a real bonding experience for all of us, and the first moment I started to feel comfortable with everyone in the house.

**"My least favorite period was the episode with Bill, the *Real World* director. I felt really embarrassed and strange about that. As far as I was concerned, it was no one else's business, even though being on the**

**"If you do the show, you have to be prepared to suffer the consequences... in all ways. It's not a vehicle for promoting a public image. You're not going to be able to 'front,' as Heather would say. You're going to be exposed."**

**KEVIN: "I think Becky had a tough adjustment to the real world after *The Real World,* like a lot of our cast—myself included. She and I talked several times after the show about supporting our creative career, doing jobs like waiting tables, while simultaneously being a *Real World* celebrity. You know, it's not easy taking a lunch order when the customer also wants your autograph. I know she went out West to get away from it all. But, I've heard she's back East pursuing her music again and I'm glad to hear it. She's a real talent and I wish her well."**

**show made it everyone's business. I just felt like no one should put their morality on two consenting adults, even if it is a TV show. And on top of that, I felt really bad that Bill was fired.**

"I guess that's one piece of advice I'd give future *Real World*-ers. If you do the show, you have to be prepared to suffer the consequences...in all ways. It's not a vehicle for promoting a public image. You're not going to be able to 'front,' as Heather would say. You're going to be exposed. So, if you don't want that to happen, don't do the show.

"Has *Real World* helped my music career? A little. Sometimes, people come to my concerts just 'cause they've seen me on the show. And some fans wrote to me about a song of mine that played on the show. But on the other hand, a few musicians and record people dismiss me 'cause they think I'm just some TV personality. *Real World* was about seven people living in a loft. Not about my music.

"I love looking back on *The Real World*. It's like my own not-so-little home movie. It was a bit overwhelming at the time. But now, I think back on the show as a wonderful experience—an experience, for better and worse, that I'll never be able to escape."

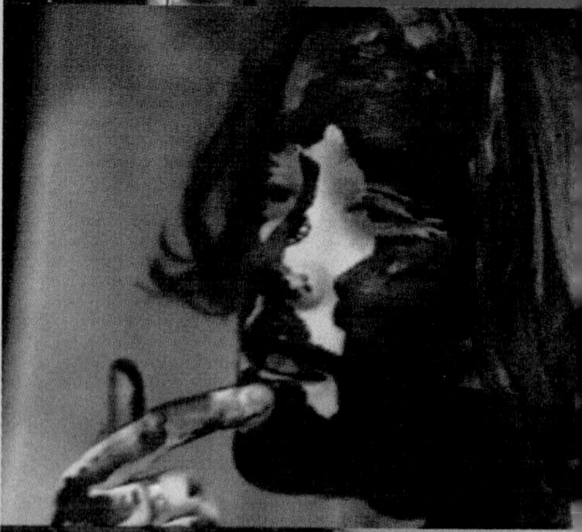

JULIE: "I've never had the hots for Eric. That was definitely sensationalized.... Eric has gotten older, smarter and more pleasant to be with since we lived together. I know he used to worry that people were jealous of him 'cause he'd gotten the *Grind* stuff going. But he's gotten so much more comfortable with it all."

NORMAN: "I think Eric has done the Hollywood thing and is now finding a purpose in his life. He sees the influence he can have and I think it's great. I wish him the best of luck."

**"No one comes up to me in the street and says, 'Hey, there's Eric from *The Grind.*' It's always, 'Hey, there's Eric from *The Real World.*' That's what I'm known for.**

"If you watched our shows, you know exactly who I am. You know where I live. You know who my mom is. You know what I look like in my underwear. You know far more about me than I do about you. I don't even know if you have something positive or negative to say about me.

**"We were really *the* guinea pigs. After the producers got through with us, they were like, 'Okay. Let's take what we've learned from the first group and apply it to the second, the third and so on. We'll add a little more drama, sprinkle in some more conflict....**

"When we did *The Real World,* we had no idea of how it was going to turn out. No one told us how they were going to piece it all together. No one showed us how they were going to edit the interviews in with the live action. So, I feel like we kind of solved *The Real World* for everyone else, especially future participants. Forever after, people knew how it worked.

# Eric

**"Some things in the second season really kind of disappointed me. I thought the L.A. house totally blew things out of proportion when they kicked David out. What David did was all in fun. He didn't attack Tami, especially with a bunch of cameras in his face the entire time. So for Miss Beth to cry "rape" and for the house to vote him out like that, well, I just**

**JUDD (S.F.): "Eric is the nicest guy. I didn't think we'd get along at all before I met him at the reunion, but he's just the nicest guy."**

**thought it was unfair, selfish, rude and insensitive. *Real World* is the opportunity of a lifetime. You shouldn't deprive someone of such an experience, just like that.**

"I think *Real World* cast members forget we have a such a great opportunity to promote a positive message. What we say and do is projected to the rest of the world. There are a lot of problems out there for teenagers and young adults, like drugs and violence. I kind of wish we focused more, both on and off-screen, on actually helping these kids, instead of just thinking about making money.

"The show helped teach me to keep an open mind. Don't

## "We were really *the* guinea pigs."

dismiss somebody the first time you meet them just 'cause they eat with their fingers, brush their hair differently or act weirdly. Accepting people for who they are is crucial for surviving on *The Real World*, and an important thing to remember in the real world.

"Unfortunately, I haven't been able to keep in close touch with my fellow cast members, except through the reunions. I've just been too busy working on my career and trying to stay in contact with my own family and friends. But I always enjoy seeing the gang whenever we get the chance. I wish it were more often, but you know, I work in a crazy business and you just have to go on with your life."



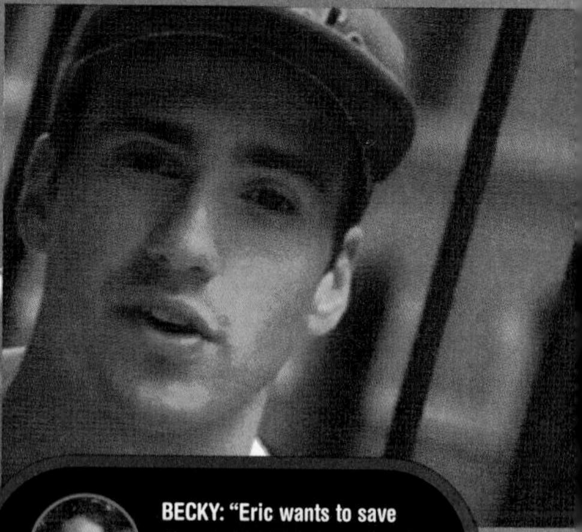

**BECKY: "Eric wants to save the world, which is a very nice thing. You know what? I'd like to save the world, too. But I don't think we ought to use *The Real World* as a vehicle for doing it, as he does. Listen, I know Eric is sincere about helping people. I guess I just don't have the ego to tell other people what to do.**

**"But I definitely think Eric has softened up a bit since our days on *Real World*. He's been around the block some and there's a lot more soul to him. That was always the one thing that I thought was missing in him. I'm glad to see he's changed."**

# Heather

**What was your favorite season of *The Real World?***

"Of course, I think we were the best. It wasn't so much the people, 'cause we didn't always get along. No, it's because we worked things out. And to me, that's life in general. You just can't say, 'Get out! We don't want you here any more,' like the other houses did. That's not real. Not to me it isn't. You just can't do that in the real world."

**How would you compare your season to the ones that followed?**

"I consider us the realists. We just didn't know what was going to happen. The other casts might say, 'Oh, but I never watched the show.' But that's bulls**t. Because even if you didn't 'watch yourself,' you knew somebody else who did. Fact is, if you knew nothing, you wouldn't have been auditioning in the first place.

"I'll be honest, I just thought the second and third casts didn't have a choice but to be phony 'cause they knew what was going on. They already knew the show was going to make them 'stars.' We just went into it raw and natural."

**How did you get picked for the show?**

"My manager told me that MTV was holding auditions for something called *The Real World*. I went to my audition with another one of her clients, this guy, but he didn't get past the first round. When they asked him about a dream date, he said he wanted to date the secretary in the office.

"Anyway, I just hit it off with the interviewer. I was like, 'Man, you're telling me I get to live someplace for free? I don't care who you put in there with me. I'll do it!'"

**JULIE: "Heather is the best. I don't think anyone understands just how hilarious she is. She and I have phone bills to prove how close we are. We ought to be spending the money on airfare to see each other, instead of talking on the phone all the time."**

**What would have happened if you all lived together for six months, like the subsequent seasons, instead of three?**

"I still don't think anybody would have gotten kicked out. I think the opposite might have happened. We would've had more time to resolve our differences and become closer friends."

**Are you still friends with anyone in your cast?**

I'm friends with Kevin, Norman, Julie and Eric. The only reason I don't say Becky and Andre is because I don't talk to them as much. But we're cool with each other."

**What was it like seeing everyone at the last reunion?**

"Our group really likes each other, unlike some of the other casts. We don't have time to argue. We're too happy seeing each other and catching up. But maybe that's a function of time. At our first reunion, which opened the second season, there was still a lot of bitterness and tension in our group. You could just feel it."

**Were there any cast members from other seasons you wanted to meet at the last reunion?**

"The ones that got kicked out of the house—David and Puck. That's it. Everybody else is just like everybody else to me. But I couldn't believe those people were kicked out. I mean, nobody paid rent. How could they put somebody out like that? The whole show is about learning to deal with people unlike you. Not about putting them out."

**Could you have "dealt" with Puck?**

"If Puck had gotten his ass kicked a couple of times, he would've been all right. I just think his housemates were scared of him. Nobody said nothing to him because they thought he was crazy or something. But he's not crazy. He's like the school bully. He knows who to pick with and who not to pick with.

"I can tell you this much, Puck wouldn't have gotten away with that s**t in New York. And I know he wouldn't have acted that way with me. I'd have killed him if he'd tried. For real. I'd have punched him right in the face. Nobody talks to me like that. Nobody!"

**What did you think of David after meeting him?**

"I liked him a lot. I think it's cool that he's no longer bitter. He's got his comedy and he's just moved on. He's gotten over it and I really respect that."

**Was there anything about *The Real World* you found difficult getting over?**

"I think what bothered everyone the most was the period right after we lived together. We were like...stuck. We didn't know which way to turn. Should I go follow this television career? Do I go back to what I was doing before? A lot of us went out to L.A. to find agents. I didn't even know what the hell an agent was. And I'm out there listening to these people, saying to myself, 'What am I doing here?' Not until I finally decided to leave that stuff alone and go back to me before the show, did I return to normal.

"We all figured that since we'd done *Real World,* we were

**JUDD (S.F.): "To call Heather blunt is an understatement. Heather is just this wonderful ton of bricks. She doesn't care. And that's just what she keeps telling you. She finishes every sentence with, 'I don't care...I just don't care!'"**

supposed to have this big career in TV. But that's not the way it happens. It's not going to happen, unless you make it happen for yourself. *Real World* doesn't make you a star. You better have something to work with. And if not, you'd better develop it first. Because if you don't, you're going to come back two, three years later a sad, miserable person and blame MTV and *Real World* for f**kin' up your life."

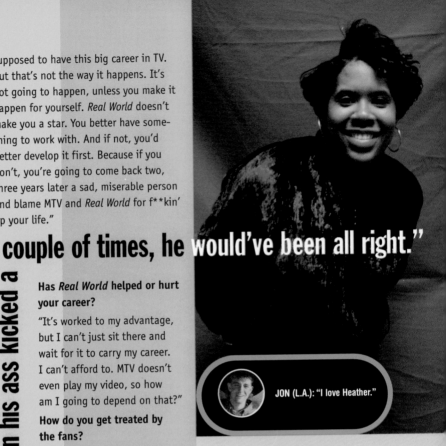

**"If Puck had gotten his ass kicked a couple of times, he would've been all right."**

**Has *Real World* helped or hurt your career?**

"It's worked to my advantage, but I can't just sit there and wait for it to carry my career. I can't afford to. MTV doesn't even play my video, so how am I going to depend on that?"

**How do you get treated by the fans?**

"Everybody is real cool. They just come up to me and say, 'What's up, Heather?' Everybody feels like I'm their homegirl."

**Do you ever tire of it?**

"No, because I don't get fans like Eric must. You know the ones—girls that ask the craziest questions. The kind you just want to say, 'Get out of here' [laughing]."

**JON (L.A.): "I love Heather."**

**Do you miss *The Real World?***

"I don't really miss it, but sometimes I think about all the funny things that happened. Back then, I just didn't have anything to do. I was like a chicken running around with my head cut off. All I had to give was me—just Heather. That was it. I didn't have anything else to focus on. The music was there, but I wasn't into it the same way I am now. Now, I no longer have the time to sit around with six roommates and gab. I've just got too many things to do in the real world."

**WOULD YOU DO IT AGAIN?**

**"I wouldn't do *Real World* again 'cause I'm having too much fun doing what I'm doing now. I've got other friends and I've got other things to do. And I don't want to live with six people no more. It was a passing phase."**

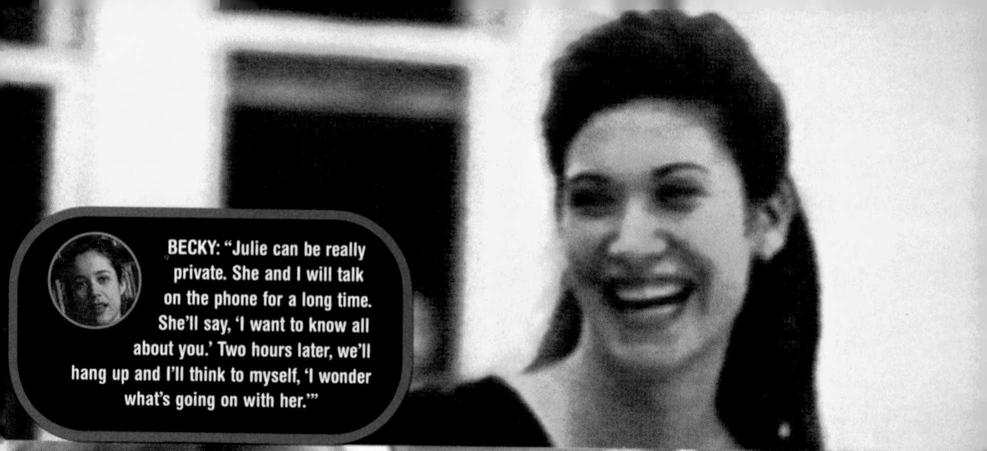

BECKY: "Julie can be really private. She and I will talk on the phone for a long time. She'll say, 'I want to know all about you.' Two hours later, we'll hang up and I'll think to myself, 'I wonder what's going on with her.'"

**"Listen, our cast is just better. We can't help it. We're not mad about it. We're not coming down on anybody. We just are. Things are hard that way. And I'm sure it's insanely hard for all those other seasons to live up to our high standard, just knowing the level of talent, the beauty and the strength we all had. Gosh, it must be hell to reckon with. You know, guys, I feel bad for you. Really, I do [laughing].**



"And moreover, **Puck should have lived with us.** I know he and Andre would've gotten on extremely well. And boy, would I have loved to see some good Heather-Puck fights. Not to mention Puck interacting with Norman's cast of characters. Now that would've been complete entertainment. **I think Puck would've gotten thrown out of our house for having too much fun.**

PUCK (S.F.): "Julie is cool, man. She's down. She got naked and went into the pool after the reunion show. I dig that. She's also honest and sincere. She'll sit and listen to your story and give you back an honest, concise response."

"But seriously, a major reason why I enjoyed *The Real World* so much was because of the group we had. Had I lived with any other cast, I'm certain I wouldn't have liked them nearly as much. The latter casts have just taken themselves way too seriously. I mean, come on, it's cable TV.

"No doubt, we were the 'realest' of all the casts. Perhaps, it's because we had the advantage of not knowing what to expect. **I could never imagine signing up for *Real World* after having seen it.** I'm glad I didn't know the repercussions. The only advantage to knowing would be knowing to take a little more care with your hair products and makeup.

"I was as real as I could be. But I admit, I did sell out for my audition. Yes, I was willing to clog on my videotape application just to get noticed. And I even told a story about menstruating on a rock in the water, which I think is what got me cast. **In fact, if you want to get cast on the show, I suggest you tell a really disgusting period story about yourself [laughing]. That'll do the trick every time.**

"People still stop me to talk about the show. The only time it bothers me is when it's an obnoxious fan. **An 'obnoxious fan' is someone who tells you they hated you and every reason why, reciting every word of every episode. All I can say is, 'Hey, then turn the channel.'**

"Most fans ask me questions, like, 'Can you really be yourself in front of the cameras and crew?' The answer is yes. When you see how insanely hard they work, you feel like you're all in it together. The cameras are like having a kid—you still shop at the same grocery store, but now you've got to remember to bring the kid along.

# Julie

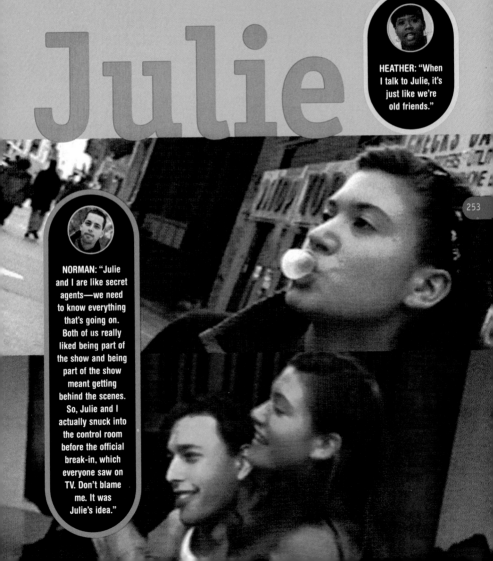

**HEATHER: "When I talk to Julie, it's just like we're old friends."**

**NORMAN: "Julie and I are like secret agents—we need to know everything that's going on. Both of us really liked being part of the show and being part of the show meant getting behind the scenes. So, Julie and I actually snuck into the control room before the official break-in, which everyone saw on TV. Don't blame me. It was Julie's idea."**

# "The latter casts have just taken themselves way too seriously."

And instead of a screaming kid annoying everybody, it's a sun gun with a huge light [laughing].

"It was also fun playing practical jokes on the crew. Whenever we got bored, one of us would walk around the column in the middle of the loft and sit back down. Of course, the cameraman would have to follow. Then five minutes later, another one of us would walk around the column again. And again, the cameraman would follow. Eventually, we'd done it so many times the camera cord would be wrapped tightly around the column and they had to untangle it.

"In a way, that was what made *Real World* such a special experience. The seven of us will always have these unique memories to link us together. That's why I enjoyed seeing our cast at the last reunion. It was like a family reunion. Your sister might've stolen your favorite shirt a few years back, but now you've gotten over it. Any grievances our cast once had have been swept under the rug.

"After we finished taping the reunion show, we all ran back to the hotel to change clothes for a big party. Well, everyone from the New York season changed into T-shirts and jeans. But all the other casts put on high heels and tighter clothing. It was like they raided the MTV VJ closet. I was, like, 'Oh, my gosh. What are they doing?' I think that alone said a lot about how real the people from the other seasons have been.

"To tell you the truth, I feel like that was my last *Real World* reunion. The whole thing has gotten too massive! **I just feel like everyone and their brother has now been on *The Real World*. We're everywhere. It's like a zoo!"**

**JON (L.A.): "I can't figure Julie out. I mean, I would think that Julie and I would have so much in common just being from the South and being on *Real World*. I would think I could just sit down with Julie and talk for hours. Just go, 'You know, that happened to me, too.' But Julie and I are very separate and very different. Even though we're the same stereotype of people, what's acceptable to her is totally unacceptable to me."**

# Kevin

"I've spoken to more than 150 colleges during the last four years and a lot of kids—white and black—say, 'You're nothing like you were on MTV!' Well, one, I was 25 and a starving writer at the time. And two, *The Real World* just showed a small part of who I am. But I don't regret having done the show. **I didn't love being portrayed as the angry black man. But as Heather once said, 'How can I be mad, if we gave them what they used?'**

**"Now, I do regret the fight I had with Becky. That one got me the most grief from my mother. She berated me soooo bad for that. 'How could you call that girl a bitch on national TV?' She's right. I shouldn't have said that.**

"I accept the fact that some people will forever see me as my 'character' on *Real World*. That's part of the power and problem with TV. A lot of viewers get trapped inside these little historic memory boxes. What they see on TV defines who you are.

**BECKY: "Out of everybody at the last reunion, I was the happiest to see Kevin. Even though we had a really heated argument on the show, we never became enemies. Anyway, sometimes fights create better friendships than peaceful coexistence. When I saw Kevin, I just gave him the biggest hug. He's so intelligent. He's so successful. He's so handsome."**

**"I didn't love being portrayed as the angry black man. But as Heather once said, 'How can I be mad, if we gave them what they used?'"**

"I wished the last reunion show had focused a bit more attention on who and where we are *now.* But instead, they wanted to relive the past, not to move us forward. I mean, since *Real World* I've done cover stories for *Rolling Stone* and *Vibe,* published a book and sold a screenplay. But somehow, that never made it on the air [laughing].



**"Listen, I'm a classic Gen X-er, who grew up on a lot of television. So, being on a TV show was a dream come true. In fact, I recently went to the Museum of Television and Radio in New York to check out some old TV shows. Of course, I paid to get in just like everyone else. Well, someone from the museum came up to me and said, 'Why are *you* paying? You're Kevin from *The Real World.* You're *in* the museum.' It was hilarious.**

"Man, the recognition I've gotten from this show is astounding sometimes. I've had LL Cool J and Damon Wayans say to me, 'Yo, I really liked you on the show.' Can you believe that? They're saying they liked *me.*

**"I'm known from *Vibe* magazine for interviewing Tupac Shakur. Well, he was like, 'Yo, dog. I had your back on MTV. I supported you, man.' And I was like, 'Uh, excuse me, Mr. Shakur. I would like to interview you.'**

IF *REAL WORLD* WAS MADE INTO A MOVIE, WHO WOULD YOU WANT TO PLAY YOU?

**KEVIN:** "Larenz Tate. He's got passion. He could pull off the angry-black-man stuff and I am the angry black man [laughing]."

"The hardest part of *The Real World* was the period after it started airing. On the one hand, all these people were running after us, screaming our names. At the MTV Video Awards, the kids treated us like we were the f**king Beatles. 'Oh, my God! It's Norm, Eric, Kevin, Julie, Heath, Andre, Becky.....Aaaaahhhh!'

"But on the other hand, we were all completely broke. I went back to my $300-a-month, roach-infested apartment. And I was experiencing serious 'telegenic withdrawal.' It was crazy. It was nuts. It was horrible [laughing].

"Right after the show ended, none of us knew what the f**k to do with our lives. Becky, Norm and I were the oldest, so we had some ideas. But Julie was just 19. And Andre was in a serious band, which a lot of people began to believe had actually been invented by MTV. I think he felt like Reigndance had been turned into the f**king *Monkees.*

**HEATHER: "I often see Kevin walking down the street in New York. And, I mean, it's like we don't even talk about the show. We talk about other things."**

"But what's past is past. Everyone is doing pretty well now and all of us can be proud of what we accomplished.

When Julie went with the homeless woman, I mean, how many kids would have done that? And look at all the *Real World* imitators, from *Friends* to *Reality Bites*.

"Speaking of imitations, during the summer of '94 I rented a big RV with two friends—a photographer and sketch artist—and we drove cross-country, filming interviews with Gen X-ers. We talked to like fifty, sixty kids. Well, I ran into Jon Murray, one of the *Real World* cocreators, when we arrived in L.A. Jon asked me what I was doing and I told him about our road trip. A few months later, I heard he and Mary-Ellis Bunim were starting a new show called... *Road Rules*. What a coincidence [laughing]!

"You know, if they'd really wanted to create something interesting, they should have sent the New York cast on a road trip."

**JON (L.A.):** "I'd never met Kevin before the reunion show. I didn't think he was going to be as laid-back as he turned out to be. I figured he'd be, 'I'm here, I'm me, and that's that.' He pulled me aside and said, 'I really admired you for sticking to your guns...you've got to stand for something and you're doing it.' And I said to myself, 'Man, I didn't expect that coming out of Kevin's mouth.' I just never thought we had anything in common. I'd never met him, but he knew exactly what I was going through."

## *KEEPIN' IT REAL*

**(Kevin on his book)**

**KEVIN:** "Being on *The Real World* made me want to confront some personal issues with my writing as well. That's why I wrote, *Keepin' It Real,* which contains four long personal essays in the style of Joan Didion, Hunter Thompson and James Baldwin. In a lot of ways, the book is my answer to being seen as an angry black man. There haven't been a lot of personal testimonies from Gen X-ers, particularly from my background and point of view. So I can't wait for you all to read it and let me know what you think. Incidentally, it's in stores now."

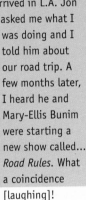

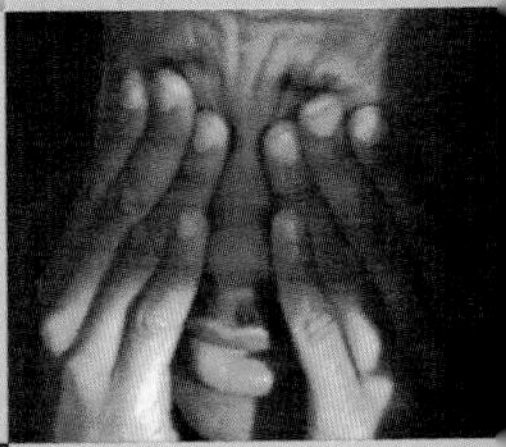

# Norman

"**H**ave I ever dated someone who sent me a fan letter?

"Not just one, man. I've gotten so *many* dates. When Julie was working at MTV, I used to go over there and snatch the mail. She and I would go through boxes and boxes of stuff. It was so much fun.

"Naturally, the *Real World* people warned me to be careful about how I responded, that there were bound to be psychopaths out there writing to me. And I was like, 'Well, if they're fans of mine, they're all gonna be psychopaths [laughing].' In fact, I told MTV that I was the crazy one they ought to be worried about. I'm liable to answer the mail, track down the sender and move into his, or her, house.

"I really do enjoy it when people write to me or recognize me on the street. It's been one of the best things about the show. *The Real World* turned my world into a small town. I consider the fans of the show my friends.

"And I felt the same way about the cameras during filming. They made me feel like I was really special, like I was doing something so important that people *wanted* to watch me. They gave me the feeling I could do anything.

**RACHEL (S.F.): "I love Norman. We get along great. He's really bright and he's up for anything. I just get a really good vibe off him. But Norm is not a good dancer. He's kind of stiff. On the other hand, Eric is a good dancer. I feel very inadequate dancing next to him."**

"When the show started, I was totally nervous about being openly bisexual on the air. But eventually, I gained the confidence to come out and even have a relationship on the program. That might seem common now, but back then a real-life gay relationship had rarely been portrayed on TV.

"I still remember that first instant when I walked into the loft. I recall seeing all the cameras and fellow cast members standing around, just kind of dazed and confused. It was the beginning of a whole new chapter for everyone involved—cast and crew. And it was the beginning of a whole new chapter in my life.

"But I'm one of the few from the New York cast, who thinks the integrity of the *Real World* experience has *increased* as the show has progressed. A lot of people come up to me and say, 'Your cast was great because the other seasons fought all the time. You guys were happy and we like to see happy people.' **I think one of the major reasons we got along so much better than the other seasons is that we were together half as long as the other seasons.**

"But had we filmed six months instead of three, I don't believe I would have signed on. Too much stress. I do wish, however, that our show had traded some 'happiness' for a lot more dimension. We were a bit single-dimensional compared to later casts, but I suspect that's largely a function of the added time.

"I confess, I did dread the thought of going to the last reunion. I wanted to see my fellow cast members, but I had no desire to see the others. The last thing I needed was to deal with all their

**"I've gotten so *many* dates."**

**JULIE: "Norm says that he and I have a 'hot line.' If we don't hear from each other every couple of days, we panic and have to find out where the other one is."**

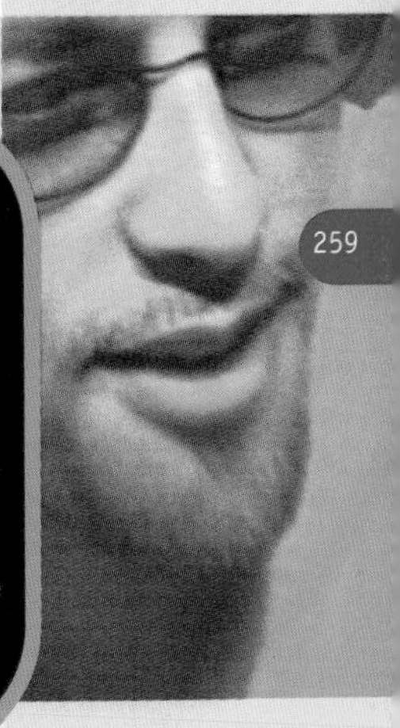

**ERIC: "I thought Norm had an incredible personality and attitude. He was happy, jolly, and all those good chipper things."**

JUDD (S.F.): "Everybody knows Norm. Norm is like this big yenta, who seems to know three-quarters of the people who have ever been involved with *The Real World.* I thought it was a big deal to know a couple people in the other casts. But Norm knows just about everybody."

baggage and anger. But it turned out okay. It was actually enjoyable meeting all of them.

"Okay, truthfully, the one person I really didn't want to see was Tami. Of course, when I went to lunch that first day, who should be seated next

## "I'm one of the few from the New York cast, who thinks the integrity of the *Real World* experience has *increased* as the show has progressed."



to me, but Tami and...David. I was like, 'I'm going to die.' But you know what? We had ourselves a little diplomatic moment, kicking each other under the table, as if to say, 'Let's not create a little Puck moment here. Let's learn to love each other.' And all was right with the world.

**"You know what else, I feel like I could've lived with any one of those people, including Puck. In fact, I'd have loved to live with Puck. I'd have even shared a room with him. We could've learned a lot from each other."**

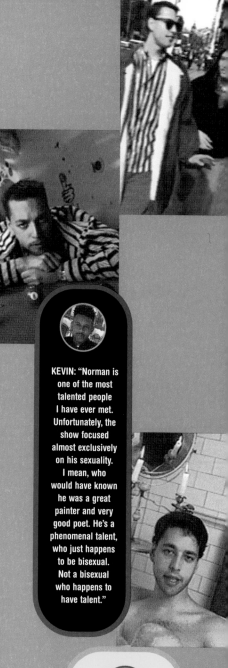

KEVIN: "Norman is one of the most talented people I have ever met. Unfortunately, the show focused almost exclusively on his sexuality. I mean, who would have known he was a great painter and very good poet. He's a phenomenal talent, who just happens to be bisexual. Not a bisexual who happens to have talent."

WOULD YOU DO IT AGAIN?
"Oh yeah, I'd do it again. In fact, I think our gang should do it forever. It would be kind of like *60 Minutes.* We could just travel around and air it every Sunday night after football."

## THE REAL WORLD–NEW YORK

## CAN WE TALK?

I have learned so much watching *The Real World,* especially the New York season. I just loved that one. I never missed it, of course, how could you when MTV repeated every single one sixteen times? I've seen it so many times, in fact, it prompted me to offer the cast some advice on how to live in complete harmony.

The first person who desperately needs my advice is dear Eric. You're gorgeous, but Eric, get a grip. Get a life. Get a shirt! Understand, Eric, the only people who parade around in their underwear are hookers and Madonna. There's more to life than great pecs. When I find out what that is, I'll get back to you. In the meantime, I recommend at least a tank top during blizzards and three sets of twelve to fifteen reps on the Abdominizer.

As for you, dear Julie, the "virgin" from Alabama. Oh please! I believed that one like I believe Pamela Lee's marriage will last. Julie, virgins don't go to New York. They go to convents. The only virgins left in New York are pregnant women who aren't showing yet.

As for Heather, I really don't want to give you any advice because I'm afraid you'll deck me, too. Well, okay. Heather, you've got to realize that rap music does not lead to career longevity. Ask the Notorious B.I.G. about that. I think you ought to ease out of rap and into country music. You can still use the same lyrics, something like, 'I just want to kill, 'cause my old man's drinkin' and my baby's ill.' Don't bother to thank me.

Kevin, you won't thank me either because I have no advice for you. All poets ought to be angry. If I was taking home six bucks a week, I'd figure I had every right to be angry, too.

And Norm, why did you have to be a bisexual artist? Break the stereotype, Norm. Be a bisexual Teamster or a bisexual pipe fitter. Or how about something really impossible to accept—a bisexual gay person? By the way, Norm, I really love your paintings. I have one of them at home...and you can hardly see the numbers.

As for you, sweet Becky, take a bit of advice from the mother in me: be careful who you go out with. When someone asks a bartender, 'You got something cheap?' you don't want him answering, 'Yeah, Becky from New York!'

Aw come on, you guys, you know I'm just crazy about ya'. You too, Andre. But that hair? My goodness, I know musicians are supposed to wear it long, but you look like a cross between a country singer and a virgin.

Oh, that's right, they had one of those the next season....

—Joan Rivers

### *REAL WORLD–THE PILOT*

**Long before Eric, Julie, Kevin and Heather, there was an Eamee, Tracy and Dizzy. Who, you ask?**

### Welcome to *Real World–The Pilot:*

**"Had they actually been wise enough to use us, I believe we'd have gone down as one of the more interesting casts *The Real World* has ever seen," laughs Tracy Grandstaff, one of six strangers cast in the pilot episode of *Real World.***

**In 1991, the creators of *Real World* assembled Grandstaff and five others in a New York city apartment. The sextet, which included two dancers from the show *Club MTV,* were filmed living together over a long weekend.**

**"We were all completely paranoid," recalls Grandstaff, now the voice of Daria on the *Beavis & Butt-head* spin-off. "We thought there were hidden cameras and 'bugs' everywhere. We checked the bathroom, inside the refrigerator, anywhere you could think of. We just didn't know what to expect."**

**But even though the pilot was picked up by MTV, the original six were not. "We were told we could re-audition," Grandstaff recalls. "I did. But I lost out to Becky." But no hard feelings, she says. "I couldn't have taken all that terror. And I'm no Becky. She was such a drama queen!"**

# Quiz
## NEW YORK

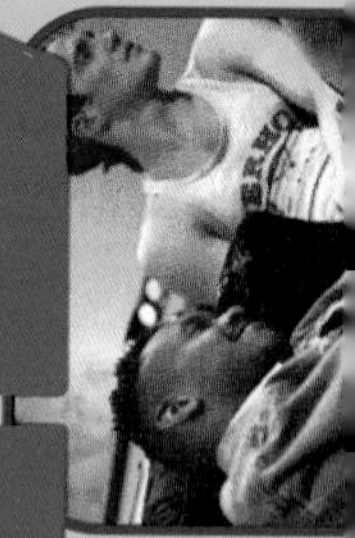

## MULTIPLE CHOICE

**1. What did Becky wear as a bra when she went to the Limelight nightclub?**
a. Ice cream cones
b. Paper cups
c. Nothing

**2. What did Andre find in the street and return to its owner?**
a. Lars' bike
b. A stray dog
c. Becky's homemade bra

**3. What famous basketball player did Heather have a crush on and get to meet?**
a. Larry Johnson
b. Dennis Rodman
c. Lisa Leslie

**4. For what violation was Eric on probation?**
a. Indecent exposure
b. Fooling around on a photo shoot
c. Selling steroids

**5. For what special cause did Norm paint an "800" number on the loft wall?**
a. Hair Club for Men
b. Jerry Brown for President
c. Dial-a-Mattress

**6. For what product did Eric do a commercial that was deemed "too steamy" to air?**
a. Jovan Musk cologne
b. Calvin Klein jeans
c. Carrier air conditioners

**7. What song did Andre's band, Reigndance, make into a video during the show?**
a. "Why Can't We Be Friends?"
b. "Love Me Tender"
c. "Lazybones"

**8. What did Julie claim Kevin threw at her?**
a. A candlestick
b. A biography of Malcolm X
c. A copy of *Vibe*

**9. Why did the police question Heather during one of the cast's house parties?**
a. She slugged a guest
b. She did an obscene rap
c. She was starring in an episode of *NYPD Blue*

**10. What did Heather say was the reason none of the roommates had sex with each other?**
a. "Our religious convictions prevented us from having premarital sex."
b. "We must be in love before we'd ever consider a sacred union like that."
c. "Everyone is ugly!"

## DID THEY REALLY SAY THAT?

Which lines were really said by the cast members on *The Real World–New York* and which lines are fake?

11. BECKY: "Mom, it's just like any other place."
12. KEVIN: "Most men are dogs."
13. ERIC: "My Dad is a better NBA referee than your dad."
14. JULIE: "Why are boys so horny?"
15. NORM: "I'm a Pisces. I'm always out there looking for another fish."
16. ANDRE: "I must be left alone when I'm eating."
17. HEATHER: "Tell the policeman I'll be right down."

## MULTIPLE PLACES

**18. In what part of New York City was the *Real World* loft located?**

a. Soho
b. Noho
c. Hoho

**19. What was the name of the shanty town where Julie befriended Darlene, the homeless woman?**

a. Reaganville
b. Realityville
c. Reachoutville

**20. Where did Kevin perform his poetry readings?**

a. At *Yo! MTV Raps*
b. In the Nuyorican Poets Café
c. On the New York subway

**21. What was the principal reason the girls got a trip to Jamaica?**

a. To meet men
b. To train for the bobsledding team
c. To foster relations with the crew

**22. Who refused to go nude on the beach?**

a. Becky
b. Julie
c. Heather

**23. Whom did Becky hook up with on vacation?**

a. Bob Marley, the singer
b. Norm, the roommate
c. Bill, the director

**24. Where did Becky and her beau hang out when they returned to New York?**

a. Dew Drop Inn
b. Don't Drop Inn
c. Don't Drop Inn Unless You Really Have To

**25. What New York museum has the first season of *Real World* in its collection?**

a. Museum of Modern Art
b. Museum of Television and Radio
c. Madame Tussaud's Wax Museum

### SCORING GUIDE

20-25: Bravo! You've just won the admiration of the entire Big Apple.

15-19: Hooray! You've just won yourself a shiny red apple.

10-14: Fine! Would you settle for a bite of an apple?

5-9: Ugh! You'd be lucky to get the stem.

0-4: Duck! Here comes a rotten apple.

ANSWER KEY: 1.b 2.b 3.a 4.c 5.b 6.a 7.c 8.a 9.a 10.c
11.did 12.did 13.did not 14.did 15.did 16.did 17.did not
18.a 19.a 20.b 21.a 22.c 23.c 24.a 25.b

# BOSTON

| IS *REAL WORLD* A SOAP OPERA OR A DOCUMENTARY? | WHAT DO YOU REALLY THINK OF THE OTHER *RW* SEASONS? | WHO'S YOUR FAVORITE *RW* CAST MEMBER FROM ANOTHER SEASON? |
|---|---|---|
| "They shoot a documentary. They edit a soap." | "I liked London the best, especially Jacinda, Neil and Sharon. I thought the New York cast was very boring." | "I connected with Rachel the most. She was a Catholic schoolgirl from a very strict upbringing and so am I. She pierced her belly button and I pierced my eyebrow. She spread her wings and so did I." |
| "It's supposed to be a documentary, but we acted like we were in a soap. I'd call it a docu-drama." | "Compared to the Miami cast, I think our group was a bunch of losers." | "I related to Julie the most 'cause she came from the South and went up North. I think we both experienced a lot of culture shock." |
| "There was so much drama in our house, it felt like a f**king soap." | "The Miami cast fought about a lot of stupid, childish s**t. If we'd thrown the 50 grand to Syrus and let him promote clubs, we would've made a s**t load of money. But to have gotten the girls to agree on that would've been a chore." | "I thought Puck was full of s**t! I'd really like to meet Kevin of the New York cast 'cause he did spoken word and writes for *Vibe*. I heard he's a cool guy." |
| "It intends to be a documentary, but you're bound to get drama when you cross seven different lives. And we certainly crossed each other some." | "New York is my favorite season 'cause they started it all. They were the 'Oh, gee, *Real World*-ers.' My least favorite season was London. All they did was sleep!" | "I liked Heather from New York the best, because she's so up-front. She was really loud and really funny." |
| "There were no scripts, no rehearsals and no, we didn't play for the cameras. So, in that sense it was a documentary. But my life was a soap opera before I even got to Boston." | "New York and San Francisco were my favorite seasons, but I thought the London cast was super boring." | "I liked Dominic, Julie and Norm. All of them got goofy— the way I like to get." |
| "It's a combination of both. They pick the seven people. They put you in a kick-ass house. They give you a vacation. But they don't influence us while we're here. They let us do our thing and film it. It's hard to believe, but that's really the way we are." | "I liked the L.A. season the best. I thought the Miami group was a bunch of turds for not getting their business going. I could've gotten everyone to work together. But then again, it's always easy to second-guess. I'm sure people look at our show and say, 'What the heck were they fighting about?' You never really know unless you're there." | "I thought Dominic was cool. I'd have liked him a lot. But I would've hated Puck." |

**SYRUS**

"I don't like soap operas, so I hope we're not a soap."

"I liked the group in 'Frisco and the Miami house. Their house was phat. Living in that place would've been hot."

"I liked Mohammed a lot. I also liked David, the comedian, even though he was a d**k. He didn't try to change for the house. He was, like, 'F**k it! I'm a d**k. Get me up out of here if it's going to be like that.' I also respect Puck for not giving a damn. But, I would've whipped his ass if I'd have lived with him."

# MIAMI

**CYNTHIA**

"It's a real-life soap opera. It trips me out seeing it on TV."

"I'd love to meet Mohammed. That would work. I'd love to to know all about his experiences, and love to know if he saw mine. He and I are in the Bay Area, so it might happen."

**DAN**

"One of the reasons I did the show was because I had the biggest crush on Norm when I was in high school. And then I got to meet him at a casting session [sighing]. It was a dream come true. I want to meet Heather. I love f**king Heather from New York. She's the coolest. And Cory from San Francisco seemed so real. Not neurotic."

**FLORA**

"All soaps are documentaries of someone's imagination."

"I've seen repeats of the Pedro episodes. Those shows taught kids about AIDS and all that. Our shows taught kids how to drink, how to party and how to be sexual."

**MELISSA**

"I never call it a documentary. Never! I don't think it's anywhere near that. The show just skims the surface. I'd say it's a soap opera about Gen-X. It's like *Melrose Place*."

"I think San Francisco was the best ever. The best, by far. The whole Puck thing, the Pedro thing. Every person they cast that year had something to give. They weren't a bunch of airheaded Gen-Xers. They were a cast of substance."

"Norman! He's so delicious. Definitely! He's soooo cute. It's between him and Pedro. But Pedro, forget it. I'd have never had a chance with him. He'd have said, 'Sorry, you're not a guy.' At least with Norman I'd have a shot. God, I nearly forgot Lars. He's soooo beautiful. It would be between Lars and Norman. Eric never did it for me. He's too pretty. I need a scar, something to make 'em human. He's just too perfect."

**IS *REAL WORLD* A SOAP OPERA OR A DOCUMENTARY?** | **WHAT DO YOU REALLY THINK OF THE OTHER *RW* SEASONS?** | **WHO'S YOUR FAVORITE *RW* CAST MEMBER FROM ANOTHER SEASON?**

**MIKE**

"Definitely a soap. It's not scripted, but a documentary shows everything. This is heavily edited. We were there five and a half months, and they shot almost twenty-four hours a day. Yet, there are only twenty-two episodes lasting a half hour. That's eleven hours of footage. So, to me, that's kind of soap opera-ish."

"Julie from New York. She's a hottie!"

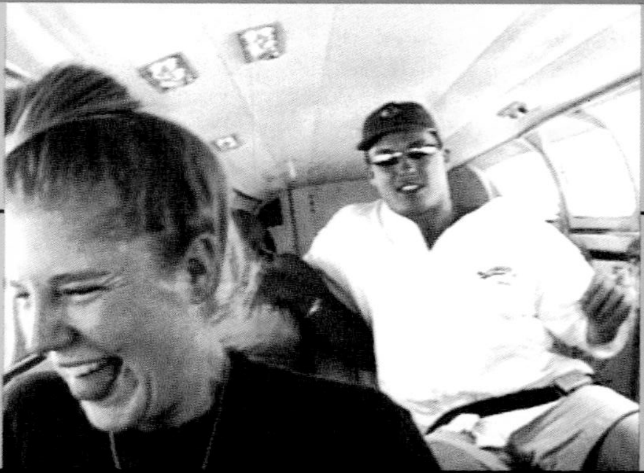

**SARAH**

"A little of each. If seven names were put in a hat and randomly drawn, then that would be different. But there's a screening process and we're put together. You have to remember that. It's not seven strangers, well, to each of us maybe. But, we're seven picked people. It might've been a completely different season if just one person had been different."

# LONDON

**JAY**

"It's a documentary. But it's not a documentary about seven people living in a house—it's a documentary about seven people living in a house and trying to pretend there aren't cameras following them around."

"The only thing I ever saw on the Miami show was sex. Did they do anything else in that house? Perhaps, if our cast had lived in Miami, we'd have had a lot of sex, too."

"I really wanted to meet Tami, because her husband is Kenny Anderson of the Portland Trail Blazers—my favorite basketball team. Well, I saw the two of them outside a movie theater in Portland a while ago, so I went up to her. At first, she was taken aback—the way I always am when strangers first approach. But, when I explained who I was and that I'd been on *The Real World*, too, she was very warm and friendly. She even introduced me to her husband, which was a thrill."

**LARS**

"It's a mixture of both. It's a show that MTV is doing. They want to make money. They're not going to put some ugly person on with loads of zits. So, it's not totally real."

"I got to see the Miami house before the cast moved in. That was a great house. They had windows and air-conditioning, too. We didn't have a single window that could open. From April to May, it was unbearably hot in our place."

"Mohammed and Rachel were the first people I met at the MTV Movie Awards. I just thought they were really cool. We have the music interest in common."

**MIKE**

"Soap opera. If they wanted to do a documentary, they would've shown me and Jay watching TV for twenty-four hours a day, not 'Oh, I need Ranch dressing.' Of all the things to show. They wasted a half hour of some poor viewer's life."

"I prefer *Road Rules*. I'd drive the truck. They have better-looking girls on *Road Rules*. Name one good looking *Real World* girl? Melissa? Oh, no. Jacinda? Too tall. Too skinny. Not my type."

"Dan called me up one day, I think, just to talk about Dan [laughing]. No, actually he was looking for some information about a colleague of mine. Dan seemed okay."

**NEIL**

"To me, *The Real World* is a fascinating meeting of fact and fiction, reality and hyper-reality. The production team brings as much, if not more, to the show as the actual events and actions of the participants. The show employs a highly trained team of 'story editors' to construct this soap opera. The vignettes of 'reality' must be punchy and direct. This inevitably occurs at the expense of subtlety."

**SHARON**

"We give them the raw thing and they polish it up into *Melrose Place*."

"You don't have to be a brain surgeon to know a lot of tension will come about when seven people live together and work together. The Miami group didn't have a chance."

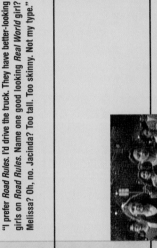

"Dan and I went to the East Village for Wigstock. I dressed him up in drag—fake eyelashes, eyeliner, blue eye shadow and lip liner. He was gorgeous! I was this cheap, nasty hag. Dan was a diva. I had a white bob; he had a purple one. We went to this gay club. There were, like, two women in the entire place. And this guy comes up to me and says, 'Oh, my God. Are you Sharon from *The Real World*?" I'm, like, 'How the hell did you recognize me?'"

# SAN FRANCISCO

**CORY**

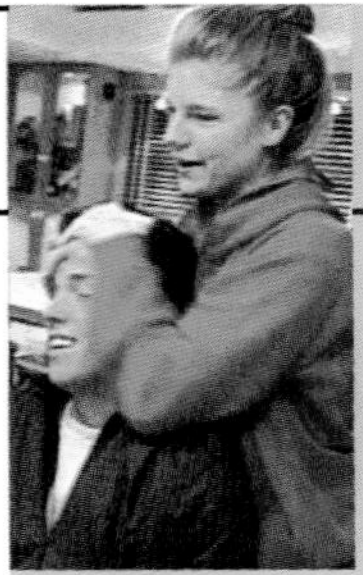

"I could've lived with any of the people who have ever been on *The Real World*. I just think it's the combination that matters the most."

**JUDD**

"They shoot it in a documentary style, but ask a documentary filmmaker about *The Real World* and they won't stop throwing up."

"Pam and I stopped watching the Miami show after the second episode. It just got too uncomfortable to watch. I mean, those people were having fifteen-round, drag-'em-out fights. Were they nuts? Half the time, I watched their show wondering, 'Don't these people know they're on TV?'"

"I can't pick one favorite, 'cause I liked so many of them. Norm was great. So was Beth A., and Kevin, too. And I liked Julie a lot. I wish I'd gotten the chance to talk with her at the last reunion. I would also like to speak with Sarah from the Miami cast. She's a comic book editor, so that would be fun. Get me on the phone with her."

SAN FRANCISCO CONTINUED

| | IS *REAL WORLD* A SOAP OPERA OR A DOCUMENTARY? | WHAT DO YOU REALLY THINK OF THE OTHER *RW* SEASONS? | WHO'S YOUR FAVORITE *RW* CAST MEMBER FROM ANOTHER SEASON? |
|---|---|---|---|
|  MOHAMMED | "I think it's a flight into voyeurism." | "I watched one of the New York shows for about ten minutes and I couldn't understand why a group of people just sat around arguing and no one left. Well, I learned why, the hard way." | "Cynthia from the Miami show. Someone's got to give her my number. Let's hook it up." |
|  PAM | | "Some people I know consider the Miami show to be *The Real World's* equivalent of *Elvis-The Fat Years.* I can't say much for that cast, but that house was incredible. That was a place to play. We're all so jealous." | "I liked Kevin from the New York cast a lot. I've never met him, but I've heard a lot about him from friends of friends. I never felt like we really got to know him from the show." |
|  PUCK | "*Real World* is real, man." | "I wish I could've lived with New York, man, 'cause all those kids are cool. But no way I could've lived with L.A. I'd have gotten the boot. I can't live with cops, man. And the London group? I'd waste that racing dude on any track. Give me a car. Give me a motorcycle. Give me anything. I'd whip his butt." | "I think all the other people who've ever done *The Real World* suck! I wish I had cast the shows." |
|  RACHEL | | | "I like Norm a lot. I talk to him often because he lives with Cory. And I think Eric is real cute. He and I had a lot of fun together at the reunion." |

# LOS ANGELES

| | IS *REAL WORLD* A SOAP OPERA OR A DOCUMENTARY? | WHAT DO YOU REALLY THINK OF THE OTHER *RW* SEASONS? | WHO'S YOUR FAVORITE *RW* CAST MEMBER FROM ANOTHER SEASON? |
|---|---|---|---|
|  BETH A. | "It's a TV show. It's a show created by people who want to pay bills. It isn't a documentary meant to enlighten people. You have to look at it from a business perspective. It's being portrayed as real life and it's called *The Real World.* So hopefully, they find people with some social responsibility." | "I haven't seen any of the other seasons, but I saw *Road Rules.* I'd love to be on that show." | |
|  BETH S. | "Oh, God. It's a soap opera. Definitely a soap." | "New York was my favorite season 'cause they all seemed to become really good friends. The friendships on the other seasons have seemed forced and unnatural to me. I thought the Miami cast was a bunch of whiners." | "Here's how I rate them as sex gods: 1. Eric 2. Lars 3. Jon 4. Dan—Man, was I heartbroken when I heard he was gay." |

| | | | |
|---|---|---|---|
| DAVID | | "They should've put me in Miami. I would've been kicked out for being too normal. One of those people would've said, 'Dave doesn't want to be bisexual with us in the Jacuzzi. Get out!'" | |
| GLEN | "I think it's a documentary. No one will deem it that. Maybe in ten years, they will. I'm surprised no one else has copied it." | | "I'd love to hunt Puck. Set him free on an island and let us hunt him. He's crazy! Our cast had a great time playing survival games. I'm sure Puck would have loved it too. It would have been fun to see how many people got hits on him." |
| IRENE | "It's a soap opera. I watch *All My Children* and I see things on that show that we did on *The Real World.*" | "I would never have wanted to live with the Miami cast, but I would've loved to live in their house." | |
| JON | "It's both. The editors don't use stuff that didn't happen. But they soap opera it up more." | "The London house was the house of love. I met them at the reunion and I could've lived with those people a lot easier. As for the Miami show, that got a little immoral. I think the viewers were going, 'This is kinda stupid.' Those people...I just didn't get them." | |
| TAMI | | "Heather made a comment that everyone after the New York season was fake, that we all put it on in front of the cameras. I was a little offended by that because I tried to be myself at all times. I don't know about anyone else, but I was being me. To say we were fake offends me. In fact, there were times I watched their show and thought, 'Oh, they're just doing that for the cameras.' So, they can't judge anyone else." | |

## NEW YORK

| | | | |
|---|---|---|---|
| HEATHER | | "I thought what the L.A. cast did was bulls**t. I mean, a girl has an abortion but then throws someone out of the house because he pulled a blanket off of her. What the f**k is that? That is 100 percent dumb." | "I don't know who my favorite is, but I can tell you my least favorite. When I met Tami at the reunion, I was prepared to give her the benefit of the doubt. I'd heard she was a bitch, but I wanted to make up my own mind. Well, she walks in, sits down next to me and starts talking, like, 'Oh, yeah. Heather, you were like the ghetto queen.' I was, like, 'What the f**k is a ghetto queen?' Man, if she looks at me as a ghetto queen, she must be trying to be everything but that. Whatever! I really don't care enough about her to make a statement." |

NEW YORK CONTINUED

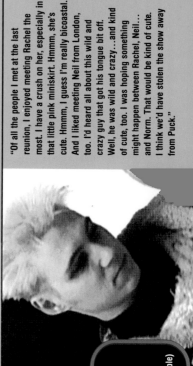

| | IS *REAL WORLD* A SOAP OPERA OR A DOCUMENTARY? | WHAT DO YOU REALLY THINK OF THE OTHER *RW* SEASONS? | WHO'S YOUR FAVORITE *RW* CAST MEMBER FROM ANOTHER SEASON? |
|---|---|---|---|
|  JULIE | "I don't know what you'd call it exactly, but I don't think it's real. It's not real time. It's edited. I wouldn't have gone to Jamaica. I don't usually walk around with great music accompanying my movements. Nor do I appear in a bunch of really weird angles. Real life just isn't like it is on TV." | "One of the first times I tuned in to see the L.A. show, Tami was having her mouth wired shut. I was like, 'Off you go, TV.' I don't need to see any of that. It was clearly some ploy to get more airtime. And that blanket incident was so pathetic, to boot. If I'd been in that situation and wasn't comfortable with someone in the house, then I think I ought to be the one who has to go." | "I was so psyched to meet Puck at the last reunion. And boy, did he live up to every expectation. He's perfect. He's the best. He didn't let me down a bit. Just the fact that he came out and started this whole big scene. He's like fire. He needs oxygen to keep going and his housemates just feed his fire with more and more oxygen. If you thought he really meant any of that crap, you're stupid. He's just getting a rise out of everybody. I don't know why they don't ignore him." |
|  KEVIN |  | "I don't really care for the shows after us. I thought L.A. was a big letdown after New York. The blanket incident with Tami was a mountain out of a molehill. Frankly, I don't have a lot of respect for her after that, that's all I have to say. Saying 'rape,' that stuff sticks with you. I thought the London show was borrrr-ing. And Miami? If they'd charged us with doing a business, we'd have done it. But I liked the San Francisco season because of Pedro." | "Puck is not my favorite, but the writer in me wants to sit down and have a back-and-forth with him. I thought he was f**ked up for dissing Judd and for dissing Pedro in death, but I've always identified with those guys who want to be rebellious." |
|  NORMAN | "How real is *The Real World*? Aren't people teaching courses on this now? Why is it so important that everyone needs to know if *The Real World* is really real? If it's entertaining, that seems real enough for me." | "The San Francisco house just knew how to push each other's buttons. And they surely did."  | "Of all the people I met at the last reunion, I enjoyed meeting Rachel the most. I have a crush on her, especially in that little pink miniskirt. Hmmm, she's cute. Hmmm, I guess I'm really bicoastal. And I liked meeting Neil from London, too. I'd heard all about this wild and crazy guy that got his tongue bit off. Well, he was wild and crazy...and kind of cute, too. I was hoping something might happen between Rachel, Neil... and Norm. That would be kind of cute. I think we'd have stolen the show away from Puck." |

**JON MURRAY (executive producer of *The Real World*) PICKS HIS FAVORITE EPISODES FROM SEASONS PAST AND PRESENT:**

NEW YORK **Episode 1 (Julie's arrival from Alabama)** LOS ANGELES **Episode 11 (Tami's abortion)**
SAN FRANCISCO **Episode 19 (Pedro and Sean's commitment ceremony)** LONDON **Episode 7 (Neil's tongue)**
MIAMI **Episode 14 (Sarah takes over the business)**
BOSTON **Episodes 9, 10 (Syrus dates after-school parent and Genesis overhears a child say she hates gay people)**

# *The Real World* According To...

While some may consider this a trip down memory lane, *The Real World* According To... is presented more as a community service. Think of it as a helpful guide for future crises in case you find yourself trapped in a shower with two other people; stuck in a hospital with your tongue bitten off; or in desperate need of Ranch dressing. If you've already experienced all these moments in your life, perhaps you don't need to read on. But if not, here's a sampling of how the roommates of *Real World* have talked themselves into and out of thick and thin.

## On Attraction

"I tried to explain to everybody how come there is no sex in the apartment—everybody is ugly...That's why there's no sex."

—Heather explains the birds and the bees in *RW-New York.*

## On Bird Watching

"We were supposed to come down here to Jamaica 'cause we're desperate to meet men...we come to Jamaica, and there's a bunch of loser birds flying all around these trees."

—Julie laments migration patterns on vacation in *RW-New York.*

## On Bunny to the Rescue

"You reek of broads. You got cooties, man. Bunny, help me! Bunny, save me!"

—Sarah calls in reinforcements against Mike in *RW-Miami.*

## On Cabin Fever

"I'm starting to die 'cause I haven't been around a gay person since I've been here...I'm in a f**king house full of straight people and I'm beginning to wonder if I'm turning straight myself."

—Genesis sounds the Firehouse alarm in *RW-Boston.*

## On Car Pooling

"My boyfriend, Louis, had to go to the hardware store instead of driving me to the emergency room and that kind of sucked." —Flora laments Louis' priorities in *RW-Miami.*

## On Changing the Sheets

"She's into all this college Republican this and that, and I'm a bed-wetting liberal, so there might be trouble later."

—Judd discusses with Rachel in *RW-S.F.*

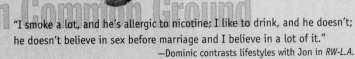

## On Common Ground

"I smoke a lot, and he's allergic to nicotine; I like to drink, and he doesn't; he doesn't believe in sex before marriage and I believe in a lot of it."

—Dominic contrasts lifestyles with Jon in *RW-L.A.*

# On Coping

"When I get in a mood like this I just want to do something like pierce something or dye something."
—Kat channels her anger in *RW-London.*

# On Dating

"Dinner and a movie don't get you no ass!"
—Cynthia describes the value of a cheap date in *RW-Miami.*

# On Democracy

"I say that whenever more than four of us are going out and you come along, we vote on whether you have to take a shower or not."
—Pedro calls for a referendum on Puck's hygiene in *RW-S.F.*

# On Dieting

"I got force-fed a lot of their parents' ethics."
—Puck refuses the house specialty in *RW-Reunion.*

# On Dilemmas

"It's hard to be wacky and silly when all you want to do is watch television and pout."
—Judd animates to Cory in *RW-S.F.*

# On Doing the Crew

"The only sin you could've committed on *The Real World* was to snatch somebody that was holding a camera... That was like the cardinal sin. And she did that. So Becky was like the black sheep from that point on." —Heather counts sheep in *RW-Vacations.*



# On Doing What You Gotta Do

"You gotta do what you gotta do, y'know? You gotta please the women. That's my job."
Eric serves womankind in *RW-New York.*

# On Drawing the Line

"Y'all can look at it, but I don't want any bodily fluids on it."
—Genesis shares her adult magazine with the guys in *RW-Boston.*

# On Ethics

"I'm thinking we should just take the money and go to Vegas."
—Dan shares his business plan with Cynthia in *RW-Miami.*

## On Expectations

"They wanted sex on *The Real World* and instead they got us." —Heather delivers the bad news at the end of *RW-New York.*

## On Firsts

"I've never seen drunk people be so crass and vulgar in my entire life. Not even during Spring Break." —Elka rates Sean and Montana in *RW-Boston.*

## On Forever

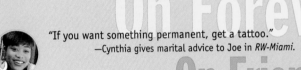

"If you want something permanent, get a tattoo."
—Cynthia gives marital advice to Joe in *RW-Miami.*

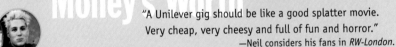

## On Friendship

"They just decided to be friends 'cause nobody was talking to either one of 'em."
—Tami on Beth A. & Glen's relationship in *RW-L.A.*

## On Full Days

"I had a very trying day.
I went to jail and got hit by a car."
—Puck greets the roommates at the beginning of *RW-S.F.*

"What a day. A cat barfed on me, I got my hair cut like this, and I'm getting married."
—Puck unwinds days later with his roommates in *RW-S.F.*

## On Getting Your Money's Worth

"A Unilever gig should be like a good splatter movie.
Very cheap, very cheesy and full of fun and horror."
—Neil considers his fans in *RW-London.*



## On Going Native

"It saddens me to a certain extent that people
still haven't embraced English culture...
but on the other hand, Mike uses the word wanker,
so that's a step in the right direction."
— Neil looks at the bright side in *RW-London.*

## On Good Advice

"Never shave angry."
—Judd cautions Pedro about shaving his goatee in *RW-S.F.*

## On Gross National Products

"What kind of country doesn't have garbage disposals?"
—Mike laments the decline of the Royal Empire in *RW-London.*

## On Guys

"You can look up "guy" in the dictionary and there's this big picture of Mike with a can of beer in his hand, grinning."

—Dan thumbs through *Webster's* in *RW-Miami.*

## On Having Something in Common

"You think about hooter like I think about hooter. We both love it."

—Sean finds common ground with Genesis in *RW-Boston.*

## On "Honey, I'm Home"

"I come home and the first thing I see in the house is penis."

—Flora greets Mike and company in *RW-Miami.*

## On "I'm Not an Elephant, I'm a Man"

"People take different attitudes toward people who are actors and models... in reality, we're no different than anybody else—we're humans too."

—Eric appeals for understanding in *RW-New York.*

## On Knowing Thyself

"I get bored with people, I get bored with things. I think maybe it's because I hate myself."

—Glen gets to the heart of the matter in *RW-L.A.*

## On Laxatives

"I'm involved in lots of different sorts of music....One of them I like to describe as progressive assquake, the idea being to create the right frequency of noise to cause people to s**t."

—Neil paints a pretty picture in *RW-London.*



## On Marcia, Marcia, Marcia

"Look at us—I mean, we're like the mutated Brady Bunch."

—Aaron tells the story on *RW-L.A.*

## On Married With Children

"Mike's family is like the Bundys, but with more money."

—Neil crosses himself off another Christmas list in *RW-London.*

## On Men

MONTANA: "It's hard to be a girl and not have issues with men. Men are basically weak, stupid, base..."

KAMEELAH: "And they're everywhere."

—Montana and Kameelah compare notes in *RW-Boston.*

## On Men Behaving Badly

JULIE: "Why are boys so horny?" BECKY: "Boys are horny 'cause all their equipment is on the outside, ours is on the inside."

—The pair discuss indoor vs. outdoor plumbing in *RW-New York.*

## On Morality in Music

"He's rude, he's obnoxious, he's profane.... I think that it's all that rap music he listens to because you don't see people who listen to country music running around that way."

—Jon raps on David in *RW-L.A.*

## On Multiple Personalities

"I almost feel two-faced because I see everyone's point of view."

—Genesis comes out to Jason in *RW-Boston.*

## On 9-1-1

"The fashion police need to come and arrest her."

—Cynthia cuffs Joe's girlfriend, Nic, in *RW-Miami.*

## On Nutrition

"If I were stuck in the middle of nowhere with a toothpick and a can of water, she'd be the person I'd eat first."

—Neil opts for the soup du Sharon in *RW-London.*

## On Organ Donors

"Please, please tell me my favorite organ is okay."

—Neil relives a penis-scare from the past in *RW-London.*

## On Pilgrim Pride



"I knew this lesbian couple, where one of the women was inseminated with a turkey baster and her kid was born on Thanksgiving."

—Montana carves a tale on *RW-Boston.*

## On Positive Developments

GENESIS: "I could just run up and down the stairs, and jump up and down, and they don't move."
MONTANA: "You're lucky, man. I wish I didn't have to wear a bra...in sixth grade."

—Genesis and Montana size up the situation in *RW-Boston.*

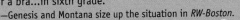

## On Pub-ulation Growth

"I really enjoyed living in England. There are more pubs here than people."

—Kat performs her census in *RW-London.*

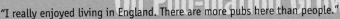

# On Prime Time

"You just have to sit back and watch Flora. She's like a sitcom, you know."
—Sarah reviews the fall lineup in *RW-Miami.*

# On Reality

"Real people pay rent!"
—Judd sets it straight on *RW-Reunion.*

# On Reality Bites

"It hasn't affected my relationship with Chrys too badly. However, cunnilingus is out of the question for a while, which may cause problems later on..."
—Neil ponders his tongue lashing in *RW-London.*

# On Receiving Is Better Than Giving

"My sex life is going to be great, even if I have my mouth wired. I won't have to do anything and I can get everything done to me."
—Tami kicks back and relaxes in *RW-L.A.*

# On Reunions

"I wanted to meet the other bitch from the other episode."
—Rachel to Tami in the *RW-Reunion.*

# On Rhymes with Show

"Joe, you a ho!"
—Cynthia after learning about Joe's two prom dates in *RW-Miami.*

# On Roll Over Beethoven

"It's a fine line between making the noise that you want to make and making the noise people want to hear."
—Neil straddles the line with his music in *RW-London.*

# On Rollerblading

"I figure Rollerblading is kind of like sex. The first time's a little difficult."
—Judd crashes on his date with Jessica in *RW-S.F.*

## On Sharing

"I'm getting my own food now. I'm buying my own peanut butter and everyone else can kiss my mutt."
—Puck lays down the law in *RW-S.F.*

## On Sharing Hobbies

"Both of 'em are looking for women, so they've got that in common."
—Dominic finds common ground for Beth A. and Glen in *RW-L.A.*

## On Standards and Practices

"The women are starting to look better, or maybe my standards are dropping."
—Mike checks the meter in *RW-London.*

## On Stardom

"A bike messenger is a pretty revered thing here in San Francisco."
—Puck describes the view from the top in *RW-S.F.*

## On Sticky Fingers

"He walks right by me, puts his finger in the peanut butter, just licks it and goes on. That is the same hand that he was wiping on his shirt because he got... snot all over it."
—Pedro ducks Puck in *RW-S.F.*

## On Strengths and Weaknesses

"Intelligent people want to do the things they're least cut out for, so being a rock 'n' roll star is quite a challenge for me."
—Neil endears himself to rock stars everywhere in *RW-London.*

## On Stupidity

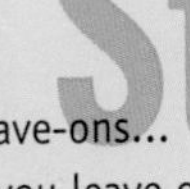

"I hate it when stupid people in positions of power make me cry."
—Pam rages after being rotated out of her rotation in *RW-S.F.*

## On Style

"Those shoes are leave-ons... those are the ones you leave on when you're doing it."
—Cynthia gives fashion tips in *RW-Miami.*

## On Supply and Demand

"I'm glad to see you still have something to squirt after all this time."
—Neil discusses Ranch dressing with Mike in *RW-London.*

## On Telling It Like It Is

"Girl, you acted like a ho' tonight. I'm not gonna talk behind your back. I'm gonna give it to you straight to your face."
—Cynthia grounds Flora after first date with Louis in *RW-Miami.*

# On Telling Time

"You know anything after 11 o'clock ain't nothin' but a booty call."

—Cynthia to Melissa about late-night phoning in *RW-Miami.*

# On the Laws of Physics

"I don't know what Flora and her breasts were thinking when they tried to squeeze through that window."

—Dan ponders a brief history in time in *RW-Miami.*

# On the Meaning of Life

"I can't live without Ranch dressing. That's like lifeblood."

—Mike draws the line in *RW-London.*

# On the Meaning of Love

"You say you love me, but you're friends with loose women and you won't bring them over."

—Judd questions Rachel's devotion in *RW-S.F.*

# On the Miami Sound Machine

"Flora and Mitchell are meant to be together. To hear them fight is like music. It's, like, back and forth; I mean, there's rhythm to it."

—Melissa feels the rhythm of the beat in *RW-Miami.*

# On *The Real World*

"I do feel like I'm in prison part-time. And part-time, I feel like I'm in *Romper Room.*"

—Syrus bristles full-time over house rules in *RW-Boston.*



# On the Theory of Relativity

"Did I say I had a good sex life? Well, I'm not going to Jamaica, so apparently I have a better sex life than them."

—Andre finds relief in *RW-New York.*

# On the Truth About Cats and Dogs

"When you deal with women, you're used to honesty and openness. When you deal with men, it's totally different."

—Kameelah to Genesis in *RW-Boston.*

# On the Truth About Dogs

"Most men are dogs."

—Kevin lays it all out in *RW-New York.*

## On the Value of a Good Education

"Joe's knowledge of sexual ability does attract a lot of women. I, for one, am attracted to him for that."

—Cynthia tells it like it is in *RW-Miami.*

## On the Value of Prior Experience

"Dealing with Puck really reminds me of some psychiatric patients that I've dealt with."

—Pam compares notes in *RW-S.F.*

## On the Voice of America

"I'd never wire my mouth shut 'cause I like for people to hear what I'm saying."

—Jon broadcasts his opinion on Tami in *RW-L.A.*

## On Trust

"My boyfriend, Mitchell, definitely trusts me more than I trust him. On a scale of one to ten, he probably trusts me a four, or four and a half. I trust him one. Maybe one and a half." —Flora calculates her love in *RW-Miami.*

## On Understatement

"I was pretty nasty to live with."

—Puck sees the light in *RW-Reunion.*

## On Voltage

"Don't touch me, 'cause I'm electric."

—Puck reads his meter in *RW-Reunion.*

## On Valuables

"I want to keep my nipples."

—Rachel establishes soapbox ground rules with Puck in *RW-S.F.*

## On White Lies

"Mom, it's just like any other place."

—Becky phones home in *RW-New York.*

## On What's Fair Is Fair

"If he's going to show us the back, he's going to have to show us the front."

—Montana to Genesis after Sean's full mooning in *RW-Boston.*

## On Zoology

"I don't think we could be more different... unless I had antlers sticking out of my head."

—Dominic compares species with housemates in *RW-L.A.*

# Three Strikes and You're Out

## An Essay by Sean Bentz

That could have been me up there!

After watching *The Real World* for several seasons, I got the crazy idea to call up MTV and find out how I could be a part of it. I felt like I had a lot to offer. I'm drug and alcohol free. I run youth events for the kids in San Diego. I've traveled around the world. I was an intern in President Bush's Office of National Service. I'm as real as they come.

So, I called *The Real World* information hot line, which said the next season was going to be in London. Hello, London! I made a videotape—a little long—but the show must have liked it 'cause I made it to round two. Awesome! And my brother got rejected right off the bat. Too bad for him.

I filled out the 13-page written application and sent it along with my resume and lots of pictures of me. I didn't hear anything back for several months, until Christmastime, when I received my own rejection letter. What? They must have made some kind of mistake. But the letter did say I was among the Top 200 candidates. That made me feel a lot better.

I watched the London show and tried to enjoy it. It didn't help that a lot of people told me how much they thought I looked like Lars. How nice for me.

When casting for the following season started up, I decided to reapply because I heard the Miami group was going to start a business. Well, I'm studying International Business. Hello, Miami! I couldn't miss this time. I even wrote a business plan. I got out the old video camera again, and overnighted my tape. I got a response the very next day asking me if I could come in for an interview in a few days. I didn't even have to check my calendar. Just tell me the time!

I arrived at my interview early. I was nervous, but everyone put me at ease. It was like they all knew me. I thought, this is sooo cool. My bags were practically packed for Miami. I knew my one-hour interview with the casting director went very well. But, when he turned to me at the end and said he was "glad good people like me were still in the world"...well, I just wanted to run out and buy tanning oil.

Then, nothing. Months passed without a word. Nothing until around Christmas (I'm starting to hate December) when I got yet another rejection letter. This time it said I'd made it to the Top 45. I guess that was some consolation—I was getting closer.

The big question was, could I put myself through this again? Well, when I heard the group in Boston was going to help run a youth center, I figured, WOW, that's me. I've been helping kids and running youth activities since 1989. Hello, Boston!

Again, I put together a video and sent it in. Naturally, I just assumed a written application would arrive in the mail. None came. I called the hot line, which mentioned that an open call was being held in San Francisco—in just two days. Well, I scraped together the $200 plane fare and flew up from San Diego.

The interview lasted five minutes, and it did not go well. Okay, I'm not what they're looking for. That's all right. I may never get on the show, but I still think *The Real World*—even the experience of trying to get on—is awesome!

SEAN BENTZ is a San Diego-based student, aspiring model, graphic artist and youth activist. And he still has no idea why he wasn't selected.

# How to

## get on *The Real World*

To apply to be on *The Real World*, you need to show us that you are an open, honest and sincere person who's dealing with issues of concern to *The Real World* audience. How can you do this? Read on for step-by-step directions. **1. Call *The Real World* Hotline: (818) 754-5790.** This number will give you the latest information on applying. It will tell you where to send your application and when the deadlines for the next season are. Be sure to call this number first to get the most up-to-date information. **2. Write a cover letter.** We want you to tell us a little bit about yourself. Why do you want to spend six months in a house full of strangers? What activities will you pursue? Please also include a snapshot of yourself in this cover letter. **3. Make a videotape.** We would also like to see you as well as hear from you. Make a ten-minute videotape of yourself talking about whatever you think makes you a good candidate for *The Real World*. Remember, we want to see if you are a person who is open and willing to express what is important to you. Sometimes the best videos are very simple: someone sitting on their bed talking about what makes them tick. Try to be honest, and sincere. Don't overthink it. (Also make sure there's enough light on your face and that you are close enough to the microphone to be heard.) **4. Fill out the enclosed application.** Answer all of the following questions as best and as honestly as you can. Please keep your answers to a paragraph in length. And please be sure to type your answers or write legibly.

# APPLICATION FORM

THE REAL WORLD

DATE RECEIVED

NAME

ADDRESS

PHONE | E-MAIL ADDRESS

BIRTHDATE | AGE

SOCIAL SECURITY NUMBER

PARENT'S NAME

ADDRESS

PHONE

SIBLINGS (NAMES AND AGES)

ARE YOU OR HAVE YOU EVER BEEN A MEMBER OF SAG/AFTRA? | HAVE YOU EVER ACTED OR PERFORMED OUTSIDE OF SCHOOL?

**EDUCATION** NAME OF HIGH SCHOOL | YEARS COMPLETED

NAME OF COLLEGE | YEARS COMPLETED AND MAJORS

OTHER EDUCATION

PARENTS' OCCUPATION(S)

WHERE DO YOU WORK? DESCRIBE YOUR JOB HISTORY FOR THE LAST YEAR. LIST COMPANY, IMMEDIATE SUPERVISOR AND PHONE NUMBER.



WHAT IS YOUR ULTIMATE CAREER GOAL?

WHAT ARE YOUR PERSONAL (NOT CAREER) GOALS IN LIFE?

TELL US ABOUT WHAT PART OF YOURSELF YOU ARE MOST INSECURE? (EXPLAIN)

WHAT PART OF YOURSELF ARE YOU MOST CONFIDENT IN? (EXPLAIN)

DO YOU USUALLY HANG OUT WITH A GROUP OF FRIENDS OR FOCUS ON ONE FRIEND AT A TIME? (EXPLAIN)

WHAT ABOUT YOU WILL MAKE YOU AN INTERESTING ROOMMATE?

IF YOU'RE LIVING WITH A ROOMMATE, HOW DID YOU HOOK UP WITH HIM OR HER? TELL US ABOUT HIM OR HER AS A PERSON. DO YOU GET ALONG? WHAT'S THE BEST PART ABOUT LIVING TOGETHER? WHAT'S THE HARDEST PART ABOUT IT?

HOW WOULD SOMEONE WHO REALLY KNOWS YOU DESCRIBE YOUR BEST TRAITS?

HOW WOULD SOMEONE WHO REALLY KNOWS YOU DESCRIBE YOUR WORST TRAITS?



DESCRIBE YOUR MOST EMBARRASSING MOMENT IN LIFE:

DO YOU HAVE A BOYFRIEND OR GIRLFRIEND? HOW LONG HAVE YOU TWO BEEN TOGETHER? WHERE DO YOU SEE THE RELATIONSHIP GOING? WHAT DRIVES YOU CRAZY ABOUT THE OTHER PERSON? WHAT'S THE BEST THING ABOUT THE OTHER PERSON?

HOW IMPORTANT IS SEX TO YOU? DO YOU HAVE IT ONLY WHEN YOU'RE IN A RELATIONSHIP, OR DO YOU SEEK IT OUT AT OTHER TIMES? HOW DID IT COME ABOUT ON THE LAST OCCASION?

DESCRIBE YOUR FANTASY DATE:

WHAT DO YOU DO FOR FUN?

DO YOU PLAY ANY SPORTS?

WHAT ARE YOUR FAVORITE MUSICAL GROUPS/ARTISTS?

DESCRIBE A TYPICAL FRIDAY OR SATURDAY NIGHT:

WHAT WAS THE LAST UNUSUAL, EXCITING OR SPONTANEOUS OUTING **YOU** INSTIGATED FOR YOU AND YOUR FRIENDS?



OTHER THAN A BOYFRIEND OR GIRLFRIEND, WHO IS THE MOST IMPORTANT PERSON IN YOUR LIFE RIGHT NOW? TELL ME ABOUT HIM OR HER:

WHAT ARE SOME WAYS YOU HAVE TREATED SOMEONE WHO HAS BEEN IMPORTANT TO YOU THAT YOU ARE PROUD OF?

WHAT ARE SOME OF THE WAYS YOU HAVE TREATED SOMEONE WHO HAS BEEN IMPORTANT TO YOU THAT YOU ARE EMBARRASSED BY, OR WISH YOU HADN'T DONE?

IF YOU HAD TO DESCRIBE YOUR MOTHER, (OR YOUR STEPMOTHER, IF YOU LIVED WITH HER MOST OF YOUR LIFE AS A CHILD), BY DIVIDING HER PERSONALITY INTO TWO PARTS, HOW WOULD YOU DESCRIBE EACH PART?

IF YOU HAD TO DESCRIBE YOUR FATHER, (OR YOUR STEPFATHER), BY DIVIDING **HIS** PERSONALITY INTO TWO PARTS, HOW WOULD YOU DESCRIBE EACH PART?

HOW DID YOUR PARENTS TREAT EACH OTHER? (DID YOUR PARENTS HAVE A GOOD MARRIAGE? WHAT WAS IT LIKE?)

DESCRIBE HOW CONFLICTS WERE HANDLED AT HOME AS YOU WERE GROWING UP (WHO WOULD WIN AND WHO WOULD LOSE, WHETHER THERE WAS YELLING OR HITTING, ETC.)

IF YOU HAVE ANY BROTHERS OR SISTERS, ARE YOU CLOSE? HOW WOULD YOU DESCRIBE YOUR RELATIONSHIP WITH THEM?

DESCRIBE A MAJOR EVENT OR ISSUE THAT'S AFFECTED YOUR FAMILY:



WHAT IS THE MOST IMPORTANT ISSUE OR PROBLEM FACING YOU TODAY?

IS THERE ANY ISSUE, POLITICAL OR SOCIAL, THAT YOU'RE PASSIONATE ABOUT? HAVE YOU DONE ANYTHING ABOUT IT?

DO YOU BELIEVE IN GOD? ARE YOU RELIGIOUS OR SPIRITUAL? DO YOU ATTEND ANY FORMAL RELIGIOUS SERVICES?

WHAT ARE YOUR THOUGHTS ON ABORTION?

OTHER SEXUAL ORIENTATIONS?

WELFARE?

AFFIRMATIVE ACTION?

DO YOU HAVE ANY HABITS WE SHOULD KNOW ABOUT?

DO YOU: SMOKE CIGARETTES?

DRINK ALCOHOL? HOW OLD WERE YOU WHEN YOU HAD YOUR FIRST DRINK? HOW MUCH DO YOU DRINK NOW? HOW OFTEN?

DO YOU USE RECREATIONAL DRUGS? WHAT DRUGS HAVE YOU USED? HOW OFTEN?

DO YOU NOW A LOT OF PEOPLE WHO DO DRUGS, OR NOT? WHAT DO YOU THINK OF PEOPLE WHO DO DRUGS?



ARE YOU ON ANY PRESCRIPTION MEDICATION? IF SO, WHAT, AND FOR HOW LONG HAVE YOU BEEN TAKING IT?

HAVE YOU EVER BEEN ARRESTED? IF SO, WHAT WAS THE CHARGE AND WERE YOU CONVICTED?

WHAT BOTHERS YOU MOST ABOUT OTHER PEOPLE?

DESCRIBE A RECENT MAJOR ARGUMENT YOU HAD WITH SOMEONE. WHO USUALLY WINS ARGUMENTS WITH YOU? WHY?

HAVE YOU EVER HIT ANYONE IN ANGER OR SELF-DEFENSE? IF SO, TELL US ABOUT IT (HOW OLD WERE YOU, WHAT HAPPENED, ETC.)

IF YOU COULD CHANGE ANY ONE THING ABOUT THE WAY YOU LOOK, WHAT WOULD THAT BE?

IF SELECTED, IS THERE ANY PERSON OR PART OF YOUR LIFE YOU WOULD PREFER NOT TO SHARE? IF SO, DESCRIBE (I.E. FAMILY, FRIENDS, BUSINESS ASSOCIATES, SOCIAL ORGANIZATIONS, OR ACTIVITIES)

IS THERE ANYONE AMONG YOUR FAMILY OR CLOSE FRIENDS WHO WOULD OBJECT TO APPEARING ON CAMERA? IF SO, WHY?

ARE YOU NOW, OR HAVE YOU EVER SEEN A THERAPIST OR PSYCHOLOGIST?

WHAT IS YOUR GREATEST FEAR (AND WHY)?

IF YOU HAD ALADDIN'S LAMP AND THREE WISHES, WHAT WOULD THEY BE?

**PLEASE RATE THE FOLLOWING ACTIVITIES/PASTIMES USING THE FOLLOWING SCALE: N: NEVER S: SOMETIMES O: OFTEN A: ALWAYS**

| | RATING | COMMENT |
|---|---|---|
| READ BOOKS | | |
| SLEEP 8 HOURS | | |
| WATCH TELEVISION DAILY | | |
| SHOP | | |
| SOCIALIZE | | |
| SPEND TIME WITH FRIENDS | | |
| SPEND TIME ALONE | | |
| WORK/STUDY | | |
| TALK ON THE PHONE | | |
| COOK | | |
| CLEAN | | |
| ARGUE | | |
| WRITE | | |
| READ NEWSPAPERS | | |

| | RATING | COMMENT |
|---|---|---|
| STATE OPINIONS | | |
| ASK OPINIONS | | |
| CONFIDE IN YOUR PARENTS | | |
| VOLUNTEER | | |
| PROCRASTINATE | | |
| EAT | | |
| DRINK ALCOHOL | | |
| DIET | | |
| SMOKE | | |
| CRY | | |
| LAUGH | | |
| CINEMA | | |
| THEATRE | | |
| CONCERTS | | |
| CLUBS | | |
| PARTIES | | |

**LIST 4 PEOPLE WHO HAVE KNOWN YOU FOR A LONG TIME AND WILL TELL US WHAT A GREAT PERSON YOU ARE (EXCLUDING RELATIVES)**

| | | | |
|---|---|---|---|
| 1. NAME | ADDRESS | PHONE | HOW DO THEY KNOW YOU? |
| 2. NAME | ADDRESS | PHONE | HOW DO THEY KNOW YOU? |
| 3. NAME | ADDRESS | PHONE | HOW DO THEY KNOW YOU? |
| 4. NAME | ADDRESS | PHONE | HOW DO THEY KNOW YOU? |

HOW DID YOU HEAR ABOUT OUR CASTING SEARCH?

I ACKNOWLEDGE THAT EVERYTHING STATED IN THIS APPLICATION IS TRUE. I UNDERSTAND THAT ANY FALSELY SUBMITTED ANSWERS CAN AND WILL BE GROUNDS FOR REMOVAL FROM THE APPLICATION PROCESS AND FROM YOUR SUBSEQUENT PARTICIPATION IN THE FINAL SERIES. I FURTHER ACKNOWLEDGE AND ACCEPT THAT THIS APPLICATION FORM AND THE VIDEOTAPE I PREVIOUSLY SUBMITTED TO MTV WILL BECOME PROPERTY OF MTV AND WILL NOT BE RETURNED. BY SIGNING BELOW, I GRANT RIGHTS FOR MTV/BUNIM-MURRAY PRODUCTIONS (BMP) TO USE ANY BIOGRAPHICAL INFORMATION CONTAINED IN THIS APPLICATION, MY HOME VIDEO OR TAPED INTERVIEW, AND TO RECORD USE AND PUBLICIZE MY HOME VIDEO TAPE OR TAPED INTERVIEW, VOICE, ACTIONS, LIKENESS AND APPEARANCE IN ANY MANNER IN CONNECTION WITH *THE REAL WORLD*.

SIGNATURE DATE

THANK YOU FOR YOUR TIME AND EFFORT IN COMPLETING THIS FORM